Play Therapy

Play Therapy

A Comprehensive Guide

O'Dessie Oliver James, Ed.D.

JASON ARONSON INC.
Northvale, New Jersey
London

Director of Editorial Production: Robert D. Hack

This book was set in 11 pt. Adobe Caslon by Alpha Graphics of Pittsfield, NH and printed and bound by Book-mart Press of North Bergen, NJ.

Library of Congress Cataloging-in-Publication Data

James, O'Dessie Oliver.
    Play therapy : a comprehensive guide / O'Dessie Oliver James.
       p.   cm.
    Includes bibliographical references and index.
    ISBN 0–7657–0052–2 (alk. paper)
    1. Play therapy. I. Title.
RJ505.P6J35 1997
618.92´891653—dc21   96–45165

Printed in the United States of America on acid-free paper. For information and catalog write to Jason Aronson Inc., 230 Livingston Street, Northvale, New Jersey 07647. Or visit our website: http://www.aronson.com

To Doddie Baccus Oliver
who inspired;
To W. Maye Oliver
who nurtures;
To Vernon James
for his love and support;
To Debbie, Cindy, and Hunt McNabb
who are in the center of my heart;
To Kate, Harry, Trevor, and James
who are the future.

Contents

PART III—PHASES AND STAGES

PART IV—OUTCOME AND FOLLOW-UP RESEARCH

PART V—CASE MATERIAL

Preface

Play therapy is not about play. It is about life and death. It is about hope and dreams. It is about learning and growing. It is about strength and survival. Play therapy is the vehicle I have used for thirty years to communicate with hundreds of boys and girls. Play therapy has given me a way to be with children and to demonstrate to them that there is a place where they can be heard, and understood, and supported while they are vulnerable. The playroom has been a sanctuary where I have developed personal insight. It is the space where I have daily discovered the human spirit in its purest form—the spirit of a child.

Acknowledgments

The author gratefully acknowledges all the assistance I have received in writing this book:

research assistance—Debbie Hanks, Kandy Wittenberg and Daniel Sweeney; *technical assistance*—Raymond Wei and Brianna McZeal Wallace.

I

Essential Elements

The Child

Children are brought to play therapy because they need relief from pain, which has developed from multiple etiologies. They are also brought to play therapy because of the suffering they inflict on their caretakers. Children who come to play therapy tend to cluster into the following categories:

1. Children who have attachment issues with their primary love object(s);
2. Children who have been inconsistently conditioned;
3. Children who have biological differences (including illness);
4. Children who have experienced trauma;
5. Children who experience social or cultural change and shock.

CHILDREN WHO HAVE ATTACHMENT ISSUES WITH THEIR PRIMARY LOVE OBJECT(S)

The concept referred to as attachment has been defined in several ways. Ainsworth (1964) described it as a two-way interactional process, while Kennel (Klaus and Kennell 1976) defined attachment as the unique emotional relationship between two individuals that is specific and endures through time. While many may use different words to explain the phenomenon known as attachment, the underlying similarity is the notion of security. Children's attachment behavior becomes more noticeable when they are around strangers or in other anxiety-provoking situations. The exhibited behavior is usually that of the child seeking a sense of physical and emotional security from the caregiver. Positive attachment or bonding experiences with the caregiver allow children a sense of confidence so that they may go on to explore their external world with little anxiety.

Attachment between children and caregivers is influenced by psychological, biological, and cultural factors. Yet, despite the presence of individual predisposition or external forces, the goal of the child–caregiver relationship always remains the same. Mahler and Pine (1975) described the goal well in saying that the mother should remain "quietly available" for the child. This type of relationship fosters an exploratory nature in the child. It allows children freedom to separate from the caregiver and explore their surroundings, knowing that at any time they can return to the caregiver for comfort.

D. James (1979) and V. James (1979) studied mother–infant pairs in doctors' offices. The babies were observed with their mothers at the time of their first medical checkup after birth. Based on those observations, they developed the James' Nurturing Assessment Scale, which divided maternal nurturing behaviors into six categories of behavior (see Appendix). The use of the scale allowed professionals to make assumptions about the quality of nurturing that was occurring between mother and infant. For example, in this study it was determined that some mothers provide quality nurturing when the child is not in need. These mothers were identified as voluntary nurturers. The second group of mothers attended to their baby when their baby was in need, such as feeding, changing, and general protection. The third group of mothers provided minimum caretaking even when the baby was demanding care. The implications of the use of this scale were that some mothers appear to have natural instincts to stimulate and embrace their children in attachment, while other mothers provide nurturance and care but do not seem to naturally stimulate without the children's requesting such. The third group of mothers appeared to be a group who needed the assistance of professionals in terms of emotional support and educative training. Over the years, the use of the scale indicates that parents do not have the same emotional or cognitive capacities for assisting their child. This finding has added to the belief that the development of a program to involve parents has to be prescriptive. This decision is based on the observed level at which the parents are operating in their attunement to their child and in their own cognitive and emotional stage of development.

Adequate attachment paves the way for future cognitive, behavioral, and social development. Many psychologists have noted that good bonding can lead to more compliant infants, toddlers who are more likely to explore, and school-age children who have advanced cognitive skills. The latter age group was the focus of research by Tizard (1977), who found that children who had not formed healthy attachments with a caregiver were more attention-seeking, restless, disobedient, and unpopular in school.

Under optimal conditions, infants and caregivers have a relationship in which reciprocal interaction takes place. This type of relationship naturally lends itself to attachment. Lack of reciprocal interactions can foster feelings of helplessness, fearfulness, and insecurity in a child. For example, an overprotective caregiver can suppress a child's desire to separate. This results in anxiety because the child cannot function with any autonomy. Other types of childhood dysfunction may emerge, depending on the underlying reasons that initially hindered attachment.

CHILDREN WHO HAVE BEEN INCONSISTENTLY CONDITIONED

The children who are having life problems reflected in this category are brought for therapy with a multiplicity of symptoms, including socialization issues in school and institutions, management problems in home and school, interactive problems between parents and the child, frustration, depression, withdrawal, regression, or failure to meet developmental milestones at expected times. These presenting problems represent the "red flag" of despair. Often parents will recognize the problems early in the child's life, when the parents are having trouble with management issues. Frequently, children are brought to therapy at the insistence of their school program. Grandparents and extended family members enter the picture often as advocates of the intervention. On the other hand, they may see the intervention as intrusive to the dynamics of the extended family circle and discourage outside influence because of fear of change. The reason for the problem is only clear after a careful overview of the child, the dynamics within the family of origin (including the extended family), and the societal institutions that interact with the child.

The significant others in the child's life will eventually surface within the therapeutic milieu as either advocates or adversaries to the growth process (depending on the individual needs that the therapy is likely to enhance or jeopardize). In the best-case scenario, all the adults in the life of the child are of like mind and wish only that the child have optimum opportunity for growth and development. However, this is generally not the case when the problem grows from confused parenting.

Children are often referred for behavioral problems because the parents or the school personnel feel that the children do not recognize limits and adhere to those limits. By the time a family brings such children to the therapy setting, the parents often state that they have "tried everything" to discipline the children and the children are still in control. Parents often state that these children are strong-willed, do not obey, do not comply with the family value system, and cause family embarrassment; they even state that the children are so "different" they do not seem to be members of the families. The children are often overwhelmed and frightened by the power and control that the family has assigned to them. They have developed many erroneous assumptions about their place in the family and are often confused about their role.

These children often are set up by the family dynamics to "act out" a particular theme and serve various roles for the different family members at large. Frequently, children are reinforced for certain behaviors because of the unmet needs of a parent, a grandparent, or a caretaker. For example, children of the Great Depression often overindulged their own children in an effort to make up for their own lost childhood. Children of divorce often compensate for their own hurt inner child by providing a totally protected environment for their own child, frequently not allowing the child to assume any responsibilities. The role of money in the family is often a reaction to the way in which grandparents or parents experienced their own wealth or monetary deprivation. Health issues and the way these issues are dealt with in families frequently are communicated to the child. In these cases, children often present with somatic symptoms or learn to ignore biological problems. Children seem to have an uncanny sense about how "pooping and peeing" will influence the emotions of their parents or grandparents.

Children have sensitive antennae and know when a parent and grandparent are in discord over parenting issues. They seem to know when mother and mother-in-law are in conflict. In these cases, the child may unconsciously use this knowledge to become a powerful member of a triad in which age-old conflicts are acted out, often resulting in the symbolic dismemberment of one of the adults involved. Generally the children are hurt in the process because of their role in the dangerous games played out by these adults. Frequently, a child will be identified as more like one or the other and will be "cast off" with the adult who loses power. This is often seen in divorces in which the mother and child are cast out of the life of the paternal grandmother when she takes back her son.

When parents themselves are in overt conflict (as reflected by arguing over issues or even by divorce) the child recognizes a new power, or else total helplessness. The parents may choose to hurt each other by providing unhealthy parenting to the child. Often parents are so regressed at the time of a divorce that they do not recognize that they are capable of destroying their children in order to punish or control an ex-spouse.

Children frequently become enmeshed within the dynamics of a dysfunctional marital relationship. They are the pawns used by one of the marriage partners to create suffering in the other partner. When a father is a misogynist, he may reinforce in his son his own anger and disrespect toward women in order to further demoralize his wife. The child acts out the father's anger and disrespect toward the mother and she is unable to manage the child in order to raise him. This type of father can also reinforce an identity confusion in his daughter that will ultimately result in negating the female bonding between mother and daughter. The lack of bonding leads to anger and disrespect from the daughter to the mother, eventual conflict between the mother and child, and finally demoralization of the parent figure of the mother. In these cases, the father is a silent conspirator in the triad. When examining the situation, the father may be aware of his anger towards his wife but may not be aware of the reinforcement and its negative influence upon the growth and development of his children. Less often, but resulting in the same lethality, the father imparts his confusion and anger toward men onto his children. This is frequently evidenced when the father has not resolved his own anger toward his father or to authority figures in general. When this occurs, the father will send messages to the child that these figures are to be disrespected and manipulated in order to disempower them. An example of this is when the father constantly negates the positive influence of structure within the society by rescuing the child from the consequences of negative behavior that has resulted in a transgression against societal norms. One can see these parents expressing disrespect toward institutions (such as schools), negating the influence of authority figures.

The mother may be employing strategies to serve her own feelings toward men or women through unconscious or conscious manipulation of her children. When the mother feels anger toward her husband, whether it is realistic or displaced anger toward her own father, she may have a propensity to teach her male child to assist her with her dilemma. This may take the form of not allowing her son's own masculine identity to develop, using emotional castration to punish the father by turning his son into a person the father will reject, thus further binding the son to the mother. Some mothers reinforce the rebel behavior in their sons, which will ultimately disempower the father. Again, when the dynamics are uncovered, the mother may be aware of anger or fear of her father, brother, husband, or men in general, but she probably is blinded to the relationship between the behaviors she is reinforcing in her son and the consequences in his life.

Mothers who have unresolved issues with their own mothers frequently bind their children to them so that they can live out the perfect mother–child relationship. This often results in putting unrealistic burdens on the children, and prevents them from experiencing socialization with other children in ways that will allow them to have fun and grow and develop as children, instead of living as distorted mini-adults developed to serve their mothers' needs.

When a mother has unresolved issues with her own past, she may reinforce behaviors that result in her daughter's life being lived to serve the mother's own unmet needs. This situation is often seen in the child who is being conditioned to live out the role of the beauty contestant, the most popular, the best dressed, the social butterfly, or the perfect student.

Mothers may also reinforce the daughters to be traditional to please the past generation or to be nontraditional to punish the past generation. In this area we find the family "prince" or "princess" syndrome, in which the child has been reinforced for qualities they actually do not possess because of the family need for a "pretty toy." These children are lost, hopeless, and even angry when they meet with society at large because their parents are not the king and queen of the world and thus the child has to face reality with few functional tools.

Children are often molded in their view of self and of others in the world based on their positions in the family and what they see as their defined roles in the family of origin and also in the extended family. Based on the dynamics of the family and the power represented by the different value systems within the members of the family, children will frequently define themselves based on the "boxes" the family has selected for each member. The pairings and bonds within the family also define what children value or negate within themselves. These dynamics ultimately result in the manipulations that children may eventually employ in order to function and cope with the world. When the family of origin is fraught with traps and distortions, children will have trouble in generalizing functional coping strategies to the world at large.

CHILDREN WHO HAVE BIOLOGICAL DIFFERENCES

Much has been written about the influence of biological conditions on the development of self-concept and a sense of personal power. The condition itself may interfere with the progress the child needs to make in a central area of development (cognitive, emotional, social, academic, or physical) to keep up with peers. This can clearly be seen in the case of a child who is confined to a wheelchair, which frequently interferes with the child's being able to play with other children and socialize comfortably. Being hindered in this way may also result in negative attitudes toward risk-taking or body concept, thus thwarting clear perceptions of self in the world.

Children who have developmental delays or learning disabilities frequently are unable to meet their developmental milestones at critical periods. An example of this is seen when children have reading disabilities. They cannot read, they feel demoralized when their peers move ahead of them, and they tend to generalize this inability to many other areas of their life. Often, when they do not read at a critical time in their lives, they miss opportunities for acquisition and expression of knowledge. This results in a loss of power among peers or devaluation by their teachers, siblings, or parents. Frequently, the entire family will become involved in protecting the children so that they will not have to experience the pain of their lives. This sometimes results in infantilizing children so that they are unable to use their own resources in solving their problems, because they have parents who are continuously compensating for them. In therapy, parents will frequently be reluctant to allow the therapist to intervene in calling up the healthy part of the disabled child.

It is well understood that most disabilities result in related emotional symptoms. For example, deaf children or children with auditory processing problems often experience disassociation interpersonally, or even some suspiciousness. They may not understand what others are saying, frequently developing fears that others are talking about them. At times children with auditory perceptual problems may hear what is said but misinterpret the meaning, thus storing unclear or distorted messages about self in relationship to the world.

De Wet (1993) stressed that children who are deaf have severe problems with language, speech, and communication. Their emotional strength and their social and educational functioning are hampered because of their hearing problems. Frequently it is difficult to use standardized psychological tests with a deaf child to determine personality variables that are influencing their life. Because of their deafness the therapist must use techniques that allow such children to express themselves through visualization and motion. De Wet stresses that one of the important strategies to use with a deaf child is play therapy. The goal of play therapy is to offer the child security, structure, and routine, and to teach the child how to communicate feelings.

Children who are blind have multiple fears about safety and lack of control. When children feel that they have little control over their environment, they frequently demand control in ways that are troublesome within the family. This need for control derived from fear is also seen in diabetic children, children with multiple physical disabilities, or chronic medical problems.

CHILDREN WHO HAVE EXPERIENCED TRAUMA

Children who have experienced trauma come to the playroom for safety. These children present with fear, anxiety, regression, anger, and depression due to the loss they have experienced. These traumas range from being victims of war, child abuse, injury, severe illness, death, divorce, sudden panic, or phobic reactions. One important first step in the treatment of these children is to obtain a comprehensive list of the child's recent regressions and his current fears. These lists can be used later to assess change in the child and relief of symptoms.

Much is written about the use of play therapy in the treatment of these children. If their parents have not been damaged by the same trauma, they can generally be engaged in the treatment of their child so that the therapy can potentially extend beyond the playroom.

CHILDREN WHO EXPERIENCE SOCIAL/CULTURAL CHANGE AND SHOCK

Some children are brought to therapy because of the stress of a move. Often children are overstressed when they are switched back and forth between two parents who have established new homes. Children have said, "I just want my bed and my toys to be the same," or, "I want my life to be like it was." In an effort to accommodate the change in societal norms and the disintegration of the family unit, child developmentalists will frequently state that change is good for children and that this change will result in increased flexibility in the child at later stages of development. It is crucial that we recognize that children need external consistency and predictability. Even in extreme cases, where family units have to change, it is still highly difficult for the children and produces anxiety and grief in most. It is not at all unusual for an abused child who is removed from parents to yearn for them and to grieve for the lost family, even though the pathology in the family was lethal.

Children whose parents are suddenly uprooted because of a job change or job loss have critical needs for comfort and reorganization through therapy. An even less recognized therapeutic need is when the family is upwardly mobile and the child is expected to continuously adjust to a new set of friends or social mores. Moving across the country to communities with different operational styles produces stress, fear, and loss of self-esteem in many children. As we move from a highly complex, nationally mobile society to an internationally mobile society, children will potentially have increased needs for a place to deal with issues of identity. It is not unusual to see children in the playroom who have more than one stated nationality, carry two passports, and have multinational parents and grandparents. As our society evolves to become increasingly one world, we will need to assist our children in adjusting to the concept. It is true that children are flexible at birth and do not have innate prejudice. However, they are narcissistic at birth and can only expand their view of the world as they cognitively develop to accommodate the construct. Thus, children learn about the world first centering on themselves, then by centering on their parents, followed by family, neighborhood, the community at large, and finally by developing a more complex understanding of the world. Children want to belong. They need stable enculturalization in order to incorporate societal norms. They want to know who is who and what is what. They want to know: (a) are we there yet? (b) what day is it? (c) where is Dad? (d) where are my toys? (e) when will you be here to pick me up? (f) will we be able to buy ice cream in our new town? (g) will we have a bed there? Once children move to a new city or to a different culture, they often try many superstitious behaviors in order to determine how to act like their new associates. Often they are far off the mark, and seriously misperceive the norms. This frequently results in pain and loss. Children have been known to decompensate because their clothing was too different from their new peers. We must remember that it is difficult for a young child to feel secure when Dad flies to Australia to work for a week, and the child has never walked outside the family yard. The playroom can assist such a child to work through the fears of the unknown. Parents of such children can also be engaged to assist their children to grasp these changes within their cognitive abilities. But the issue to be addressed is that children have emotional needs that have to be addressed at these important junctures in their lives, else the transitions may be unbearable.

When lightning strikes, when a tornado hits, when a bomb blasts, when an airplane falls from the sky, children begin to experience trauma and fear of loss, which has to be addressed intensively and immediately. After a hurricane, children grieve for their lost neighborhood or their lost toy (even though it is replaced). One child whose home was destroyed in a hurricane repeatedly described his lost truck. It was not the loss of the truck that was the issue, but the loss of control that caused the anxiety and depression in the child. The truck was symbolic of the "way things used to be before we lost control." One small boy was seen because of the sudden onset of panic attacks. He had been playing in his "safe" yard with an older brother (whom he loved and trusted) when he ran into a bench and broke his leg. His statement in the playroom clearly described his lack of trust when he said, "There I was, in my own yard, just having fun—and suddenly I had a broken leg. If such a terrible thing can happen to me at home in my own yard, anything can happen, and I am not safe anywhere."

CHILDREN WHO HAVE BEEN DESCRIBED IN THE LITERATURE

Throughout the literature, therapists have described a number of different problems with which play therapy has been used.

Anna Freud (1951) developed her technique to be used primarily for infantile neurosis. She reported working with phobic children, obsessional children, hysterical children, and those with neuroses and anxieties. Klein (1927) reported working with very young children. One child whom she discussed was 2 years and 9 months old. Klein stressed that all children could benefit from analysis and suggested that it should be a regular part of the work of the educational system. She indicated that children have suffered from improper rearing in one form or another, or at one stage or another. Therefore, she concluded, analysis should be provided universally.

Conn (1948, 1952, 1955) discussed working with a variety of types of children. He discussed using the structured interview play technique with the fearful child (1941b), the timid, dependent child (1941a), the child with castration fears (1955), and the anxious child (1952).

Conn (1955) described the method of play interviews as applied to the specific problem of castration fears in children. In working with a 13-year-old boy with castration fears, he used a specific technique that he arranged for this particular problem. The child was a passive and dependent boy. Conn encouraged the boy to talk about his fears through a doll to other dolls. Conn worked with the boy in fifteen-minute play sessions. He reported that, at a fifteen-year follow-up, the young man had assumed a masculine role.

Conn (1941b) indicated that the attitudes, feelings, imaginations, and motives of children are closely associated with their life situations and actual experiences. He used these life realities in planning a series of play interviews that give the children an opportunity to express themselves. The procedure uses the capacity of children for self-scrutiny and provides for a personal reorientation and synthesis of hitherto unrelated experiences. For the first time, the children can view the whole story and see themselves as others see them. Conn stressed the importance of allowing children to find and express themselves in the presence of an appreciative adult. This adult can listen to the parents and yet continue to like the children. There is no attempt to arouse antagonistic or hostile feelings. Guns, pistols, knives, and soldiers are not included in the play materials. Conn tells the parents to stop their criticism and nagging.

Solomon (1948) discussed types of children who would benefit from treatment. He differentiated the type of treatment that these "reaction-types" are likely to need. The "aggressive-impulsive" group includes those children who show overt hostile or overt affectionate behavior. They clown and try to get attention. Solomon described these children as being potential delinquents and stressed that they need carefully defined and restrictive limits.

The "anxiety-phobic type" presents a predominant emotional tone of fear. These children have weak ego structures and suffer from strong superego demands and strong id impulses. Because the parents generally are punishing, something should be done to lessen the pressures at home. The child is anxious and guilt-ridden. Care in the imposition of limits has to be taken or else the child will become more repressive. Solomon described the third group as the "regressive reaction-formation group." This group includes those cases where the original anxiety is replaced to a great extent by various types of defense mechanisms (1948). The fourth group is described as "schizoid-schizophrenic." Solomon suggested that play techniques furnish a method for breaking through these "autistic barriers" (1948, p. 409).

Moustakas (1951, 1953, 1959b) discussed his work with the following types of children: the disturbed child, the normal child, the adjusted child in conflict, the creative child, and the handicapped child.

The disturbed children have lost touch with themselves. These children no longer have confidence about the world. Through the safety of the relationship, these children are able to reexperience themselves for a time and to reinstate a personal identity.

In describing his work with normal children, Moustakas said that the process of the therapeutic relationship with an insightful adult offers the children a unique opportunity for growth. The children are allowed to become more aware of themselves and to explore their feelings in reference to others. The normal child generally begins testing limits and examining the setting immediately, and expresses negative feelings clearly and directly. The full, enriching experience provided by this type of hour offers concentrated time with an adult. This is different from other relationships with adults in that adults often are too rushed and busy to be with a child (1951, 1953).

The adjusted child in conflict is one who is generally normal but, because of a stressful situation, needs help in working through it. Such conflicts as divorce, a new baby in the family, or death can be worked through effectively because of the relationship with the therapist. Moustakas felt the technique provides the child with an opportunity to work out temporarily disturbing feelings and so removes the possibility that these feelings will be repressed. If not dealt with, these feelings will distort reality and eventually even damage the child by creating free-floating anxiety.

Moustakas indicated that the therapist–child relationship can be a very enriching experience for the creative child.

The handicapped child was described by Moustakas (1953) as a child who must be worked with using all of the basic principles of child therapy. In addition, the process must be adjusted for the child's handicapping condition. The therapist must be flexible and willing to believe that the child is a whole person of immeasurable potential. The therapist cannot be beneficial if he does not perceive the child as whole in spite of the apparent physical handicap.

Axline (1947, 1948, 1949, 1950b, 1964, Axline and Rogers 1945) described the use of play therapy with a wide variety of children and referred to difficulties as well as to age. She reported working successfully with the retarded reader (Axline 1947, 1949), the handicapped child (Axline and Rogers 1945), the child with speech problems (Axline and Rogers 1945), the depressed child, the emotionally disturbed child (1964), the socially maladjusted child (1948, 1950b), and the retarded child (1949). Axline and Rogers (1945) reported the case of a child who had difficulty speaking due to a constriction in his throat (anxiety). The child's teacher acted both as a teacher and as a teacher-therapist. Axline concluded that it would be possible for a person to be both teacher and therapist to a child.

Landreth (1991) indicated that play therapy has been shown to be effective with children of all diagnostic categories except the completely autistic and the "out-of-control schizophrenic" (p. 42). Landreth described his work with a child who had cancer and subsequently died. Landreth (1988) states that working with children under situations of extreme stress can have strong impact on the therapists. Kottman and colleagues (1987) indicated that play therapy is very appropriate with children between the ages of 3 and 10, but it also is useful with preadolescent and early adolescent children, especially if play media are included in the playroom that would be helpful to those children. Kottman has stressed that play therapy is a viable vehicle for children who have difficulties within the family infrastructure. She uses play therapy to assist children to develop more accurate perceptions of their place in the family and to assist them to resolve the misperceptions that they have developed within the family constellation.

In the last fifteen years, there has been intense interest in working with children in play therapy settings. The body of literature has grown to the degree that it is impossible to summarize every article related to types of children seen in the playroom setting. A recent book published at the University of North Texas references types of children seen, approaches used, settings involved, and authors prominent in the field. *The World of Play Therapy Literature: Definitive Guide to Subjects and Authors in the Field* (Landreth et al. 1995) gives a current, thorough description of the types of maladies in children that have been shown to respond to the techniques of play therapy. A new text by Landreth and colleagues (1996) has provided a summary of the current literature. It is impossible in this book to summarize all the material that is now available; however, these two books provide that summary.

The following sections do not provide a comprehensive review of all of the articles in print about the way in which children with different presenting problems respond to play therapy. However, they are meant to provide readers with a sampling of the material that can be found to assist them with the children they see. For a comprehensive reference and summary of current material, please refer to Landreth's work.

CHILDREN WITH SPEECH PROBLEMS

Some articles have been written about the usefulness of play therapy in providing remedies for speech difficulties. The case of a 7-year-old child whose problem was a stuttering speech defect was presented by Reynert (1946). He reported that, as a result of nondirective play therapy, the child was able successfully to overcome the stuttering.

Dupent and others (1953) suggested child-centered therapy as a treatment method for delayed speech in which emotional disturbance was considered a causative factor. In a study that involved two therapists, the investigators conducted forty-one interviews over a year. The therapists' observations of the child indicated improvement in emotional adjustment and in intelligibility of speech. The improvement in the mechanics of speech occurred without speech instruction, because the child received no speech therapy. The authors suggested that the results reinforce the hypothesis that child-centered therapy can be an adequate treatment for some types of delayed speech. They further suggested that there was evidence of the potential value of further research.

Homefield (1959) investigated the effect of creative role playing as therapy for stuttering children. His basic hypothesis was that catharsis could result from a limited reexposure of the disturbed child to the types of emotional situations with which he had been unable to cope. The function of masks in this procedure was also studied. Eighteen stuttering boys of elementary school age were divided into three groups that met once weekly for hour-long role playing sessions. One group never used masks, the second group used masks during the first weeks only, and the last group wore masks during the second eight-week period.

As a test procedure, the children were shown pictures and were asked to tell what they thought was happening. The investigator established that the permissive atmosphere provided a situation in which creative role playing could provide catharsis. Homefield contended that most children speak more fluently during role playing than during their regular speech. This fluency is increased if the children play an authoritarian role or one in which they engage in bodily motions. Masks used in the initial stages of role playing accelerate the actor's ability to sublimate personal identity and to approximate the character of the role.

Sokoloff (1959) compared the gains in communicative skills resulting from group play therapy and individual speech therapy among a group of nonseverely dysarthric, speech-handicapped cerebral-palsied children. He concluded that group play therapy was more effective than individual speech therapy on the factors measured. Twenty-four children were divided into two groups. The experimental group received thirty one-hour sessions of group play therapy. The children in the control group received thirty one-hour sessions of group play therapy as well as thirty half-hour sessions of individual speech therapy. It was found that the children in play therapy made significantly more improvement than did the children in speech therapy in the areas of speech and communication, social development, and personality factors. Sokoloff concluded that play therapy aids the development of communicative skills without formal speech therapy.

CHILDREN WHO HAVE LEARNING DISABILITIES

Landreth and colleagues (1969) suggested the use of a team approach when working with the learning-disabled child. Much research indicates that certain biological conditions, neurological differences, developmental delays, speech and hearing defects, emotional problems, and reading difficulties frequently occur concomitantly.

The play therapy as described by Landreth and colleagues (1969) was nondirective. Within an atmosphere of acceptance and broad limits, children are allowed to use their most natural medium of communication, play. This allows them to express their feelings, both positive and negative, and explore new ways of reacting to themselves, to others, and to the environment. Children learn to be responsible for their feelings and their actions at home, in the playroom, and at school.

Siegel (1970) investigated the effectiveness of play therapy with other modalities in the treatment of children with learning disabilities. He used a variety of treatment experiences with a sample of children diagnosed as having learning disabilities. Primary intervention experiences such as a special class or tutoring were educational. Secondary intervention experience, such as play therapy, parent counseling, or a combination of play therapy and parent counseling, was psychotherapeutic. The hypotheses of the study were designed to examine the effectiveness of the primary and secondary intervention.

Forty-eight children in grades two to five were selected. It was found that children in the special classes improved more than did children who had tutoring. However, in comparing the effectiveness of the secondary intervention, it was found that the high levels of therapist-offered conditions provided to parents and children were the critical variables. Whether the therapy was directed toward the child, the parent, or the combination of child and parent, significant improvement on all three factors was found when this group was compared to a group who did not receive counseling.

CHILDREN WHO HAVE READING PROBLEMS

The case study method to describe the treatment of a reading problem through nondirective play therapy was used by Bixler (1945). Through a series of twenty interviews, the author succeeded in helping the child to overcome a reading problem by the use of nondirective play therapy technique. No reading instruction was given.

In articles on understanding and helping reading problems in children, Axline (1947, 1949) presented case studies of children of above average intelligence who had reading difficulties. Two of the children had reading problems and one substituted the fantasy world of reading for friends. Axline reported that, during therapy, it became apparent that the children's emotional problems contributed to their reading problems. Axline stressed that, if children are given the opportunity, they can help themselves. She indicated that the play therapy experience enhances children's chances for helping themselves.

In an article describing four alternative ways to help children learn to read when they are having difficulty, Mehus (1953) stressed that care must be taken so that no relapse occurs in the progress in reading. She contended that if children have failed using one method, then a different experience for remediation is required. She indicated that psychotherapy can be effective in preparing children to accept learning to read. Often when this stage is reached, the children have to acquire techniques of reading and, in order to do so, they have to return to the same unacceptable environment, thus generally regressing. Mehus proposed that, rather than preparing children to read through psychotherapy and then providing tutoring, an alternate plan would be to provide the two simultaneously by the same therapist.

According to Mehus, there are generally two types of children having reading difficulties. In one type, emotional difficulties have prevented the child from accepting reading, and in the other type of child the technical difficulties of reading have proven too much and the child has become emotionally involved so that the disturbed feelings are projected onto the inability to read.

Mehus suggested four approaches in working with these children, which include applying play therapy and allowing the school to teach the children on their own levels (providing the school individualizes to this degree), involving the use of play therapy in developing responsibility in the child, or having reading and therapy carried out simultaneously (the therapist providing both services). The fourth alternative would be to provide supportive therapy within the reading situation.

The effect of nondirective play therapy on maladjusted junior high school boys was investigated by Pumfery and Elliot (1970). The eight socially maladjusted boys were of average intelligence but were retarded in reading progress. Modifications in adjustment and reading attainment both at the end of therapy and on follow-up one year later were measured. A limited number of play therapy sessions did not produce a significant overall improvement in social adjustment. However, on a one-year follow-up, eleven of sixteen students in the experimental and control groups combined had improved in adjustment. There was no significant improvement in reading attainment in either group at the end of treatment.

Bills (1950a) reported a study designed to assess the relationship between personal adjustment and reading achievement. Using a group of eight poorly adjusted, 8- to 9-year-old retarded readers for his study, he designed the experiment so that each child was her own control by dividing the period of ninety school days into three blocks of thirty school days. This included four testing sessions. Reading tests were given six weeks before beginning therapy, immediately before therapy, immediately following therapy, and six weeks after therapy. The gains made on reading scores by the therapy group during the six weeks after therapy were significantly greater than during the initial control period. Bills concluded that significant changes in reading occurred.

In another article, Bills (1950b) described repeating the study using a group of well-adjusted readers. He hypothesized that therapy would not improve the reading ability of a group of children who exhibited adequate emotional adjustment. As a result of the findings in both studies, he suggested that the gains in reading achievement in the first study (involving poorly adjusted children with reading difficulty) were related to the children's improvement in personal adjustment. He further concluded that play therapy may be helpful to retarded readers who are emotionally disturbed but not necessary for all retarded readers.

In discussing the effectiveness of play therapy in helping poor readers, Axline (1947) reported a study of fifty second-graders listed as poor readers by their teachers. They were given a reading test, and the thirty-seven children who received the lowest scores were placed in a special class. The group consisted of eight girls and twenty-nine boys whose intelligence scores measured by the Stanford-Binet ranged from 80 to 140. These children had all of their schoolwork in one room with the same teacher. The reading problems were considered to be a part of the whole child. The children were given the opportunity for ample emotional expression, and their feelings and attitudes were accepted and clarified. No remedial reading instruction per se was given. At the end of the semester, three-and-one-half months later, intelligence and reading tests were administered. Axline reported that twenty-one children gained more than the maturationally expected 3.5 years in vocabulary. Four subjects are reported to have gained in reference to the intelligence score.

Winn (1959) investigated the influence of play therapy on personality change and the consequent effect on reading performance. The data were collected through the administration of pretests and posttests on twenty-six children. The children were randomly assigned to two groups of thirteen each, with the experimental group being given weekly individual play therapy for sixteen weeks.

Results indicated that the experimental group showed a significantly greater improvement in personality change than did the control group. However, the experimental group did not show significantly greater improvement in reading than did the no-therapy group. Possible explanations could be that personality change has little or no bearing on reading improvement. The author suggested that possibly the existence of reading skills in children has a bearing on the degree of reading improvement brought about by personality gains.

CHILDREN WHO ARE BLIND

Rothschild (1960) discussed his work in play therapy with blind children at the Service Bureau for Blind Children in Brooklyn, New York. The parents of these children were seen by social workers in a rather formal manner. He suggested that working with blind children in play therapy requires certain modifications in facilities and media. The range of materials that can be employed is reduced because many toys require vision for manipulation. Locomotion is often more difficult with impaired vision; the area of the playroom should be smaller.

The medium of play is not as natural a medium to the blind child as it is to the sighted child; therefore, the therapist must first spend time in an introductory phase before play. Peacefulness in play is essential in working with a child. Often, the blind child has not developed this peaceful feeling in playing with toys. This presents the therapist with the task of helping the child to overcome the inability to play and of further enabling her to solve problems in play in the context of her relationship with the therapist.

Rothschild suggested that the fully nondirective approach may not be the best approach for the blind child because of the nature of the physical handicap and the imposed limitations. A considerable amount of direction on the part of the therapist is indicated. The therapist has to establish herself as a helpful and kind companion in the child's world through interested participation in the child's play. The child gradually learns that this is a new and different relationship from any that has previously occurred.

Because a thorough understanding of the effects of blindness on the child is critical, much preparation on the part of the therapist is needed prior to beginning therapy with a blind child. Blindness continues to pose limitations and deprivations throughout the child's life. It affects the way in which the child perceives the environment and the way in which the environment reinforces the child. Release therapy is not appropriate for this type of child. The child needs support as she tests and experiments with her environment. She needs instruction in the development of skills and interpretation of her environment which allows her to gain insights into the world.

Raskin (1954) suggested that work with blind children in play therapy is basically the same as work with a sighted child. The therapist has to view children as persons with their own individual rights to development. The therapist gives children the right to express themselves and to grow in a unique way. It is the responsibility of the therapist, in as nondirective a way as possible, to allow children to experience and feel. The therapist is further responsible to children to limit actions that would interfere with their safety and the comfort of others. Children should be given the opportunity to find themselves and to grow on their own terms.

Jones (1952) described his experiences in working with blind children at the Perkins Institute for the Blind. He suggested that the study of play therapy in its adaptation to work with blind children is necessary. Evidence pointed to the fact that handicapped children are subjected to different parental attitudes (overprotection or rejection) much more frequently than are physically normal children.

CHILDREN WITH SEVERE EMOTIONAL DISTURBANCES

Nonspeaking children in play therapy were described by Jackson (1950). Two of the cases she described were of childhood schizophrenia. Jackson reported that at the end of the play therapy experiences the children were showing trends in a positive direction.

Jackson also described two cases of neurosis or severe behavior disorders, a 5-year-old child and a 4-year-old child. Jackson attributed her success to the intensive work done with the parents by a psychiatric social worker. Jackson did not indicate that the children were "cured" but that the condition was reversed. She suggested that the evaluation of the process could occur only as one watched the way these children dealt with the future tests of adolescent adaptation—choice of a career and of marriage—without a major breakdown.

Rosenzweig and Shakow (1937a) discussed the rationale for using the play technique for adult schizophrenia and psychosis. The justification was that the immaturity found in the schizophrenic is "childlike," in that behavior is characterized by egocentric and irresponsible behavior. The patient is dependent mainly on more mature adults. Because these patients tend to function more like children and have fewer verbal skills, the authors suggested that the use of play media would facilitate the process in work with them. The authors contended that the play lives depicted could be regarded as representations of the fantasy lives and as samples of their intellectual functions. The play could also be used diagnostically in order to find the level of construction at which the patient is working. The experience would provide catharsis and an opportunity for social reeducation because, in play, the entire world of social experience can be represented.

Rosenzweig and Shakow (1937b) reported a study in which they tested the applicability of the play technique to working with schizophrenic and psychotic adults. The researchers expected the results would involve a description of the form of construction rather than an interpretation of the content of material used. The method involved the use of a specially designed playroom, which was divided into three parts, including a table with toys, a table for construction, and a room for observation. A one-way mirror was used. The adult subjects consisted of ten paranoid schizophrenics, ten diagnosed as hebephrenic schizophrenic, and ten normal individuals.

The findings indicated that the schizophrenic patients responded favorably to the form of play technique used. Typically, different patterns were discernible for the three groups of subjects in respect to the general characteristics of their constructions. The researchers contended that individual cases yielded some material of psychiatric interest even in a single session. They indicated that this can be used productively, not only diagnostically but also therapeutically, with psychotic adults who exhibit childlike behavior.

CHILDREN WHO PRESENT WITH PSYCHOSOMATIC PROBLEMS

Miller and Baruch (1948) reported the use of play therapy with six children in order to treat the symptoms of allergy. The young children failed to respond to medical treatment and were selected for play therapy. Miller and Baruch reported, "As patients blocked the outflow of troubled feelings, allergic symptoms increased. As feelings were brought out, symptoms decreased. At least five of the six children showed improvement in therapy" (p. 14).

Jessner and colleagues (1951) cited case studies to support their theory that play therapy can be used effectively to treat children with asthma, ulcerative colitis, and other psychosomatic disturbances. The children treated were aged 5½. They had above average intelligence and were capable of verbalizing, although anxiety made verbalizing difficult for them. The authors suggested that play therapy was the treatment of choice.

CHILDREN WHO ARE RETARDED

Maisner (1950) theorized that there is a circular relationship between intellectual and emotional functions in the retarded child. The child is not only having difficulties in the three R's but is also having difficulty in an additional R, relationships with others. Maisner suggested that "underlying the motor or symptomatic manifestations of each of these inefficiencies is the child's inadequate perception of his physical or social world" (p. 263), and she contended that the play therapy experience can help these children "reorient their concepts of themselves in relation to the institutional community and the school in order that they might more effectively use the growth-producing resources at their disposal" (p. 237).

Maisner (1950) discussed an attempt made at a training school, which was labeled "Special Personality Reeducation Program." This program involved a psychologist who attempted "to establish close rapport with a given child and to help the child use this relationship in learning how to relate more effectively to the rest of his environment" (p. 238). This special intervention method is considered to be a "wedge" in that its aim is to get an "in" with the children and to reverse the vicious cycle of their negative responses. This enables the constructive cycle to begin so that the rest of the training at the school can be effective. As a part of this program play therapy was used in individual sessions. The sessions were conducted in a building set apart from the school in a room large enough to accommodate the movement of hyperactive children. Leland and Smith (1962) recommended the use of the unstructured play therapy experience with neurologically impaired, retarded children. They suggested that this was a positive therapeutic practice in that the needs of children with this syndrome fall in three primary areas: the need to establish a level of self, the need to establish impulse control, and the need to establish social interaction. The authors stress that the play therapy setting in which the therapist uses unstructured materials and loosely structured procedures gives the children with these types of problems an opportunity to meet those needs.

The unstructured nature of the materials teaches the children that they gain acceptance for using their imagination and creating play activities. This allows children more avenues for carrying this learning to their environment than does the limited, structured toy. Included in the therapeutic concepts is the process of conditioning, which is closely in line with the theory of the learning theorists.

Axline (1949) reported examining stenographic therapy protocols of fifteen 6- and 7-year-old children who were in play therapy because of behavior and speech problems. The children were seen in eight to twenty sessions. On the basis of the pre- and posttest therapy scores, the children were categorized into three groups: children who showed no significant change in intelligence scores after therapy, children who showed significant gains in intelligence scores after therapy, and children with average intelligence both before and after therapy.

Axline did not state the conclusions of her study explicitly, nor did she answer the question posed by her title, "Mental Deficiency, Symptom or Disease?" She did, however, point out that the retarded children who showed no gains in intelligence score did not complete their therapy, while those who gained in intelligence score did complete it. She did not claim that play therapy raised the intelligence of these children but rather that the emotional relief attained in therapy enabled them to express more adequately their true capacities. The children in group three, who had average intelligence before and after therapy, were included in the study to indicate that behavior problems stem more from emotional deficiency than from mental deficiency.

OLDER CHILDREN

Much material has been written about using the playroom and play materials with older children. Most authors suggest that adaptations should be made in the types of media used with the older child.

Ginott (1961a) suggested that different materials should be used for older children. He recommended painting, model building, woodwork, leatherwork, and similar activities for fearful and withdrawn older children. The pugnacious older child can effectively use a play therapy setting that allows for safe and respectable expression of aggression; otherwise, the child is likely to be very destructive. Ginott reported Slavson's recommendation that the older child be provided with media such as penny arcade machines, rifle galleries, table bowling, and boxing machines. He further recommended that an activity room be designed for the older child that includes machines, tables, and so on. This room should be five times the area of the furniture necessary for work.

Schiffer (1957) suggested that a room of about 600 square feet is optimal in size, and materials suggested are a rectangular table, 7 feet by 3 feet, an isolated table, 3 feet by 2 feet, a round table, a woodwork bench with two vises, a cabinet for supplies and unfinished projects, and a pegboard for tools. In addition, there should be hammers, nails, saws, clamps, files, planes (for woodwork), wooden mallets, and ashtray molds for metal work, tools for leather craft, and a typewriter and paper.

Schiffer (1957) further suggested that, in working with the older child in a school setting, special materials should be provided. He suggested woodworking tools and games designed for older children. He would also include the traditional toys recommended by the nondirective therapists.

Mendes and Maria (1966) described their work with a group of pre-adolescent girls in Lisbon. They saw play as a symbolic language and looked for free-floating communication through the play themes and conflicts having a manifest and latent content. The authors discussed the application of group analytic concepts to play therapy. They used permissiveness and support only as a means of uncovering unconscious and repressed content.

The girls seen in the play group consisted of a group of six who had behavior problems and school difficulties. The facilities consisted of a former kitchen that had been divided into two rooms. One room was furnished with adult furniture, a couch, chairs, and tables, and was attractively decorated. The other room was furnished as a playroom with toys and pre-school material. No structure was placed on the group as to where it would meet. For the first thirteen months, the girls used the playroom exclusively; then, gradually, they moved to the outer room and became a verbal group. During the period of transition, there was a good deal of movement between the rooms. The therapist followed the needs of the group as to the setting. While the group worked in the playroom, they acted much like younger children. They never verbalized situational problems. Play was characterized by sudden motor outbursts, fantasy play, and nonverbal expression of primitive impulses. The therapist began interpreting the play and indicated that the turning point into the meaningful material began at that time. Gradually, the girls moved to the "adult room" and began verbalizing their situational difficulties. The group became a talk group. At this point, more mature behavior was noted in the members in their interactions.

The dynamics and needs of latency-aged children are unique, according to Meeks (1970), who stressed that children in this stage of development like games that are organized in nature, competitive, realistic, and have definite roles. Children at this stage have a need to improve their skills and try to win. Meeks contrasted the latency period with the period that immediately precedes it, the oedipal. During the oedipal period, the play has as its aim granting children their wish to do as the adult they envy. The play of the oedipal period is fanciful, charming, and unrealistic. Meeks added that the games of checkers, chess, and cards offer excellent media for children in the latency period because they are trying to overcome the fantasy of the oedipal and move toward realism.

Often, the therapist will work with children in the latency period who have suffered such a loss of self-esteem at earlier stages of development that their behavior is compensatory. This is particularly evident with children who have experienced school failures. Children with a poor self-concept are so fearful of loss of self-esteem that, instead of competitively trying to win according to the rules, they practice cheating. Meeks stressed that this will occur after good rapport has been established. Children expose typical ways of handling other experiences in their lives. Every time such children have an opportunity to develop a new skill, they are so frightened of losing self-esteem that they bluff or cheat their way out, so that they can maintain the false stance of omnipotence. In this way, they continue to deny themselves the opportunity to develop skills and, thus, the ego strength that accompanies this skill. Meeks contended that it is important to allow full elaboration of the cheating before the therapist intervenes. If the therapist intervenes too early, children will stop because of superficial conformity, and the underlying fantasies and meaning will then be lost. The therapist's goal in the situation is to increase children's realistic awareness of their capacities and their limitations. In so doing, children can learn to assess realistically where their skills lie in a given area. From this knowledge, they will be able to move forward.

Loomis (1957) and Loomis and colleagues (1957) suggested that, for older children, the use of a checker game is an excellent way for them to play out and disclose their resistances. Hawkey (1951b) contended that the use of puppets is particularly valuable in working with older children who feel that playing with toys is babyish. Puppets allow children to express fantasy when they feel too old to engage in toy play, because older children can project their feelings onto the puppet and do not have to acknowledge them as their own.

A review of the literature about the types of children who will respond to play therapy would be limitless. Since 1975, the body of literature has exploded. Most of the material written about types of children seen is technical in nature. Very little research has been reported that supports the efficacy of one model over another.

2

The Parent(s)

Parental involvement is a necessary component of the total treatment plan when using play therapy. The age of a child who is seen in play therapy always dictates that they are a part of a larger system. This can be a traditional family unit or a nontraditional family unit. Included in this category can also be a foster home. Additionally, children are generally members of larger groups, such as schools or daycare centers. In some situations, the child is interacting with a larger unit of an institution such as a court or social services. For the purposes of this chapter, the issue of the relationship between the child, the therapist, and the traditional or nontraditional family unit will be addressed.

It is essential that the child therapist recognize that change within an individual does not occur in isolation. Individual change always has an interactive relationship with other components of the total system. When a treatment plan is developed, the therapist must be prepared for the interactive influence of the change in the child on the other parts of the system. Further, the therapist must be prepared to predict the positive or negative influences of the family members on the therapeutic process of the child. Family intervention becomes an integral part of the planned therapy with the child. The strategy chosen will depend on the needs of the child and family as well as the stage of development of the family. Additionally, the stage of development of the therapy of the child will also indicate what the family might potentially need. It is generally impossible to determine in advance what strategies for the family should be implemented. The critical issue is to assist the family to develop trust in the therapist and to enter the therapeutic milieu (from the beginning) with the empowerment that they (the family) are an integral part of the work with the child.

LEVELS OF PARENT INTERVENTION

As the therapist develops a plan of treatment to involve the parents and family it is important to recognize that certain levels of involvement will be more comfortable for many families. It is important to remember that the least threatening strategies are usually educative. The least threatening strategies also tend to be those that involve both parents, rather than putting the burden of the problem on one parent. The second level of intrusion into the safety zones of the family involves family therapy. The next level would be intervention that involves each parent and the child. The fourth level would be interventions that are individual in nature and designed for the parent, to work on personal integration. Frequently, parents are in such pain that they are not resistant to a treatment plan that recommends individual therapy for the parent. However, the fear or courage may not be immediately apparent. This is the reason the therapist must take time to understand the child and the family before making treatment plans and recommending them to the family.

EDUCATIVE INTERVENTIONS

One educative strategy frequently recommended to parents is that they enter into Parent Education Classes. One such system is referred to as Systematic Training for Effective Parenting (STEP), which is reported and described by Dinkmeyer and McKay (1989). Using this approach, parents are involved in planned educative sessions that are cognitive in nature and are designed so that systematic material is presented on parenting. Many parents will feel comfortable with this as a first step in family intervention.

Play therapists will often encourage parents to read materials about a particular set of symptoms in order to assist the parents to gain information and comfort about the problems they are having with their child. Many play therapists conduct parent group meetings that are mandatory for parents to attend.

Play therapists will be wise to request regular private sessions with the parents to deal with emotional issues that involve their feelings and worries about their child. This can begin at an educative, child management-focused level and then proceed to dealing with the emotions in the parents that surface when they are discussing their child and the implications of these problems with their child in their individual lives, in their marriage, and in their family. This type of therapy is considered to be mandatory and should be scheduled on a regular basis with both parents.

EMOTIONAL INTERVENTIONS

Another type of intervention that might be indicated would be marital therapy. It is more appropriate that this therapy be conducted by a person who is trained in marriage therapy than it is by the child's play therapist. If marital therapy is being conducted with this family, then it is critical that the play therapist not allow the parent sessions to be turned into marriage therapy. When this occurs, the play therapist can be drawn into a triad with the marriage partners, negating the ability to work with the child in a noncontaminated manner.

Frequently, the entire family will need to be engaged in family therapy. It is important that the family be referred to a family therapist. The play therapist remains the therapist for the child. Generally, as the child changes, the family will need a way in which to work through feelings in order to allow for these changes. At times, the child in therapy is the presenting symptom of a dysfunctional family. After play therapy, a child is able to function with more strength in such a family, but it is hard for such a tender little person to maintain a sense of self within the same pathological system. Once the family therapist suggests that change has occurred in the dynamics of the dysfunctional family, and the play therapist feels that the child is ready, then it is helpful for the family therapist, the play therapist, the family, and the child all to work together as a group. During such a session, the play therapist will be the voice or supporter of the child.

In many cases, after the play therapist has gained the trust of the parents, individual therapy for one or both of the parents is indicated and should be recommended. This therapy is not to be conducted by the play therapist.

One model for assisting the parents and the child to begin to work together so that the power of play therapy can be enhanced is filial therapy. Using this model, parents are supported both individually and through

group work. They are trained so that they will be able to engage in therapeutic play with their children. Used correctly and with insightful parents,
this will serve as a potent addition to the play therapy process. It is appropriate for the play therapist to teach this model to the parents of the child
patient when they are ready.

FILIAL THERAPY

Guerney (1964) and Guerney and colleagues (1966) described the development and implementation of the technique in parent work that they
label *filial therapy*. Andronico and colleagues (1967) further discussed the
relevance of the combination of didactic plus dynamic elements in the training of parents for filial therapy.

Guerney (1964) and Guerney and colleagues (1966) described filial
therapy as a new psychotherapeutic method that "extends specific Rogerian
approaches to the training of parents for treatment of their own young
emotionally disturbed children" (1966, p. 8). They based their assumptions
on the effectiveness of this treatment method on the facts that (1) the parent has more emotional significance to the child, (2) anxieties learned in
the presence of parents can be most effectively extinguished in the presence of parents, and (3) the parent can be actively involved with children
as they assess their original perceptions and, with the help of the parent,
make an accurate resynthesis of the original material. The parents can be
taught effective ways to deliver the services to their child and to grow in
the process as a consequence.

Another desirable consequence of filial therapy is that it makes for a
more efficient utilization of the professional therapist's time by extending
portions of his role to a nonprofessional. In addition, there remains less
chance that the parents will be threatened by the therapist–child relationship if they are actively involved and in fact are the deliverers of the service. The parents do not maintain guilt and hopelessness because they are
actively involved in the remediation of the difficulty. Finally, the parents
develop new behaviors at the same time as the child does. In this way, the
entire family dynamic structure is influenced with the same amount of the
therapist's time.

Andronico and colleagues (1967) describe the methods involved in
the training of parents for filial therapy. This process is defined as a "method
of teaching parents of emotionally disturbed children to relate empathically

to their children for prescribed periods of time" (p. 11). The goal of the play periods that eventually will be conducted at home is to enable "the child to work through his emotional problems via play in the therapeutic atmosphere of parental empathy" (p. 11). Didactic and dynamic elements are used in the education and training of the parents. Initially, the didactic method is employed. The parents meet for eight to ten weeks and are taught the techniques of play therapy based on the client-centered philosophy. The major principles stressed are:

1. The children should be completely free to determine the use they make of the time and materials.
2. The parent's major task is to empathize with the child, and to understand the intent of his actions and his thoughts and feelings.
3. The parent's next task is to communicate this understanding to the child by appropriate comments, if possible by verbalizing the child's experience to him.
4. The parent is instructed in the setting of limits.

In addition, the parents are given a format for evaluation of each of the sessions that they have with the child. During the initial weeks, the parents work with their own child or children of others in supervised play therapy sessions. Thus, the dynamic part of the training is introduced.

This combination of didactic and dynamic elements is a valuable way of working with parents. The parents' ability or inability to explore their own and others' feelings is generally critical to whether the treatment process succeeds or fails. The parents are given the opportunity to explore these capacities in themselves in a homogeneous group. Because it would be more comfortable for the parent to focus entirely on the subject matter of the home sessions, traditional therapy often fails. The group process gradually involves all of the parents at the feeling level, and thus many continue who otherwise might not.

Stover and Guerney (1967) used the concepts of Guerney (1964), Guerney and colleagues (1966), and Andronico and colleagues (1967) to evaluate the efficacy of training procedures for mothers in filial therapy. This research was designed to assess the feasibility of training mothers for the desired reflective, empathic role in conducting weekly half-hour sessions with their own children. It was hypothesized that the mothers in the trained group would increase their percentage of reflective statements and decrease their percentage of directive statements. Also included was an attempt to see whether or not the child's behavior would reflect such a change in role behavior even as early as the first few training sessions.

Structuring for mothers included asking the mothers to participate with their children in an observed, tape-recorded, half-hour play session in a playroom. They were asked to play with their children in any way they liked and to use the materials in any way they liked. On the basis of the diagnosis, the mothers were divided into three groups, two experimental groups and one control group.

Training for the two experimental groups began with a discussion of the benefits of the coming experiences for the children and the parents. These mothers observed demonstrations and were encouraged to model their own behavior after that of the group leader. They were encouraged to attempt specific techniques and to try to express empathy toward their children. The parents were provided with supervision as they worked with nonclinic children and then began working with their own children. They received feedback from other mothers and from the trainer. During these discussions, they had opportunities for discussing their feelings in relation to their children.

After four sessions, it was found that the children in the experimental group revealed significantly more verbal negative feelings than did the control group children. The trends that began to emerge showed a definite change in the mothers' behaviors. The investigators suggested that parents can learn to modify their pattern of interaction with their own emotionally disturbed children in the role behavior of client-centered therapist. In addition, it was noted that children quickly responded to the change in role in the parents.

In further research using filial therapy, Andronico and Blake (1971) investigated its effects with parents who have children with stuttering problems. They report that this method is more difficult for parents of stutterers to use because these parents tend to want to focus only on the problem. The parents were urged in this case to focus their attention on the total personality of their children rather than just on their stuttering. The investigators report that when the parents expanded their focus, the pressure was removed from the children and their stuttering pattern subsided.

Glass (1986) studied the effect of filial therapy on parental acceptance, self-esteem, parent–child relationship, and family environment. The sample consisted of fifteen parents and nine children who were in the filial therapy group and twelve parents and eleven children in the control group. The treatment included ten two-hour weekly parent training sessions. During these sessions the parents were taught the principles of client-centered play therapy and were instructed to conduct weekly half-hour play sessions at home with their own children. Based on her findings, she concluded that filial therapy does significantly increase parents' feelings of unconditional love for their children, and that filial therapy does significantly increase the parents' perception of expressed conflict in their families.

THERAPLAY

Theraplay was developed as a way to provide intense, brief relationship therapy between a mother and child when attachment and bonding have been disturbed. Within this therapy, which has been developed and described by Jernberg (1979), Jernberg and colleagues (1987), and Jernberg and Jernberg (1993), the therapists become directly involved in the relationship between the mother and the child. One or two therapists are directly involved with the child while one therapist serves as an interpreter to the parent(s). During the first four sessions, the parents are observers and are assisted by an interpreter. During the second set of four sessions, the parents begin to interact with their child in the theraplay space.

Most of the major theorists in the area of child therapy have included their views on the importance of working with the parents as they work with the children. The orientations range from suggestions that children should not be seen in play therapy unless the parents are involved in therapy to suggestions that it is beneficial but not necessary to see the parents. However, with few exceptions, both past and current therapists report that understanding the family and including the parents as a part of the therapy process are feasible when children are in play therapy treatment.

Parental involvement should be considered a positive augmentation to the treatment of the child. However, there are exceptions to this statement. When it is determined that it is in the best treatment interest of the child, then it is beneficial that this involvement be planned so as to provide optimum assistance for the specific child in treatment.

Direction for determining the appropriate treatment plan for a child, in which the needs of the parents and the family will also be considered, is often provided through the initial history-taking session with the parents. However, because the presenting symptoms are usually not central to the real emotional problems of the child, often many sessions have passed before a proper assessment of correct parental involvement can be made. An example of this is the case of a young girl whose mother said that the child was angry because her father was married to another woman. As the case unfolded, it became apparent that the child *was* angry at her father, as well as anxious that her father would abandon her in the same way that the father had abandoned the mother. In this situation it was not a simple matter of involving the father so that he could learn more appropriate and meaningful ways to communicate his love for his daughter. In order to manage the case suitably, the mother was advised to seek therapy in order to work through her own anger, grief, and feelings of abandonment regarding her past relationship with the girl's father. The father was advised to seek therapy so that he also could work through his issues that led to the divorce of his wife, so that he could approach his daughter with increased integrity. Only when both of these parents had worked on individual issues could they be trusted to assist their daughter with her pain.

Using the concept that children come into therapy with recognizable issues that point to specific categories, it is possible to develop plans that involve parents based on those categories. There are exceptions to all rules, but the guidelines proposed by this model will be described within this general frame of reference.

PRESCRIPTIVE PARENT WORK, BASED ON ISSUES IN CHILD AND FAMILY ATTACHMENT

When children present for therapy who have experienced problems at the primary attachment level, it is critical to explore the issues in the mother at the time of the birth and during the early months between mother and child. There may be multiple reasons why early attachment does not occur. These may include the mother's sense of well-being at the birth, her health during that time, and stressors beyond her control. However, the basis for the lack of attachment may be residual integrative issues within the mother. When the problems of attachment center on illness in the mother or a temporary disruption in her functioning due to situational transitory issues, the mother can be quickly assisted through individual or group therapy to gain insight about what happened early on in the relationship. After this insight occurs and the mother forgives herself for the early problems, then she can be engaged in learning experiences that will allow her and the child to develop an enriched relationship. This will then accelerate the course of therapy.

Should the cause of the attachment problems center on the emotional deprivation or disturbance of the mother during the formative weeks and months of the infant, and should it be determined that the problems within the mother continue, then the mother will need to be assisted in entirely different ways. An appropriate course of action would be to insist that the mother start to work in individual psychotherapy. Later, a parent training model can be employed that involves the mother's being a member of a mother's group or learning filial therapy techniques and then being supervised by a family therapist while these techniques are practiced. However, to put such a mother into a filial training program without her developing personal insight could prove a disaster for the child.

There are a number of clues that a therapist can observe when working with a mother who lacks attunement to her child's needs. When such a mother is exposed to an actual play therapy session involving her child, the therapist is able to watch for the "clangs" we hear in therapy that alert us to a problem. For example, I had one mother say, "I didn't realize that my child was so little." Another one said, "He never is that nice to me." Another one laughed and pointed when her son picked up a baby doll and held it, saying, "His daddy had better not see him do that." Frequently this type of problem will present when the mother reports expectations that are far in advance of the child's chronological age, such as that her 2-year-old son will not clean up his toys. Another clue that the primary relationship continues to be convoluted is when the child cries out to the therapist, to the mother, and to the world that she is emotionally starving. Clinging, whining, and demanding behaviors are often the child's way of saying, "Please validate me, tell me that I exist." Play therapy can certainly assist this little one, but the primary caregiver must grow in order that the child ultimately survive and become a well-developed person.

MANAGEMENT PROBLEMS

When children enter therapy because of the inappropriate management they have received within the family unit and extended family, a careful family assessment has to be made. It is recommended that the therapist meet with the family along with the young child at the outset of therapy. During this time, the therapist can observe the family in action and note how they treat the child. It is critical to determine the roles the family members assume before engaging the different members in a therapy plan that directly involves the child. These families generally benefit from family therapy, filial therapy, or parent education programs. Once progress is made in these settings, then the family therapist can begin to include the child in the family sessions.

If it is determined that a family member is a "silent conspirator" in negating the treatment of the child because of their own pathologies, then immediate intervention is warranted. It is critical that this person be involved in an individual psychotherapy program, or else this pathology has to be contained through family therapy intervention. If this does not occur, then the child will remain at risk of being used by the pathological member with the hidden agenda. To involve such an individual in the direct treatment of the child will only serve to provide the manipulator with an "educated costume" for doing harm.

MEDICAL ISSUES

When a child enters therapy because of a severe illness or handicap, it is generally helpful if the parents become actively involved in the treatment through filial therapy. Before engaging the parents in such a process, two things have to be explored. First, the therapist and parents must explore the level at which the parents have worked through their own pain and fear about the illness. If they are stuck in any of the grief stages (denial, guilt, anger, bargaining, blaming, or apathy) then they will need to resolve these issues through individual psychotherapy or family therapy. Second, the therapist and the parents must determine realistically how drained the parents feel because of the needs of the ill or handicapped child. If they are exhausted from the medical interventions and the physical demands of the illness or handicap, then they may not be psychologically able to also add filial therapy to their daily regimen. The therapist must be sensitive to the needs of the parents at this time. There is a possibility that another family member (such as a grandparent) can be engaged initially to assist with the filial therapy.

When a child is brought to therapy because of a recent traumatic event, then care must be taken to determine whether the parent(s) have also been traumatized. Frequently, the trauma that happened to the child also happened to the family. The child is brought to therapy because the parents may be containing their own anxiety by taking care of the child. In one case, the family home was struck by lightning, burned to the ground, and the family narrowly escaped with their lives. The parents brought in their oldest daughter for treatment. She was openly showing her pain through crying and being fearful in various situations. However, a family assessment showed that the father was leaving his workplace daily because "he was worried about his daughter." The mother had a car accident because of "her worries about her daughter," but she later said that she had been watching an approaching storm. It is clear in this case that these parents were not ready to assist in the cure. A family in this situation may benefit from family therapy. Since their pain is shared, they may be able to use mutual strength for mutual growth. This is typically more logical than individual psychotherapy for each of the adults.

OTHER MODELS FOR WORKING WITH PARENTS FOUND IN THE LITERATURE

The following section is a brief review of the literature about the way in which many therapists work with parents. The review contains both beliefs about the way in which this should be done and also some research. This summary is not comprehensive and does not describe all the existing literature, which is now almost impossible to summarize in one book. The following is meant to be a small sampling of positions on this subject.

Anna Freud (1951) involved the parents of the children she saw from the very beginning. She obtained an intensive, detailed case history of the child from the parents. In her earlier statements about parents, Anna Freud wrote that children should not be seen unless their parents have been in analysis or are in analysis. However, she later added a fourth stage in the therapeutic process, which includes counseling with parents in preparing them for the changes in the child and in educative procedures. This would help them to be healthy enough to handle the child without contributing further to the neurosis. She indicated that something must be done to "change" the outlook of the parents because it is dangerous to turn the responsibility for the newly liberated "instinctual life" over to them. There is a great risk that the child will be forced to use repression and thus neurosis again, as it was with these same parents in the same way the original neurosis started. Anna Freud (1951) indicates that in situations where the parents did not have personalities with analytical understanding, it would be more economical to omit the analysis of the child.

Miller (1986) studied the effects of parent participation in a nine-week systematic training for effective parenting (STEP) program on the outcome of individual play therapy. Thirty-two children between the ages of 4 and 8 and their families were assigned to one of three subject groups. Twelve families were assigned to a treatment group providing STEP for the parents and eight sessions for the individual, nondirective play therapy for the children. A second twelve subjects were involved only in the play therapy component. A third group of ten were wait-listed for both the STEP and play therapy, and served as the control group. No statistically significant differences were found. However, the author did indicate that nonstatistical trends of increased parent confidence in the parent training program group were reported, along with fewer problem behaviors in the children.

Working with a combination of the parents and child in the therapeutic process was recommended by Solomon (1948). He emphasized the importance of working with parents whenever possible, especially as it is reflected in the handling of the child. The problem in the very young child often dissipates when the parents develop benevolent attitudes. Even the older child will change when parental attitudes alter. However, there is a stage in the development of the child when a fairly fixed pattern of disturbed thought develops and when simply working with the parents will not affect the child enough to cause the needed change.

In this situation, the therapy is focused on the child. It is not always the relationship between the parent and the therapist that causes change in the parents. When the parents take the step of calling for help, they begin to assess themselves because they realize that they may be "objects of discussion between the child and the doctor" (Solomon 1948, p. 402). Solomon (1940, 1955) stated that parents can be sources of valuable information in that they can give the therapist another view of the activities of the home.

Conn (1941a,b, 1952) worked with both the parents and the child. The child accepts the parent–physician–patient relationship as a natural process. The parents were usually seen just before the child was seen. The parents were given the opportunity to tell their side of the story and were praised for doing their best to assist the child. The parents can be invited into the playroom while the child reviews what has been learned. From the first, the child is commended for expressing feelings, both loving and hostile, in reference to parents and siblings.

The importance of involving the parents so that they will be able to assist in the treatment process was stressed by Hambridge (1955). Parents are informed of the expected increase in the aggressiveness of children as a result of treatment. The family is told to maintain the usual restraints at home. The therapist's task is to pace the treatment so that the parents' ability to handle children at home is not overtaxed. Hambridge (1955) said that this influences the direction of the work with the children, the intensity of the work, and further aids in the diagnosis of the individual child.

The importance of parental involvement was also stressed by Allen (1942). The mother and the child come to the child guidance center together, and both are counseled at the same time. This is beneficial because they are together, yet differentiated. This is a start in the growth process of the child. The child is seen by the play therapist while a caseworker sees the mother.

Therapy might move faster if the parents were involved in counseling or therapy themselves, according to Axline (1947). But, she added, "It is not necessary for the adults to be helped in order to insure successful play-therapy results" (p. 68). Children see their environment in a different way, and as they relate to it in a different way the environment will relate to them differently. The circular pattern becomes positive, they are accepted more, and they respond positively. This causes more acceptance by others. Axline points out, however, that in the case of handicapped children, the parents should be more directly involved. These parents have trouble in accepting the handicapped child, especially in the case of mental retardation. The parents have to work through their own feelings of guilt and inadequacy before they are able to change their perceptions of the child.

In another article, Axline (1955a) discussed the value of group therapy as a means of self-discovery for parents and children. Often, the therapist is too forceful in his own philosophy and in his own value judgments. The use of groups in working with a family has many advantages, one of which is that self-disclosure within the family group offers an opportunity to experience self in many different ways within the family, as the family has often lost its individual family identity.

Therapists need to be alert to factors that usurp the intelligence of a family group and destroy independent thoughts and actions within the family. Such usurpation obstructs the development of the family's own moral values. Conformity that suffocates self-discovery is thrust on them when the unit is broken down and each member is treated individually by the therapist. The group offers the opportunity for the family to have a choice of participation and a system of checks and balances in the face of a strong therapist. Within the group, both parent and child can be involved in the constructive relationship. This occurs when the group has built-in checks for errors in interpretation and perception of actions by the different family members.

Axline suggested putting the child and the parents all in the playroom setting because it allows the child a known medium of expression. It further allows the child to begin talking to the family in a comfortable setting.

Fuchs (1957), the daughter of Carl Rogers, described a problem that she was having with her young daughter regarding proper bowel elimination. She wrote her father for suggestions in working with the child, and he suggested a play therapy treatment at home by the mother. Rogers advised her to read Axline's book on play therapy and then to get furniture, dolls (which represented family members), a toilet, potty chair, clay, and toilet paper. By providing the child with media, and by accepting and reflecting the child's fears, she would be able to help the child overcome the difficulty. It becomes a learning experience for a mother when she begins to watch her child's play and learns to listen to what her child is saying. Not only is the mother able to assist the child in problem solving, she is also able to develop observational skills for herself. Carl Rogers (1957) described in part the technique that would be included in filial therapy.

Moustakas (1959b) indicated that the best results can be obtained if the therapist works with the parents as well as with the child. He did not indicate who should see the parents, only that "someone" should see them. The alleviation of children's psychological tensions, the resolution of their problems, and their self-perception as worthwhile individuals are goals that are achieved more completely when the parents participate in the experience.

Moustakas and Makowsky (1952) presented two cases from their clinical records to demonstrate their work with parents. They suggested that one problem in working with the parents is that often the parents do not see the problem as a reflection of their own conflict and confusion. They are intellectual about the problem, or have it poorly defined in a vague way. They like to see the problem as belonging only to the child, and they come to the counselor for authoritative advice on how to handle the child. Often, when they do not get direct advice, they terminate the contract. One way to work with the difficult parent is to first focus on the presented problem and, then gradually move to the real problem. These authors stress that, in all cases, the client-centered philosophy should be used. However, in situations where parents feel that they need advice, the therapist should attempt to satisfy them to some degree and, at the same time, lead the family back to their feelings during the therapy hour.

Ginott (1957a) described differential treatment using groups. He identified the four types of groups as guidance, counseling, psychotherapy, and psychoanalysis. He suggested that the aim of any type of group is to effect change. Each of the assigned groups is the method of choice for specific persons. Group guidance is a method of choice for parents who are without serious personal disturbances yet have difficulty in getting along with their children. The group guidance experience gives the parents an opportunity to go over their troubled feelings with sympathetic group members who are "in the same boat." Pent-up emotions and guilt-charged conflicts are diminished by ventilation, while ego strength is enhanced by satisfying relationships with the leader and the other parents. This emotional relief is designed to free parents to face problems, and opens them to accepting guidance.

The basic technique generally involves a group of eight to ten parents. Sometimes it involves both parents, but it generally involves only mothers. Two basic types of composition are used, heterogeneous and homogeneous. The homogeneous group involves parents who have children of like ages or similar difficulties. The heterogeneous group involves parents with children of varying ages and difficulties. The groups are problem-centered and child-centered. The mothers learn to be aware of the effects of their own attitudes and behavior on the behavior of the children. They begin to see that the children are reacting individuals with rights, feelings, and cravings, and they are helped to realize that the problem lies in the relationship between the parent and the child, and not just in the child.

The way in which a child guidance clinic began a new service of group screening, which was necessitated by the tremendous number of persons seeking service, was described by Ginott (1956). The aim of the group screening was to render immediate initial service to those who called the clinic for help. The method used was to schedule the parent who called for help into a group. The parents sat in a small group with a leader and gave their complaints. Based on the difficulties presented and the recommendation of the group leader, a decision was made whether the child should come individually, the parents should come individually, or the parents and child should both be seen. According to Ginott (1956), the group screening allows applicants to be seen quickly and economically while they are feeling the urgency of assisting their child. When they come to the group interview, the parents have an opportunity to become acquainted with the clinic and the staff in advance of a formal session. Frequently, this helps the parents to become more comfortable sooner, which allows them to experience increased productivity early in therapy. Ginott wrote that once parents came to the group screening, they were less likely to cancel their first appointment. The parents saw that they were not so alone with their problems in that they had the opportunity to meet other parents who were requesting help from the clinic.

Ginott (1957b) described a measure used at the child guidance clinic as an attempt to combat the increased lag between request for services and the delivery of those services. Group screening and parent education groups were developed. Parent education groups differ from group psychotherapy in that group therapy is aimed at bringing permanent changes in the intrapsychic balance of selected patients grouped for the therapeutic effect that they have on each other. Parent education groups were designed to improve the everyday functioning of parents in relation to their children. The parents are helped to a better understanding of the dynamics of parent–child relations and of the basic facts of child growth and needs. This is done by "sensitizing parents to the needs of children, increasing their awareness of the role of feelings in human life, and promoting understanding of the latent meanings of children's activities, play, and verbal expression" (p. 83).

The parent education groups were composed of twenty to twenty-five mothers who meet for ninety-minute weekly sessions for a period of ten weeks. The groups were generally homogeneous—mothers of children of like ages and similar problems were grouped together. The first meeting generally consisted of all of the mothers telling their problems. After all parents told their problems, they were asked to tell their remedy or those remedies that they thought might work. The group was then asked to attempt to form reasons why they thought these measures failed. At this point, the members of the staff refused to give answers or to relieve the anxiety that mounted in the group. The skilled leader functioned mainly in a nondirective way.

Gradually, as a result of the interaction, the mothers began to acknowledge that children have feelings just as adults do, that these feelings are both positive and negative, and that the expression and acceptance of feelings are more healthful and more helpful than their rejection and denial. The mothers began to grasp the value of noncritical empathic mirroring of feelings. "Therapeutic understanding and reflection of feelings cannot be taught but it can be 'caught' by individuals who experience them" (Ginott 1957b, p. 85). Ginott concluded that the most significant effect of the group was the reported decrease in tensions and greater harmony between the mothers and their immediate families.

A study designed to determine why people fail to carry out plans for treatment after having gone to the trouble of contacting the agency was conducted by Ginott and others (1959). Because of the tremendous demand for clinical services, it is expedient that there be a way that nonattenders can be identified. In the Duval County Child Guidance Clinic, it was noted that at least one-third of the applicants did not arrive for their initial appointment in the group screening, and, in addition, a considerable number of parents attending the screening procedure did not continue. The purpose of the study was to answer the following questions:

1. What accounts for nonattendance after an appointment is accepted by the parents? More specifically, do negative feelings toward a group meeting account for nonattendance at the initial interview?
2. What accounts for the failure of some parents to carry out the next step in the intake procedure, namely returning the completed medical form? More specifically, does the initial attendance in a group setting arouse negative feelings in the parents so that they fail to continue contact with the clinic?

The method of the study involved contacting the two hundred parents who had failed to keep their initial group appointments and the one hundred parents who had attended a screening group but did not follow up on their commitments. The reasons given by parents as to why they did not attend the initial interview included transportation problems, a change in the parents' concerns about the problem, forgetting the appointment, and receiving help from other sources. The reasons for failing to return the medical forms included: they were less concerned about the problem; they had transportation problems; and, they received assistance through other avenues.

Jackson (1950) described her work through the case study method with nine children who successfully responded to treatment. She attributed much of the success, however, to the work done with parents by a psychiatric social worker. Jackson suggested that the mother of a severely disturbed child needs to exercise special skill and tact in assisting her child to socialize. This socialization will allow the child to make a better adjustment within the culture at large. Often, the mothers of such children lack this skill, knowledge, and intuition. They need warmth and support as they develop them. The mother has to be educated in awareness of the special difficulties that children with unstable heredity may encounter in early years. The treatment and support of the parents help to prepare them for the future difficulties that are likely to arise in the lives of these children.

Rothschild (1960) suggested that, in providing the play therapy experience for the blind child, work with the parents is critical. In the case of blind children, the need for "disentanglement" between the mother and child is of primary importance if the child is to learn to feel and function in his own right. Therapy with the child has to include changes in the relationship between mother and child before changes in the child can occur. This is possible often only through the simultaneous therapy of both mother and child.

The use of a playroom setting for diagnostic family interviews in which play therapy and family interviewing techniques are incorporated was described by Orgun (1973). By using this method, the diagnostic team can accumulate valuable diagnostic data on the family while causing the least discomfort and stress to the child by using the playroom and play materials. After having used this technique, Orgun suggests that it can be a useful procedure in family therapy when working with young children.

According to Gerard (1948), the purpose of therapy with children is to correct the patterns resulting from previous trauma or parental mishandling or to provide a release of energy from repression. Treatment can be carried on entirely through the medium of guiding the parents in the application of healthy training methods or in the treatment of the mother's neurosis. The neurosis of the child is closely related to the neurosis of the parent. The parent cannot make good use of the learning experience unless her own neurosis is resolved. However, if the pattern of behavior is fixed in the child, the therapist should work with the child.

In an article describing therapeutic effects of a play group for preschool children, Burlingham (1938) stated that parents should be worked with closely. Parental work is necessary in understanding the needs of children. Leland and Smith (1962, 1965) saw working with parents of handicapped children as a necessary part of the process for the children. Handicapped children have particular difficulties in self-perception, while their parents have particular difficulties in self-acceptance.

In Cameron's (1940) view, parental guidance should be a part of the total process of child therapy. Because the child's problem is often the consequence of a disturbed parent–child relationship, both parties must be involved in the process if effective change is to occur. The mother (according to Cameron), because of her own neurosis, often tends to relive her own traumatic childhood through her child. If, however, the mother is truly interested in her child, willing to look at herself, and willing to accept her own role in the parent–child struggle, she will be able to allow her child to grow as a result of the therapy. Some mothers resent the attention given to the child in therapy and will become a deterrent to the growth process. This constitutes one of the major reasons that the parent should be involved in the process. When parents are involved, they themselves will begin to take pride in the work and feel themselves to be a part of it. Cameron believes that these services to parents should be delivered by a psychiatric social worker who is a member of the clinic staff.

Withall and Reddenhouse (1955) claimed that no therapy can be really effective for a child if any members of the family are not involved. And Katz (1965) stressed that, in working with emotionally disturbed children, parental education and guidance are more important than individual psychotherapy with the child.

Pechy (1955) discussed work done at the Meyrick Bennett Children's Medical Centre in Durban, England, with mothers and children. He wrote that, in examining the cases treated there, the staff concluded that success with the young child in therapy seemed to depend not on catharsis nor abreaction but on lasting changes in the familial relationships. These changes tended to occur as a result of two factors: (1) freeing of the growth process in the child through a permissive, accepting relationship with the play therapist, and (2) application of the insight into the needs of the child and his problems gained by the parents. As this involved the treatment of the parent and the child separately, it posed difficulties that could be avoided. One of the difficulties was that a common experience of the child was not available for both therapist and parent. It was difficult for the therapist to understand the home dynamics and for the parent to make good use of the insights gained by the therapist.

The major theory of the staff was that maladjustment was the consequence of blocks and obstacles, more or less internalized, to the natural development of the child. They proposed that these blocks had arisen from disturbances in the relationship between parent and child. Therapy had as its goal the removal of these disturbances by freeing the child through play therapy and in addition the development of parental insight through increased awareness of the relationship between the parent and child. Using these concepts, the staff developed a technique where the parent, usually the mother, and the child were observed together, and the parent was trained in working with the child.

During the first part of the treatment, the mother was seen alone. The therapist functioned as an objective, sympathetic worker. The mother was initially given time to express feelings, fears, and attitudes. Later, she developed a sense of responsibility for the process. The mothers generally went through the same stages. The first part of the time was generally spent on a concentration of the symptoms and a search for nonpersonal causes. Gradually, the mothers tended to move toward the expression of guilt feelings and acceptance of a personal responsibility for the difficulties. Finally, they began to show signs of interest and eagerness to search for the disturbing factors in the relationship.

When the mother reached a stage of rapport and active participation, she was put with the child, who had been undergoing a series of diagnostic tests with another therapist. The child and the mother were observed through a one-way mirror during all of the sessions. The mother was instructed to allow the child to play any way she wanted her child to, just as she would play with her child at home. After each thirty-minute session, the therapist worked with the mother in helping her to understand the dynamics of her encounters with the child.

Basing his conclusions on numerous case studies, Pechy suggested that this method allows the therapist to view the parent–child relationship directly, placing the responsibility where it belongs (with the parent). It deals directly with this relationship and allows the parent to be involved actively in remaking the relationship.

Marshall and Hann (1965) reported an experiment designed to determine a cause of correlations between parent and child behaviors obtained earlier by Marshall. Twelve matched triads of preschool children were trained in doll play fantasy, in the use of toys, or were given no training. Frequency of dramatic play before and during training were the dependent variables. The results indicated that if an adult engages in fantasy play with a child, enacting topics commonly used in children's dramatic play with peers, the child will increase the frequency of his dramatic play with peers. Training in dramatic play was the critical factor.

The influence of the mother's presence on children's doll play aggression was observed by Levin and Turgeon (1957). Twenty children were observed in two sessions of doll play. The first session involved the child and an experimenter. During the second session, the child's mother was an audience for one group, and an adult female, not previously known to the child, watched the sessions of the second group. Each of the ten children observed by their mothers was more aggressive in the second than in the first session. Eight of the ten children watched by a stranger decreased their aggressions in the second session. The findings were discussed in terms of modifications of the displacement theory of aggression.

In a study designed to evaluate the effectiveness of play therapy, Schiffer (1967) included in his design two groups whose parents were involved in parent group therapy and one group whose parents were not. He reported no significant difference between the progress of the children whose parents were involved and those whose parents were not.

An investigation on the effects of high levels of therapist-offered conditions on parents and children was conducted by Siegel (1972). Whether the therapy was directed toward the child, the parent, or both parent and child, the conditions of therapy were the critical variables, not whether parents or parents and children were involved.

Dorfman (1958) assessed the outcomes of client-centered play therapy. She found that therapy improvements occur without parent counseling despite the emotional dependence of children on parents.

Baker (1971) found that when parents are provided with high-quality counseling, or when parent counseling and play therapy are combined, both become an effective method of treating learning disabilities in children. Forty-eight students were divided into two groups of twenty-four each. For one group of twenty-four students, there were two special classes of twelve each that involved reading and other learning instruction. The other students in the study received tutoring. These two groups were further divided to determine the effectiveness of counseling on academic and other performances of the students. As a result of the treatment methods, Baker concluded that high-level therapy was instrumental in causing a change in the parent–child relationship to a greater extent than either the tutoring or special class situation alone. The counseling of the parent, play therapy with the child, or a combination of the two proved to be a valuable treatment as an adjunct to the services of either the special class or the tutoring.

Prestwich (1969) described a study investigating the influence of two counseling methods on the physical and verbal aggression of preschool American Indian children. The purposes of this study were (1) to investigate the influence of anthropomorphic models as a therapeutic vehicle to help 5-year-old Indian children handle appropriately, and thereby decrease, physical and verbal aggression, and (2) to investigate the influence of group counseling with Indian mothers on aggression in their preschool children.

Subjects in the eight-week study included thirty children randomly assigned to three groups. In group one, children were placed in a controlled environment with human-featured life-sized dolls. Mothers of group two met for ninety minutes weekly to see films and participate in group discussion and counseling sessions. The counseling model used was perceptual modification through verbal reinforcement. Group three was the control group. Pre- and posttest observations and ratings were made for the subjects on an experimenter-designed instrument that measured quantitative aggression responses. Study results revealed no significant differences in physical, verbal, or total aggression between experimental and control groups before or after treatment. Indian mothers significantly increased verbal output during treatment, but results indicated that this change bore no relationship to children's aggressive behavior at preschool.

The importance of parent treatment to the successful outcome of therapy with children was studied by Levi (1961). It was hypothesized that the successful outcome of children's therapy is related to the concurrent treatment of their parents. The sample consisted of 314 cases. It was found that there is no relationship between parent treatment and outcome of the child's therapy. The data suggest that the most important factor in the outcome of a child's therapy may be the identity of his therapist. Length of treatment was also found to be a factor. While the superior therapist achieved as much success with his briefly treated cases as with cases that remained for a longer time, the other therapists achieved much better results with cases who remained for relatively long periods.

In summary, working with parents has been shown to be a strong enhancer of the treatment modality when planning for play therapy with children. The power of this work must be considered by the therapist. It should be planned for diagnostically and implemented based on empirical data and therapeutic clinical knowledge.

3

The Therapist

The "personhood" of the therapist has been discussed throughout the literature. It is generally agreed that the knowledge and emotional insight of the therapist has significant impact on the growth and development of the child. Relationship therapists would tend to describe the growth in the therapist and child as being interactive. Carkhuff (1973) and Landreth (Landreth 1991, Landreth et al. 1996) have shown that certain statements made by therapists in the playroom tend to have a more potent effect than other statements about process. Because of the magnitude of research that has been done on therapist variables in the last ten years, it would be impossible to describe all the components of personal attributes that a therapist should maintain.

CREDENTIALS

Models for training will not be presented here. However, it is critical to note that play therapists should demonstrate credentials and training in their field of study. For example, a child psychiatrist would have training in medicine, psychiatry, child psychiatry, and training specific to the technique of play therapy. A social worker would have training in social work, therapeutic interventions in social work, training in child therapy, and training specific to the technique of play therapy. A psychologist would have appropriate degrees in the field of psychology, appropriate internships, both pre- and postdoctoral supervision in child therapy, and in addition, specific training in the technique of play therapy. Licensed professional counselors have masters level and doctoral level training with appropriate internships and supervision, along with specific training in the field of play therapy. Registered nurses would have appropriate training in nursing and, in addition, training in the field of counseling that includes specific training in the model of play therapy.

The designation of registered play therapist (RPT) has been assigned to those persons who have had the training, supervision, and experience necessary to qualify them for membership at that level in the Association for Play Therapy. There are many persons providing services through the play therapy model who have chosen not to enroll and follow the guidelines for membership in the Association for Play Therapy at this time. When a family is seeking support for their child, it will be increasingly more important that the person they seek to help their child have credentials in this field. The Association for Play Therapy regularly publishes a journal, *The International Journal of Play Therapy.* This organization also sets forth the credentialing process for registered play therapists and lists persons who are active in the field of play therapy in this country (Association for Play Therapy 1996–1997). The theoretical orientation of the therapist dictates the nature and type of experiences that the therapist should have before they enter the play therapy room with the child. For example, the analyst has a highly structured approach in training that involves personal analysis before entering the field, which continues while the therapist is an active analyst. Jungian analysts have had years of experience, both in their own personal analysis and through ongoing supervision while they are engaging in the practice of play therapy.

Therapists maintain qualities of professional excellence in whatever setting they choose. They assume all the responsibilities of a therapist, both inside and outside of the play therapy room. The intense process of play therapy must be treated with reverence and dedication on the part of professionals who engage in such practice. They have an obligation to seek their own personal therapy on a regular basis so that they are able to clearly define which issues are their own and which issues belong to the child. In the absence of this, we must recognize that some of the work that is done in a playroom could be labeled as "junk." In working with a child in a play therapy setting, a therapist assumes grave responsibilities. Play therapy is not simply a technique, but is a planned intervention, developed and implemented by an enlightened, educated, responsible professional. The magnitude of the responsibility for the credentialing process in this field must include intensive scrutiny of the background and training of individuals and also the dedication that they evidence through their own personal therapy. There have been some studies that have attempted to determine whether or not the gender, age, or theoretical orientation of the therapist influences the process of play therapy. The issues seem to boil down to the personal insight of the therapists, the training that they receive, and the continuing growth and self-development of the therapist. These variables determine whether or not the personhood of the therapist will have a positive or negative influence on the play therapy process.

BEHAVIORS AND ORIENTATION

Harnish (1983) studied how children perceived therapist-stated conditions of empathy, unconditional positive regard, and genuineness, and determined how those perceptions influenced the process and outcome of nondirective play therapy. Harnish hypothesized that children perceiving high levels of therapist warmth, empathy, unconditional positive regard, and genuineness would exhibit more favorable outcomes of psychotherapy, as well as change their expressions of positive and negative feelings. She hypothesized that if the child perceived these conditions accurately, these perceptions would be accurate predictors of outcome. She found that several of the outcome variables were significantly and positively related to the level of child-perceived conditions.

Martinez and Valdez (1992) discussed cultural considerations in play therapy with Hispanic children. Cultural influences and considerations are probably one of the most critical variables we must deal with in choosing a particular therapist for a particular child. It may be impossible for a therapist from a different culture to relate to a child who presents material based on their own cultural experience and background. Certainly, only therapists who have enlightenment related to a particular culture should offer themselves as therapists to a child from a different culture. The more culturally blended a child is (regardless of the heritage or background from which he comes), the more possible it is for a therapist from out of that cultural orientation to provide therapy. However, the closer the child is to his culture of origin, the more critical it is that the therapist understand the culture of origin. Carried to the extreme, the concept of matching therapist to child could be ridiculous. For example, a therapist does not have to be deaf in order to deal with a child who is deaf. However, that play therapist should have a thorough understanding of the needs of a deaf child. A therapist does not have to be of a particular religious persuasion to work with a child who comes from a different religious background. However, that therapist must dedicate herself to understanding the religious background from which the child comes and deal with her own areas of respect or nonrespect for that background. When therapists engage in their own personal therapy, they are able to determine their limitations, their prejudices, and their strengths related to persons who are different. If therapists have a fear of death and an aversion to illness, they should not be working with sick children until they have worked through their own issues related to the trauma that may be presented through play therapy. Just as therapists who work with adults should not offer themselves as therapists for the population at large, therapists who work with children must be cognizant of their own strengths and limitations in accepting the responsibility of therapy with specific children. There is some material that will be offered in this section describing investigations involving therapists and children in playroom settings.

Smolen (1959), in an article on the nonverbal aspects of therapy with children, emphasized that therapy with children is an "action cure," not a "talking cure." The therapist talks because of personal insecurity and not for the benefit of the child. In observing the nonverbal behavior of a child, Smolen said that one must place the behavior in the context of the session and of the total history of the child. In addition, one must evaluate the significance of the behavior in terms of the psychodynamic implications before verbally responding to it.

Many authors have dealt with the variable of counselor integrity. Engebretson (1973) discussed the role of interaction distance in therapeutic interventions. Because nonverbal coding of behavior is learned early in life, the therapist should be cognizant of the child's nonverbal language as expressed by distance. Stressing the relationship approach, Newell (1941) wrote that for therapy to be of value to children, they must have the experiences of relating to and of talking with a therapist who has a different attitude toward them and their problems than their parents have. Sometimes, the relationship that develops between the therapist and child represents the child's first experience with an adult who is respectful and accepting. The importance of the personality of the therapist as it influences the process of play therapy is discussed by Tallman and Goldensohn (1941). Therapists must be able to set aside personal needs in order to allow the child to loosen up in the session. This allows children to get past barriers within themselves. Withall and Reddenhouse (1955) suggested that even though nondirective play therapy may superficially appear to be simple, it is not. It should not be attempted by a novice. A person should have thorough training before attempting to work with children in a play therapy setting.

Kottman (1987) studied whether counselors who have a particular theoretical bias would be able to change that bias in individual play therapy sessions after having been trained in the Adlerian play therapy model. The counselors reported that they perceived that their behavior in the play therapy sessions had changed, to include more creative and active techniques. However, after reviewing the videotaped play therapy sessions, it was determined that many of the counselors' behaviors did not appear to have been influenced by their participation in the changing. In other words, once a therapist has determined his preferred model, it may be difficult to alter his techniques within a play therapy setting.

Siegel (1972) conducted a study to investigate changes in the client's behavior during the course of play therapy. The functions of differing levels of therapist-offered conditions were observed using sixteen children, second- and fourth-graders who were diagnosed as learning-disabled. Sixteen play therapy sessions were conducted by the same therapist. Four children receiving the highest level responses on the Carkhuff scales were correlated with the four children receiving the lowest on the scales. Statistical significance was noted in the change of behavior that occurred over time as a function of differing levels of therapist-communicated conditions. High-conditioned children increasingly made more insightful statements and more positive statements about themselves than did low-conditioned children. Occurrence of a modeling effect was noted in the children receiving high conditions of communication.

Subotnik (1966) investigated the variable of transference in client-centered play therapy in a study involving one child and the child's parents. He made an effort to identify those variables onto which a client transfers with the therapist. He hypothesized that:

1. The child's perceptions of the therapist as goal object will, as observed during the course of therapy, reach a point of significant similarity to the child's perception of the parent as goal object.

2. If the child's perceptions of the two parents are clearly differentiated, his perceptions of the therapist will more closely resemble his perceptions of the like-sexed parent.
3. During the course of therapy, the child's perception of the therapist will be modified in the direction of approach and equilibrium.
4. At the conclusion of therapy the child's perceptions of his parents will be modified in the direction of approach and equilibrium.
5. Modification will be greater in the relationship with the parent of the same sex as the therapist.

Numbers three and four were not supported by research.

The effect of permissiveness, permission, and aggression in children's play was observed by Siegel and Kohn (1959). The study involved two boys to each group in a playroom. One session involved the presence of a permissive adult, and one session involved allowing the two boys to be in the playroom alone. The authors found that the children in the presence of a permissive adult tended to be more aggressive than they were when they played alone.

Mehrabian (1968) conducted a study on the relationship of attitude to seated posture, orientation, and distance in an attempt to investigate the functional relationships of a communicator's posture, orientation, and distance from his addressers to his attitude toward that addresser. The subject played the role of the communicator with a hypothetical addresser. The latter's sex and the subject's sex and liking for the addresser constituted the independent variables. The dependent variables were eye contact, distance, head, shoulder, and leg orientation, arm–leg openness, and measures of hand, leg, and body relaxation. The findings of the study indicated that eye contact, distance, orientation of body, and relaxation of body (as measured by angle of backward lean and by sideways lean) are significant indexes of a subject's liking for the addresser. The remaining measures did not yield any significant relationships to liking.

Siegel (1963) reported a research project investigating the hypothesis that the verbal behavior of adults will vary as a function of the linguistic level of children. Two adults were assembled in a series of permissive play-therapy-like sessions. Eight children were classified as high verbalizers, and eight children were classified as low verbalizers. All were labeled as retardates. The adults were told that the children were retarded and that they could use whatever technique they could in order to get the children to express themselves. Simple toys were given to them to use in a playroom setting. An overall low adult mean length of response was observed through the use of recordings and typed manuscripts of the sessions. This was hypothesized to indicate that the adults prejudged the verbal level and ability of the children. They consequently stereotyped them all into one category.

TRAINING

Stollak (1968) reported a study in which undergraduates were trained as play therapists using a didactic procedure. This procedure included didactic lecturing, group discussion, practice, and being observed in actual play therapy sessions. The members were trained in the nondirective techniques of client-centered therapy. The author found that undergraduate students significantly change their behavior during the sessions, increasing their reflection of content and clarification of feeling statements. These statements, the author felt, effected an increase in the expression of negative feelings and leadership behavior of the children. Stollak stated that the potential for training undergraduate students to work with children was very good. He felt that their youth and malleability, their openness to suggestion, and their eagerness to learn were obvious positive characteristics. These undergraduates acted maturely and competently. They were in the fullest sense of the word "therapists" attempting to bring about change.

A study conducted by Linden and Stollak (1969) was designed to assess the changes in behavior of undergraduates trained to be reflective, noninterfering, and empathic with children. Forty-eight undergraduate volunteers were selected. The setting was the clinic playroom at a university. The playroom was 20 feet by 40 feet and contained a sandbox, chalkboard, doll house, and toys as described by Axline (1947). Two training procedures were used—didactic and nondirective.

In the didactic training procedure, the Axline paradigm of play therapy was used. The trainer told the students the principles of nondirective role playing, observed each student in a series of play therapy sessions, and gave feedback.

The nondirective training experience involved telling the students that they were being used in an attempt to answer the question, "Can twelve intelligent college students—by playing with children, observing each other, and discussing among themselves what had been done—figure out an ideal sensitive way to work with children?" The leader summarized, integrated discussion, and reflected comments and questions as this group met together for discussions. No lecture was given. The students worked with children and discussed problems in the nondirective discussion group.

The results indicated beyond a reasonable doubt that students trained didactically reflect significantly more feeling and content of behavior in play therapy. They gave less direction and unsolicited help, asked fewer questions, and restricted the children less than the other group. Other training implications would be that undergraduates and lay persons can be trained if the proper methods are used.

Guerney and Flumen (1970) suggested the use of teachers as psychotherapeutic agents for withdrawn children. They felt that the teacher was the logical person to provide therapeutic services to a child because she already knew the child and had more access to the child.

The authors hypothesized that withdrawn children would become more assertive in their classrooms when seen in therapeutic play sessions by their own teachers. In addition, the progress of the children would be correlated with the effectiveness of the teacher in her client-centered role as therapist.

The children were eight boys and seven girls from the first, second, third, and fifth grades. The teachers were trained using filial therapy procedures in training sessions that lasted twenty weeks for one-and-one-half hours each. They were trained in the Rogerian theory underlying the play therapy technique. They saw demonstrations of individual play sessions conducted by professionals and had opportunities to role-play sessions. Each teacher met with her child weekly for forty-five minutes for fourteen sessions. She was supervised during the time she worked with the child.

The results indicated increased assertiveness and significant correlation between the teacher's therapeutic role performance and the child's improvement. A need for further research in the area of delivery of services to children was indicated.

Schiffer (1960) reported a situation in which he was called in as a consultant to train volunteer teacher therapists to lead play groups within a public school setting. Interested teachers volunteered to spend one hour a day leading a play therapy group for the children in the school needing therapeutic experience. The teachers were given one hour a day release time from their classroom duties for this work.

Schiffer provided training and consulting through the use of seminars in which the teacher-therapists presented play group meeting reports that they had written after each session. In the beginning, Schiffer reported that the teachers were very dependent on the consultant for insight and interpretation. One of his goals was to help the teachers learn to look beyond the superficial behavior of the child.

The consultant tended to become less active in the seminar discussions as the teachers began to feel more confident in their assumptions. Schiffer stressed that not only the teacher-therapists and guidance workers benefited but the referring teachers who were also a part of the seminar group learned to study child behavior intensively.

The training and use of teacher's aides in a Headstart program were described by Andronico and Guerney (1969). They used the techniques they had developed for training parents in filial therapy to train teacher's aides to work with children in play therapy sessions in the program. They discussed one of the aides, who had been trained in filial therapy to work with her own child. She was a high school graduate in her late twenties who had been trained in client-centered techniques. She achieved a high degree of success with her own child, and, later, in the Headstart program, consistently with other people's children.

Members of the staff provided further supervision and training. They suggested that, in training paraprofessionals for this filial "type" therapy, the aides should be taught:

1. To try to understand how the child presently feels;
2. To accept the child's feelings no matter what they are;
3. To allow the child always to take the lead in determining how he uses his play time;
4. To enforce the rules of the session with complete firmness while remaining empathic and noncritical;
5. To demonstrate to the child that his needs are indeed being understood and accepted, by making appropriate but brief statements like, "That gets you angry," that is, reflecting feelings.

The treatment of two seriously disturbed children by their teachers in a playroom was reported by Hartley (1952). The children were seen in an institute, and it was reported that progress was noted in each case. Volunteer teachers were trained by Schiffer (1957) to be used as playgroup therapists in playgroups that met one hour a day in a school setting. The principal arranged for these volunteers to be given one hour a day for the purpose of leading the therapy groups. Schiffer was used as a consultant whose responsibility was the training and supervision of these teachers.

Much research is needed in the area of therapist qualities, as they influence process and outcome in play therapy. Training programs have the difficult task of identifying those personal qualities that students have when they enter training programs. Further, the field of mental health has yet to define personality variables and qualities that consistently allow a therapist to create a positive therapeutic interaction.

Once therapists receive training and credentials, the professional community has very little influence on what occurs between a therapist and child. However, the licensing boards and peer review systems do influence the accountability of professionals who engage in the practice of play therapy.

4

The Ethics

POSITION

Children are not little adults; they are persons in the process of developing. Many therapists tend to make the mistake of negating a child patient's unique need for expression of self by using techniques that are designed for adolescents and adults. By using play therapy, child therapists have begun to acknowledge their awareness of the developmental needs of children. Because the play therapy approach focuses on children, play therapists are often inclined to focus on the process of the relationship and do not plan for the legal aspects of a play therapy practice. A well-defined framework that ethically protects the child within his environment needs to be described and defined by each therapist who provides play therapy.

Most therapists who work with children will have their own special place in the Hereafter. It is hard, messy work. Considering the qualities of the members of this group and attempting to make a generalized statement about them, it seems that, for the most part, they are dedicated, they are child centered, and their hearts are pure. They have tempera paint on their clothing and clay under their fingernails. They probably do not knowingly make mistakes that could potentially harm children. If they do make mistakes, it is often because they are so enthralled with the child and the presented therapeutic needs that they forget that this child is also a client in

61

the legal sense of the word. It is within that context that this chapter is written.

The conceptualization of ethics that have to be maintained in play therapy is developed within the framework of the credentialing board in the state where the therapist maintains her practice. For example, a licensed social worker is a licensed social worker in the play therapy setting as well as other therapeutic settings. A licensed psychologist is a licensed psychologist wherever they work. A psychiatrist is a physician regardless of the work setting. A licensed professional counselor is also governed by a certifying board. When credentialed professionals ignore the ethical guidelines set forth by their certifying or licensing board, then they are working outside of the boundaries of the law of the state in which they are credentialed. It is possible for an individual to learn the techniques of play therapy who is not credentialed by a state board of examiners. It is not ethical for such an individual to practice play therapy unless he or she holds a recognized credential in the mental health field. Additionally, it is critical for those in the mental health field who hold state licenses or certifications to be clear about what their training allows them to do. If a psychiatrist, psychologist, or social worker has no training in the area of play therapy, it is out of the bounds of his or her training to attempt to provide such a service. The guidelines for receiving training in play therapy have been set forth by the Association of Play Therapy. The Association of Play Therapy has defined levels of service in this technique. They include providing therapy while in training, providing training as an independent practitioner, and providing supervision in the field.

Children are the clients. They are the focus of treatment. While it is tempting at times to focus only on the needs of children in play therapy to the exclusion of the parents, this type of orientation is impossible, for obvious reasons. In reality, parents are legally responsible for the child and have to be involved with the work done in therapy since they are ultimately the persons who will be living with therapeutic decisions. Additionally, they are the legal decision-makers for the child, in that the law gives the parents the right of decision-making until the child is of legal age, or unless their decisions are determined to be dangerous to the child in a court of law. Another consideration is that young children do not have the cognitive capacity to make wise decisions about their needs in areas that are related to their own social and emotional growth and development. Even older adolescents who are cognitively developed to manage abstract reasoning often cannot understand their own need for therapeutic treatment.

This is not to imply that children do not have rights, or that their wishes regarding therapy should not be heard and responded to by the adults who care for them. They should be able to express their dislike for the therapeutic process. They should also be able to express their dislike for the therapist and be free to negotiate strategies and procedures. For example, the child has to be free to simply sit in a playroom—not talk, not play, or not smile—if that is the child's desire. Children even have the right to request another therapist. Statements have been made about the developmental inability of a young child to make decisions about the choice of a surgeon, indicating that the parent has to make this decision. However, play therapy is not surgery; it is a planned therapy relationship. Within this relationship, even children as young as the age of 3 start to establish specific likes and dislikes about other people and about their own personal boundaries. As a part of this developmental process, children begin to decide whom they wish to include in their lives and whom they disrespect. We must consider that it is a violation of their rights as human beings to be subjected to a relationship that demoralizes and negates their individuality. Additionally, it is a violation of their personhood to subject them to clinical techniques that do not fit their personhood. For example, it could be harmful to a child when a therapist sits in front of a playroom door in order to keep the child there for the full course of a session when the child cries to the point of throwing up. It is a violation of their rights to manipulate them to explore hidden dimensions of their lives, until they have a desire to raise and confront those issues. For this reason, evaluations done for the court or for other legal reasons should be clearly described to the child (using child language) before they are done. Evaluations are not therapy and should not be conceptualized by anyone as such. We have to make clear distinctions in our field between evaluations and therapy.

One child who taught me about early preferences was 4 years old. He and his mother went to look at two hospitals before he made a choice about where to have his impending surgery performed. The surgeon was to be the same, and the facilities had equal reputations; therefore it seemed appropriate that the child have a say in where the surgery would occur. When they arrived at one of the hospitals, they were met by an administrator who had a professional stake in the choice. In her effort to manipulate the child, she did some rather "giddy" things. When we left that institution, the child said, "I will never come back here." When the parent asked, "Why?" the child replied, "That woman was silly." The rights of the child should be clearly communicated to the child and parents at the outset of treatment.

CUSTODY ISSUES

Most states have family law codes that should be thoroughly reviewed before a play therapist offers services to treat children. If this material is difficult to understand and apply, then the therapist will be wise to seek the consultation of an attorney who specializes in family law.

Within this body of information the therapist will find specific guidelines about the responsibility for determining issues related to child custody. Specifically, the therapist has an obligation to ascertain who is the custodial parent. This is done by asking the parents (if interviewing a single parent) and by asking them to bring the section of the divorce decree that describes issues of custody. Further, even if the child is brought by the custodial parent for therapy, it enhances the treatment of the child for the therapist to inform the custodial parent and make contact with the noncustodial parent. If possible, it is important to work with both parents in the resolution of the child's issues. Therapists should be aware that there are legal issues, ethical issues, and human issues in this highly emotional area. If every step is not planned during the telephone session and the initial parent session, the problems surrounding issues of child custody can draw the therapist into the center of parental conflicts that will make positive therapeutic outcome with the child impossible.

CONSENT TO TREAT

A document should be presented to the parents during the initial session that describes the proposed treatment procedures. The parents are requested to sign this form acknowledging that the therapist has described therapeutic methods, philosophy, and prognostic limitations. They acknowledge that they have been given the opportunity to ask questions. When parents are divorced, it is important that each parent be informed and that each sign the document. This document gives the therapist the right to treat a minor child. During the second session (that involves the child) the work that the child and therapist will do together should be described to the child and, when developmentally able, the child is also allowed to sign the consent form (see Appendix).

DISCLOSURE STATEMENT

The statement of disclosure should be presented to all parents during the initial session. It contains information about the orientation of the therapist regarding theory and techniques. It explains to the parents that neither unusual nor experimental techniques will be used with their child during the course of therapy. This document contains information about the credentials that the therapist holds. (The therapist determines that the parents understand the full range of credentials that various therapists have and how they differ.) Evidence of credentials should be placed on the wall so that there is no question about the title or credentials of the therapist. The document should describe the nature and level of training that the therapist has attained that allows them to offer their services to do the proposed work. The therapist should state any personal theoretical bias that might influence the nature of the work with the child or that might cause any member of the family to experience disrespect by the therapist. For example, if the therapist professes himself to be a "Christian therapist," then this should be disclosed to the family and the therapist should clearly explain her position to the family in advance of the therapy. Another example would be if the therapist refers to herself as a "feminist therapist." This should be clearly disclosed to the family because the father of a child under these conditions may not feel comfortable working with this therapist.

The document should contain information about the fee schedule. The issue of fees must be clarified in advance of the therapy. Issues related to potential problems when a third party payer is involved (such as insurance companies) should be clarified. The document should explain that when insurance is billed for an individual, confidentiality is broken, in that the privacy between parent, child, and therapist is violated. When insurance companies request detailed accounts of treatment progress and plans, the parents must be informed that this violates confidentiality (see Appendix).

CLARIFICATION OF CONFIDENTIALITY

The document states that confidentiality is assured. The therapist will not talk with school personnel, physicians, or any other entity about the child and the family except when directed to do so in writing by the parents. There are three exceptions to this: (1) in a case of suspected child abuse, a play therapist has the duty to report; (2) in the case of potential harm to self or others, the play therapist has a duty to warn; and (3) in the case of a court order, the therapist has to negotiate with the judge and the attorneys and may ultimately have to produce records or appear in court. Ferguson (1990) has dealt with the issue of confidentiality in play therapy. Ferguson stressed that play therapists have to deal realistically with the issue of confidentiality. The work of a play therapist continuously involves working with teachers, doctors, other professionals, and parents. These others in the child's life are continuously involved with the child and the therapist. Ferguson pointed out that in view of the current legal trends and professional qualms dealing with children, it is a challenging task to maintain confidentiality. Some of the challenges to confidentiality when one is working with children were discussed by Ferguson. It is important that children know that the privacy of their communications with the therapist will be honored. However, because adults are involved with the child, this is sometimes difficult to do. Hendrix (1991) has also dealt with the issue of confidentiality with children. He suggests that blind adherence to absolute confidentiality is neither desirable nor required. He stresses the concept that the reason for confidentiality is to benefit the client. When that benefit is overridden by other factors, child therapists must take all factors into account. The situation changes, however, when a child becomes an adolescent, because they do have increased ability to become involved in legal decisions that influence their lives. Hendrix further suggests that a therapist working with a child is well advised to seek informed consent, even when working with younger children. Noll and Seagull (1982) dealt with ethical considerations in using behavior modification and play therapy in the treatment of the enuretic child. They suggest involving the child in the discussion of procedures to be utilized. In the case of their client, the child had some choices about the treatment as it proceeded. This child also was encouraged to become involved in choosing reinforcers. Their feeling was that a child needs to feel mastery and control, even in a therapeutic relationship. To take away the child's own volition toward change violates his privacy. They further stress that, as therapists, we have the obligation to consider clinical and empirical evidence when we develop treatment plans so that therapists can provide optimum assistance to clients.

O'Connor (1990) focuses on the issue of ethical and legal dilemmas of reporting cases involving child abuse. He stresses that the law mandates that a psychologist report suspicion that an individual is engaging in a behavior defined as abusive. He also stresses that, thankfully, the law does not give the psychologist investigating power or responsibility. He clarifies that persons who are 16 and over are generally considered to be holders of the privilege when it comes to being the victim of a crime. This means they could insist that a psychologist not report the victimization. However, the conflict for a therapist arises if there is a situation of statutory rape between persons who are 16 to 18 years old. O'Connor stresses that psychologists face critical dilemmas in the area of confidentiality that must be addressed at the organizational and philosophical level. Psychologists must continue to conduct research to provide society with the data necessary to develop sensitive responses to the problem. Additionally, this information must be used in developing positions related to child abuse and reporting laws. Therapists also have the obligation to become involved and to make an impact on public policy and existing laws.

Belter and Grisso (1984) discussed research and philosophy related to the ability of children to cognitively understand the abstract concept of rights and rights violations. Their position is that even though children may not be cognitively ready to understand their rights as individuals, they should be given information about their rights. It is the responsibility of the therapist to attempt to provide information to the child at the child's comprehensive ability. The authors stress that therapists maintain a position of nurturance and advocacy toward their child patients in order to assure that children have as much information as they are able to comprehend.

The American Psychological Association *Monitor* (Seppa 1996) of August 1996 reported a recent U.S. Supreme Court ruling which upheld a psychotherapist–patient confidentiality standard in federal court. "The high court ruled that confidential communications between a licensed psychotherapist and patient in the course of diagnosis or treatment are protected from compelled disclosure under the rules of evidence applied in federal courts. The justices thus recognize the value of psychotherapy and the importance of confidentiality for success in psychotherapy" (p. 39). This recognition of privilege between a therapist and a client can potentially free therapists from many of the violations of privacy that have occurred in the past. It will be interesting to see how states and local counties deal with this, and what interpretations will be made in the interest of our clients in the future. There are, however, exceptions to this rule, and those have been described above. Of course, child abuse must be reported to the authorities, and in some states elder abuse must also be reported. Threats against the President of the United States must be divulged as well, and most state court systems have adopted precedents that require therapists to identify people who pose an immediate danger to another person. The ruling also says, "If a serious harm to the patient or to others can be averted only by means of disclosure by the therapist (which is seen as a last resort), then the psychologist has a responsibility to report" (p. 39). However, the spirit of the ruling may potentially provide latitude for the profession in the future. It is critical for therapists to know the laws in the state in which they practice. In most states, not only are the records open for scrutiny by the court, but the therapists themselves, under oath, are questioned about the child, the family, and the therapists' impressions about that situation.

The reason for requesting services needs to be established at the outset of therapy. The family should be informed that a forensic case (a case that is designed to elicit material for a potentially legal issue) should be conducted by a person who specializes in this service. This service may occur in a playroom setting, but the components of the service are specific and should be conducted by a person trained in forensic psychology. Play therapists must recognize that this is not therapy—it is assessment. This is totally different from a case that involves the therapeutic relief of pain, which would be conducted and labeled as therapy for the family and child.

Play therapists who are in personal therapy, are under supervision, are in training in a university setting, or work in settings where case conferences are held have special situations that should be addressed with the parents in advance. Children and parents should be informed in advance of such exposure of their personal lives. With informed choice, they may enter into therapy under the conditions set forth by the parameters of the described disclosure or they may seek another therapist for their work. If they choose to become involved with a therapist under these conditions, then the jeopardy to privacy should be explained. Parents should sign documents to indicate their understanding of the described limitations to privacy. The limitations should also be explained to the child in the presence of the parents and documented in the therapist's notes. However, even when all the stated precautions are taken, when therapists discuss cases in personal therapy, teaching, books, printed materials, or other educative types of settings, they have an obligation to conceal the identity of the patient.

Separate documents for taping sessions for training and supervision have been described by Daniel Sweeney, Ph.D. (personal communication, February 1996). Sweeney, who was involved in management of the play therapy laboratory at the University of North Texas has indicated that in such a setting, there are specific documents that the therapists provide for the parents in advance of seeing a child. These documents give permission for both audio and video taping of the sessions. They explain to the parents that the therapists at the Center are in training and are being provided with supervision by the clinic supervisors. The parents are informed that the material gained in the sessions with their children will be reviewed by the therapist with the supervisor. At times, material gathered from the sessions will be stated in anonymous terms so as to cover the identity of the child, and certain material may become embedded in research or written material.

Sweeney also stressed that the therapist has an obligation to describe the implications of technological advances on potential loss of privacy. For example, parents should be informed that the use of wireless telephones, cellular telephones, e-mail, and faxes have the potential for violating confidentiality. The therapist does not fax material concerning the child. The parents should conduct conversations with the therapist over a secured telephone. When a parent is on a nonsecured line, the therapist should stop the conversation and advise the parent to call back on a secured telephone.

During the first session in which the child and the therapist are alone in the play therapy room, the therapist has the obligation to clearly communicate to the child the therapist's position regarding confidentiality about the sessions that they will have together. In the situation of a typical therapy case, the therapist may wish to describe the types of issues that the therapist and parents will discuss during those "adult" sessions. Such statements like, "I will be talking about how your family solves problems," or "I will be talking about feelings in the family." It is critical at this point to help children understand that the family will need to be engaged at some level in order to assist in their growth and development. However, it is important that children understand what the boundaries of that communication involve. In this way, children will feel safe talking with the therapist and yet know that they and the therapist are not betraying the family. It is unethical to promise children full confidentiality when that will not be happening. If the situation will be a forensic one, then the therapist has the obligation to inform the child about the issues that might surround the case. These can be described in terms that the child will understand. This does often limit what the child will tell the therapist. However, it is crucial that the child not be violated by manipulating the child to share secrets within a relationship that is designed to expose forensic material.

AFTER-HOURS AVAILABILITY

If the family needs to reach the therapist for "after hours" issues, they should be told how this can be done. Frequently the therapist uses an answering service. In this case, the family should be informed of the potential violation of confidentiality. However, therapists have the responsibility to personally solicit a signed paper from the answering service that the therapist has explained the issues of confidentiality and they have agreed by their signature to uphold the confidences to which they have access. Because of the issue of confidentiality, many therapists now use answering machines.

When the therapist is out of town, it is important to have a designated colleague to take calls and to assist the family during a crisis. The therapist who has such an arrangement with a colleague has a duty to inform the family about this arrangement in that it could potentially violate confidentiality. All families with children who are in active therapy are informed when the therapist will be unavailable due to out-of-town schedules and are told who the "on-call" colleague is.

Parents are to be informed about how to reach the credentialing board that maintains control of the therapist's credentials. The parents are informed in the document of disclosure that they have the right to contact this board if they feel that their rights have been violated. The parents are asked to sign and date the document of disclosure. They are given a copy of the document for their records (see Appendix).

RECORDS

Records should be stored behind at least two locked doors (one that the cleaning crew cannot access) and in a locked file cabinet. A professional office should have a plan in place for long-term storage of and access to records as they are needed.

Records should be stored at least three years past the age of majority, in the case of a child. In the case of an adult, records should be saved at least ten years past the last date of entry into the chart. It is better to store records too long than not long enough. Most states and professional organizations provide therapists with guidelines. However, they vary from state to state, and they vary in accordance with guidelines that are designed to protect children, handicapped persons, or persons with illnesses or traumas. A therapist should be well informed about the laws in the state in which they practice. Storing records is cumbersome and costly but is important for a number of reasons. For example, therapists wishing to do follow-up studies would have the information at their disposal. If their work is questioned in the future by the children who become adults, or by the parents of the children, then they have documentation of their actual work with the children.

As a concurrent procedure, the office should have in place a plan for the safe destruction of records as they become aged. This being the case, it is logical that when a record is established on a client, the date the record is established, as well as the birth date of the child, should be put on the edge of the chart. This makes for easy accessibility when a therapist is dating and retiring charts.

It is important to go over issues related to risk management. This is usually centered on suicidal ideation and intent. However, there is also the risk of the runaway child. The therapist discusses how after-hours consultation can be accessed and clarifies arrangements for emergency care when the therapist is out of the city. The therapist discusses hospital affiliations that are maintained should the child need such care.

A thorough history is taken (see Appendix). The parents are informed about the nature of the questions and how the information will be used. Certain information is never to be disclosed to insurance companies or put in reports. The guidelines for the control of this material are clearly described in Ethical Principles of Psychologists and Code of Conduct (American Psychological Association 1992). The parents should be able to state the issues in their lives that they may wish to disclose to the therapist but that they do not wish to be put in a written history form. They should be informed that they are not required to commit to paper any information that would (in their opinion) violate their rights. Such issues as indiscretions, personal sexuality, attempted abortions, and such do not belong in a child's history form. However, in some cases, such information may be relevant for the therapist. The parents are requested to sign the completed history.

Because issues related to parental needs for therapy are frequently identified during the course of the child's therapy, it is important that the therapist and the parents discuss these issues in advance. Many therapists do family therapy and also individual therapy for each of the family members.

However, others have clear feelings about whom they will work with as their client. James (1987) has indicated that she works only with the child. She encourages the parents to align themselves with another therapist for their individual or marital therapy. Her work with the parents is confined to the scheduled parenting sessions.

BOUNDARY ISSUES

These issues generally center on gift giving and social interactions outside of the playroom. Parents and children often bring gifts, especially around holidays. The therapist and the parents can discuss these boundaries and the reasons for these boundaries in advance of therapy. In many communities, the therapist will see the family at church or on shopping excursions. The therapist, child, and parents discuss in advance how they will conduct themselves in public places so as to not violate the rights of the child and family.

INSURANCE COMPANIES

As was stated earlier, parents need to be informed in the disclosure statement that when insurance is billed, confidentiality is broken in that the privacy is violated. Bollas and Sundelson (1995) provide provocative information related to issues that therapists have to address in dealing with managed health care and insurance companies. When psychotherapists enter into a relationship with a managed care organization, they may put the client at risk. Not only are they endorsing intrusive questions about the needs and diagnoses of their clients, in most instances they are committing themselves to allowing managed care personnel to dictate the number of sessions allowed for a particular client. Bollas and Sundelson state clearly that this is an "insidious invasion" of the process that should be occurring in the therapeutic relationship. In addition, they point out that the implications in our society for the maltreatment of patients exist on multiple levels. The insurance companies and corporate America are able to access unlimited information because therapists break confidentiality when they deal with managed care systems.

As therapists exuberantly attempt to build private practices and enter into relationships with managed care companies and insurance organizations that are damaging to their clients, they must be prepared to recognize that they are putting their clients and the profession at risk, and are adding to the erosion of a component of our society that will ultimately put us all at risk. Their book is a wake-up call, and clearly describes the sellout that therapists have made in the interest of using third party payers. We have a duty to protect our clients. We have a duty to inform our clients about how they can potentially be mistreated as a result of their using insurance to pay for therapy (see Appendix).

ETHICAL CONSIDERATIONS IN SETTINGS OTHER THAN THE PRIVATE OFFICE

The current body of literature is rapidly expanding to describe working with children in settings that are not private office or university settings. This material includes working with children in hospitals and working with children in school settings. This is frequently interesting and fruitful work. However, there are legal and ethical issues that should be planned for in advance of accepting such work. Some issues to be considered in these settings in general are discussed below.

Working in these settings present variables that the therapist cannot control. When therapists work in a setting that is owned or controlled by an institution, they have to determine whether or not they can function in this setting within the ethical guidelines of their credentialing organization. If the rules of the institution are in conflict with the ethics set forth by their profession, then they cannot work within that setting.

SCHOOL SETTINGS

Counselors must determine and be assured that the work they do serves only the children and not the administration or the community. If this cannot be assured, then the counselors in those settings must redefine their roles and clearly state such to the parents and children. Because the ethical guidelines of the therapist and the mission of the institution are often in conflict, it may not be feasible that actual therapy can be conducted within a school setting. Granted, a counselor may use toys to allow the child increased freedom of self-expression, which can also result in assisting the child. However, certain cautions have to be taken before anything resembling formal therapy should be conducted. First, the issue of ownership and protection of records has to be clearly defined. Second, there has to be a safe place, free from any scrutiny, to conduct the sessions. Third, there are several potential contaminants involving work with parents that have to be considered. Therapists must recognize that when working with parents in an institutional setting, reasonable parents would likely be suspicious about who the master is. School counselors who promise that they are working for the child and the family are generally not telling the truth. Those therapists who have worked in school systems recognize that ultimately they are employed by the school district. Counselors have to inform parents to be discrete about revealing personal material. Counselors in schools should be very careful about therapeutic decisions that they make. When they find themselves in situations other than school guidance, it is strongly advised that they refer the child and the family to a private therapist where the rights of the child and the family will not be violated. Even the act of removing a child from his educational environment during the school day, in front of his peers, with the knowledge of his teacher, violates his privacy.

HOSPITAL SETTINGS

Before working in a hospital setting, it is appropriate that therapists' credentials have been reviewed and accepted. It is understood that therapists do not have admitting privileges (and must communicate such to parents) but work on specific cases under the supervision of the privileged physician. It is not possible to provide traditional play therapy in these settings without violating the child's rights and privileges. In the first place, the therapist should chart and communicate with other staff in the hospital who also work with the child. The rights of child and family may be violated by this action, and if this is the case the therapists must limit the work they do so that ethics and hospital policy do not come into conflict. These issues have to be predetermined. Hospital standards are clearly defined and have to be followed by all persons who deliver services within that setting.

Ethics of professionals who deliver services are also clearly defined by law and must be maintained wherever the service is delivered. It is the responsibility of the therapist to ensure that the two sets of laws will not come in conflict by therapist actions. Standards of care and hospital procedures are clearly described in the rules and regulations of each hospital. There are federal guidelines that control work in hospitals. It is the responsibility of the therapist to understand the rules and regulations of the hospital in which they work.

5

The Materials and Setting

POSITION

Central to the concept of the play therapy technique for use with children is that the therapist allows children to use toys and material in place of verbal language. The majority of therapists who use play therapy as a technique generally describe the toys they make available to the child. They generally have views about why these toys and materials are to be used and how the toy play will assist the child. Further, throughout the literature, therapists state a variety of suppositions about the viability of each of the materials.

A child will find a way to make a toy out of almost anything. In this writing, *toys* are considered synonymous with *playthings*. Children are capable of using something as simple as a piece of paper and imagining that it is a bear, a car, a tree, a sword, or a person. When children are free of social pressures and expectations, they create their own toys out of any material available to them. When children are placed in a free environment that contains no objects, they are capable of making believe. As if by magic, a child can develop an entire roomful of people and toys to develop his imagery about a theme even when nothing is there. Free associating is natural for a child and frequently it is his preferred state. When one places a child in a free environment that contains only one object, the child is capable of developing a wide range of toy themes. Therapists provide toys for the child to use in the playroom so that the child will have a vehicle for showing the therapist the imagery that he holds within himself without having to use words.

Everything in the play therapy room is placed there purposefully. The play therapy room is a specifically designed room for the purpose of conducting play therapy only. In order to make meaning of toy use by children, the therapist must control all of the variables that can be controlled. This concept is similar to adhering to specific conditions when conducting standardized testing in order to assess certain skills, attitudes, or cognitive profiles. Standardized conditions are critical. In play therapy, the conditions that must be standardized include the emotional well-being of the therapist, the setting, and the materials that are used. When these conditions are met, children will be freed of the confusion of external variables so that they can focus on internal processes during the session, without distractions. When children have to continuously look for an object, or if a desired object has been destroyed by another child, then this renders the play therapy room to be unpredictable and unsafe. When the child has to ask the therapist for materials or objects, then an unhealthy dependency is encouraged. When such contaminants can be avoided by planning, then the play therapy room itself does not create stress in the child.

After having been trained as a play therapist and seeking the ongoing supervision and therapy necessary to maintain emotional strength, insight, and richness, the therapist is ready to develop a play therapy setting. This setting requires the same degree of planning as designing a new building for a major corporation—and it is more important.

Choosing the size of the space for the room is highly personal, depending on the perception of space. The space must "feel right"; one approximately 12 feet by 14 feet with built in cabinetry is suitable. A chair that is on rollers and is made of durable molded plastic is helpful. This allows the therapist to unobtrusively move with the child about the playroom.

The cabinetry at one end of the room is designed much like a kitchen cabinet but is child height. It has cabinets at the top with a durable counter top and cabinets beneath. The counter top has three separate sink-like metal cavities. One sink is 3 feet by 4 feet and is filled with dry sand. There is ample counter space between this sink and the next one of the same size, which contains wet sand. At the end of this counter space is a shallow sink that is 2 feet by 4 feet with a bar-shaped water spigot that contains only cold water. Beneath the countertop are three sets of doors. The door below the water sink contains pull-out shelves with water toys. The door below the sand sink contains sand toys. The door below the wet sand sink contains many small figures and articles that can be used for sand tray play. Along one side of the play therapy room are built-in shelves that are child height. They are deep enough to hold shoe box-sized plastic containers. These containers are used to store small toys. These may be various types of animals, small dolls, cars, trucks, dishes, doll clothes, or construction toys. Each container is open or labeled with a cut-out picture of the contained objects. The facing wall is covered with washable plastic material. The painting easel is placed on this wall. The doll houses, building blocks, and larger buckets of toys are housed on the fourth wall. The floor is made of washable linoleum. The room is painted light blue. In one corner is a three-sided mirror that is child height and made of unbreakable material. The video camera is housed in one corner of the room with viewing from a private office. There is a pull-down table, which is used for older children when activity therapy is planned. Cabinets above the easel are used to store washable nontoxic tempera paint, finger paint, and nontoxic, biodegradable liquid soap. Materials in the play therapy room are designed to allow the child maximum expression with multiple uses. In order of importance the following materials are recommended: a child-sized table and chair, water, water toys, sand, sand toys, wet sand, clay, easel and paint pots (5 colors only), bop bag, plastic animals (various categories), doctor bag, blocks, doll house with furniture, multi-ethnic, multi-aged dolls, multi-ethnic, multi-aged anatomically correct dolls, multi-ethnic baby dolls and bottles, hammer (with hard rubber end), soft wood pieces, large nails, rope, small plastic or rubber gun, rubber knife, dishes, "dress-up" character hats, and vehicles of various sizes and functions (cars, trucks, cement mixer, road grader, log carrier, etc.).

The closet space above the countertop contains materials needed for activity play, which is used with children who are older than 7 years who indicate they wish to use this material. There are times when activity play should be offered for a specific child because of a special need. The activity play materials should include card games, board games, colored markers, clay, molds, and various scraps of materials that children can use to make real things like jewelry, masks, and other projects. I even have supplies for candy-making projects.

Nothing is there just because it is a toy. This is not a commercial toyland. The materials are always the same. They are placed in the play therapy room in the same order and in the same place. They are cleaned and reorganized after each session. Every child walks back into the room with a new beginning. The sand is spread neatly; the dolls are reclothed and in their beds; the dishes are cleaned and in place; the paint pots are washed and have new paint. The brushes are clean and are in the correct place. The water sink is drained and replenished with fresh water. The clay buckets are cleaned. A fresh ball of clay of each of four colors is replaced on the table. The guns and knives are placed in the proper bucket. The bop bag is restored to the correct place and has been replenished with air or replaced. The building materials are reorganized. The vehicles are back on shelves in the same place. The blocks are restacked. The easel is replenished with clean paper and the plastic that surrounds the easel is cleaned. Every object that is similar in nature is back in its own container. For example, all of the farm animals are back in the plastic tub that is stationed near the barn. The wild animals, such as tigers and lions, are placed together. The dinosaurs have their own separate space. The water animals such as sharks, fish, whales, and dolphins are regrouped at the water station. The water toys such as buckets, hoses, pistols, cups, and containers are cleaned and placed in a large container at the water table. The sand toys such as scoopers, shovels, dippers, pourers, and "gravel grinders" are cleaned and in a container near the sand box. All of the wooden people with their furniture and vehicles are back in containers and placed near the two wooden doll houses. The castle is in its spot. There are no surprises for the child who walks back into the play therapy room—even after a year. The child is not confronted with the psychological processing of the child who came earlier. Nor is the child forced to deal with the artistic renderings of other children. The child is not expected to walk back into the psychological mind-set that they experienced during the last session. They can start over. Each session is a new beginning. It is important to recognize that young children personify toys. They frequently assume the role of caretaker of these objects to which they have given special meaning. When they fear that the toys are not safe, they may also assume that they themselves will not be safe.

When a therapist has a helper in the office, he or she is hired with the understanding that the helper will clean the play therapy room between child therapy sessions. When therapists know that they will have to clean what the child messes, they may not be able to control their body signals while the mess is going on. Therefore, in order to be congruent when they say, "In here you can spend your time any way you choose," they have to control conditions so that they really mean it. They have to be free from the horror they feel when the child dumps the tiny toys onto the floor and follows this with a pot of paint. The child who uses manipulation as a coping strategy will notice the therapist's body signals immediately. Frequently, it is impossible to anticipate behaviors and set limits quickly enough to avoid the type of mess that can happen in one minute in the playroom.

There is a considerable amount and diversity of literature dealing with the selection and use of material in the playroom. It was found that people using play therapy approaches make different assumptions about what material to use, and they make different interpretations of the way in which the child uses the material.

Some of the literature stresses matching the material to specific child populations. For example, considerations in the selection of media to be used with the retarded child, the blind child, and the older child are described. Other writings focus on the selection of material to be used for specific theoretical or technical orientations. For example, the selection of material for use in structured therapy, puppet play, art therapy, and role playing are identified. The value of certain media such as masks, clay, darts, and drawing materials is also dealt with.

MATERIALS USED BY OTHER WRITERS

The following information does not represent an exhaustive search of the literature. However, it is meant to provide the reader with an overview of some of the material found in representative articles and books.

Anna Freud (1951) stressed the use of toys, especially during the introductory phase of treatment. This treatment period is described as the preanalytic period, and the major goal of Anna Freud at this time was to woo the child in any way possible. She considered play technique useful for diagnostic observation and also used drawing in the analytical phase. However, she did not elaborate on specific or nonstructured materials in her office.

In describing Melanie Klein's use of toys, Anna Freud (1951) suggested that the play technique as described by Klein is valuable for observing the child because this allows the child to establish a domestic environment in the analyst's room. Anna Freud contended that this will allow the analyst to observe various reactions that the child will express through the use of the toy. The toy allows the child to express the child's world using fantasy. Anna Freud indicated that these techniques allow a small child a way to express thoughts before they would be able to express those thoughts verbally.

Melanie Klein (1955) kept a box of miniature toys for each child in a separate drawer. The individual drawer came to signify the "private intimate relation between analyst and patient, characteristic of the psychoanalytic transference situation" (p. 227). This box, which was used throughout the child's analysis, was added to or deleted from, depending on the needs of the child in his analysis. Klein suggested the use of the following miniature toys as suitable for the psychoanalytic technique of play therapy: "little wooden men and women (usually in two sizes), cars, wheelbarrows, swings, trains, airplanes, animals, trees, bricks, houses, fences, paper, scissors, a not-too sharp knife, pencils, chalks or paints, glue, balls and marbles, plasticine and string" (p. 226). The toys should be nonmechanical. The simplicity of the toys enables the child to use them in a large variety of situations and to express many different attitudes.

Klein (1929, 1961) suggested that the equipment of the playroom should be very simple and should consist only of what is needed for the analysis. The playroom should have a washable floor, running water, a table, a few chairs, a little sofa, some cushions and a chest of drawers. Each child's playthings are kept locked in one particular drawer, and is identified as the child's own. The toys become equivalent to the adult associations, and the child shares them only with the therapist.

Bender and Woltmann (1941) stress that the same toy selected by two children may have two different meanings. Bender and Woltmann also believed that play with toys offers an opportunity for the child to create and play out all kinds of human relationships on a realistic level. This realism is a make-believe situation that reduces feelings of anxiety, fear, apprehension, and guilt, which would be present in a real-life situation.

Despert (1940) suggested that the child's use of materials is individualized. Some children will use the same toy over and over, using the same theme or varying the theme. Other children will go from toy to toy. In another article, Despert (1948) stressed that, although no play equipment is actually necessary in working with children, if the material is carefully selected it tends to increase rapport. She suggested that a great variety of toys be used but notes that children spontaneously use the equipment provided in a highly individualized manner even if the cases are similar from a psychopathological point of view.

Despert (1940) suggested that one child may be bound to one theme and one toy and use it over and over in a repetitive manner, while another child may refrain from using the toys because of the feeling that, by using a toy, they may reveal too much. Other children may fear their own aggressive nature and thus refrain from using toys. Because of these individual needs, Despert contended that children should be allowed to choose the toy and the use of it.

Bender (1937) and Woltmann (1943) stressed that materials that are plastic in nature allow for natural expression of feelings in the child. The value of the less structured medium is that it can be torn apart, restructured, destroyed, and recreated over and over without causing guilt or worry within the child. They also suggested that by observing the products a child makes with pliable materials, the observer would be able to measure cognitive and emotional growth.

Lowenfeld (1935) classified materials to be used in a child study situation into three groups. They are materials for the expression of fantasy, construction materials, and house or miniature adult material. The reader is referred to the original source for an exhaustive description of this classification system.

Moustakas (1953, 1959b) recommended that the use of unstructured materials such as sand, water, paints, and clay allow for the release of pent-up feelings. These materials can be formed, pounded, and then reformed. Using this media, the child would be able to organize the materials so as to work out multiple issues in his or her life. Moustakas suggested that these materials are valuable during the beginning sessions in that they allow the child to comfortably displace feelings onto the media. Moustakas said that allowing the use of aggressive items such as play guns, darts, and knives enables a child to express feelings of aggression in socially acceptable ways. Dolls and puppets allow the child to work out problems involving family crisis and sibling rivalry. Moustakas stressed that the use of paint, clay, and other nonstructured materials allows the child to create and to destroy. These media can be formed to represent significant others in their lives. Moustakas advocated that the therapist be nondirective and allow the child to freely choose the material and the formulation of the material.

Axline (1947) recognized that effective therapeutic intervention can occur in a number of settings such as a corner of a regular classroom, or even in a workroom. However, she stressed that optimally there should be a specific and specially equipped room designated as the play therapy room. Her suggestions were that the room should be soundproof. It should have a sink with available water, and easily cleaned walls and floors. Since she wished the child to have free selection of toys and materials, she insisted that the materials be accessible to the child. Axline suggested that these include toys to be used for aggression and family play, nonstructured materials, materials for painting and cutting, materials for water play, and various toys such as soldiers, telephones, and animals. She felt that mechanical toys were not useful in the playroom because of the limitations imposed by the structure. She also added that the child have access to a large sand box with a seat built on it. She included opportunity for dramatic play via the inclusion of a stage. Axline (1964) wrote that the room be kept in order and indicated that hiring a maid for cleaning was the best solution to keeping the room constant from session to session.

Ginott (1960, 1961a) suggested that the toys chosen for a child therapy session should have therapeutic value. He used five criteria in the selection of materials. Toys are chosen in order to

1. Facilitate the establishment of contact with the child
2. Evoke and encourage catharsis
3. Aid in developing insight
4. Furnish opportunities for reality testing
5. Provide media for sublimation.

Ginott stressed that when a therapist places correct toys in the play therapy room it facilitates the therapist's understanding of the child's issues. For example, when one allows the child the use of dolls and family objects it makes for easier interpretation about the interactions of the family.

In providing toys for catharsis, Ginott stressed that the therapist should be cognizant of what might be elicited by each toy from each child. For example, he suggested that a hyperactive child may become more hyperactive when exposed to materials that encourage freedom of expression, such as finger painting. In other children, the feelings elicited through the use of cathartic play may in fact evoke emotions that would not be therapeutic. With hyperactive children, Ginott suggested that children be exposed to toys that allow for construction in that Ginott felt that this would increase organization within the child. Fearful, fragile children should find in the playroom materials they can work with without fear of failure, such as clay, dolls, chalk, and crayons. They can use the material to practice the expression of emotions in multiple ways.

Ginott (1961a) added that sand, water, paint, and clay provide opportunity for sublimating urethral and anal drives. "Enuretic children should be given paint and running water, encopretic children should be given mud and brown clay. Children who play with fire should have cap guns, sparklers, and flashlights. All children should have miniature utensils for cooking and serving meals to sublimate oral needs; dolls that can be dressed and undressed to sublimate sexual needs; and punching bags, targets, and guns to sublimate aggressive needs" (p. 62).

Ginott (1960, 1961a) suggested that the room be about 150 to 200 square feet, and should be safe, well lighted, and easily cleaned. His list of objects in the room included both a round and an oblong table. He suggested a blackboard, a sink with running water, toys for climbing, family play, animals, hospital play, transportation play, water play, and materials to be used for art, such as paint. He included aggressive types of toys, puppets, and building blocks. He felt that homemaking equipment such as dishes should be included. Ginott also equipped the room with a sandbox and sand play materials.

Playroom materials and equipment should be chosen for their usefulness in reaching the goals set up for therapy, according to Hammer and Kaplan (1967). They indicated that materials can be used for many purposes. These include diagnosis (which uses predominately unstructured media), building tolerance (such as puzzles and model airplane and car construction), improving a sense of adequacy and sexual identification (such as tool sets and competitive games for boys and arts and crafts for girls), providing expressive and aggressive outlets (such as balloons, Bobo, toy soldiers and army equipment, transportation toys, tools for sawing and hammering, and noisemakers), promoting the therapeutic relationship (checkers and cards), and promoting sublimation (such as cooking utensils, books, toy musical instruments, dolls, and tape recorders).

Arthur (1952) suggested that play equipment should include a dollhouse, dolls, guns, snakes, horses, and plenty of creative materials. The playroom should provide enough space so that the child will be able to play in a creative manner without being restricted from normal movements.

Oaklander (1988) describes a wide range of materials and objects that she uses in her therapeutic work with children. She focuses heavily on those materials that allow a child to have a sensory experience. Her approach encourages the child to get in touch with feelings. And, using the gestalt approach, the connection between emotion and body is necessary in assisting the child to develop congruence. She uses the materials as a vehicle to assist in the integration of feelings. Further, she uses materials that allow children to express ideas so that she will be able to use the designs and objects as a road that she and the child can travel in order to get to their feelings about significant others and happenings in their life.

In describing a model play therapy room, Landreth (1991) followed Axline's description closely. However, in his discussion about the setting and the materials to be in it, he varied slightly from Axline's description of the room. In his 1991 book he elaborated his own position.

Landreth (1991) reported that not only were the toys of utmost importance, but so was the playroom and its atmosphere as well. He recommended a large space, brightly colored walls, and a large mirror because he felt it would encourage the appropriate response, with the entire effect being cheerful yet private. Landreth (Landreth et al. 1995) believes toys should be selected to encourage children to be themselves; his rules for selection of toys are as follows:

1. Toys that aid in the establishment of a positive relationship
2. Toys that help the child express emotions
3. Aggressive toys that allow for limit testing
4. Toys that allow for feelings of mastery and a good self-image
5. Self-understanding through toys of discovery, such as dolls
6. Toys that facilitate self-control, such as sand.

Kottman's (1995) Adlerian approach regarding toys is similar to that of a client-centered play therapist, but with five major divisions instead of three. Family/nurturing toys are used for eliciting information concerning the family and its dynamics. Scary toys are intended to uncover traumas, threats or illogical beliefs. Aggressive toys elicit control and trust problems. Expressive toys are for creativity expression, emotions, and relationships. Lastly, fantasy toys allow a child to investigate alternative behaviors and relationships.

Like Jungian play therapists, Oaklander (1988) endorses the use of manipulative and imaginative toys in her playroom. She wrote extensively about children's drawings, which to her serve a variety of purposes, including family information and expressions of emotions including anger, and, like Kottman and Landreth, she encourages fantasy play. Tactile stimulation through various media such as clay, water, sand, and wood is encouraged because as Oaklander said, "I find that most children who are singled out as needing help . . . have some impairment in their contact functions. The tools of contact are: looking, talking, touching, listening, moving, smelling, and tasting" (p. 57).

In addition, Oaklander encourages storytelling (either in books, video form or tape) as a means of communication between the therapist and child. This is in line with the work of cognitive-behavioral therapists, like Susan Knell (1993a,b), who encourage bibliotherapy as a means of learning new methods of behavior and coping skills.

MATERIAL USED WITH HANDICAPPED CHILDREN

In describing the reeducative process of play therapy in a school for retarded children, Maisner (1950) suggested that the room should be large enough for hyperactive children to have ample room for movement. The room used in this particular setting contained a lavatory, a drinking fountain, and a closet. Other equipment included open shelves, a sandbox, and a six-foot-tall doghouse. Media included amputee dolls, a long low table, a set of marionettes, finger-painting material, hostile weapons such as "a popgun, water pistol, rubber daggers, toy money, billy club, handcuffs and boxing gloves" (p. 241). Maisner also included dolls, a cradle, nursing bottles, a picket fence, a dollhouse, and a toy telephone.

Cowen and Cruickshank (1948a,b) reported that, in providing facilities for small group therapy for physically handicapped students, they used a vacant kindergarten classroom that was not set up for play therapy groups. It was 40 feet by 20 feet in size and contained a piano, desk, and small chairs and tables. The media available included games, puzzles, paste, crayons, blocks, and boxes and boards for building, blankets, balls, doll carriages, cabinets, beads, and a large three-dimensional doll house. Finger paints were also provided. In providing materials for the physically handicapped child the physical limitation has to be considered.

Leland and Smith (1962, 1965) discussed the use of unstructured material in play therapy for emotionally disturbed, neurologically impaired, and mentally retarded children. They suggested that proper selection of materials should be based not only on the rationale of the therapy that is being conducted but also on the specific needs of the child in therapy.

Leland and Smith suggested that the special needs of retarded children seem to center on three primary areas: the need to establish a level of self, the need to establish impulse control, and the need to establish social interaction. The authors state that these needs are best served in a situation where both the materials of play and the procedures of the therapist are fairly loosely structured. This gives children as much opportunity as possible for self-expression. The materials recommended for use in this unstructured setting include sand, water, wooden blocks, beads, pipe cleaners, snow, scraps of wood, and twigs. A minimum of tools and equipment are required. These include a sink, a sandbox, a cabinet, a table, a few containers, sponges, scissors, and a broom.

MATERIAL USED WITH BLIND CHILDREN

In an article describing his work in play therapy with blind children, Jones (1952) discussed the materials that are beneficial in the playroom. Certain considerations should be taken into account when working with the blind child. Jones suggested that toys should be of the same size as those to which the child has become accustomed elsewhere. Any toys that are to be used together, such as dolls and dollhouses, should be in proper scale. He suggested that the number of toys and the complexity and variety of toys should be limited with the blind child.

So that the blind children will know what toys are in the playroom, Jones (1952) suggested an orientation, in which children are taken around the room. The toys are described, and their various uses are discussed. This allows children to familiarize themselves with the materials and it allows the therapist to have a more accurate understanding as to why or why not certain toys are used by each child.

Rothschild (1960) suggested that practical media should be used and further developed for use by the blind child in play therapy. He suggested that suitable recordings and reading of stories can serve as valuable aids in helping blind children to express themselves. Materials need to be developed with which children can identify that they can use for self-expression.

Raskin (1954) suggested that toys that can be used in working with blind children include sand, water, blocks, clay, dolls, puppets, figures of people and animals, toy autos, and planes. There are limitations to the use of the toys and materials in that the blind child tends to make simpler uses of the toys than do sighted children.

MATERIAL USED WITH OLDER CHILDREN

Allowing older children to use materials and games rather than have talk therapy enhances the process in a number of ways. Frequently, even though a person is older than 7, or even during adolescence, they respond with more freedom if the pressure of language expression is off of them. Kids this age seem to like to relate on a number of different levels with a therapist. Often this happens within the same session. During a 50 minute time period, a 17-year-old may move from expressing childlike joy on the completion of an object modeled of clay to exhibiting highly competitive play in a game of cards. The material allows a person to move through several levels of emotional experience, thus allowing them to try on a variety of behaviors and emotions in a safe environment.

When children are moving from the fantasy level to more realistic levels of development, games with rules are helpful to them in that they have a chance to try out their skills in an accepting environment. Additionally, structured games allow the therapist to work with the older child on issues of manipulation and honesty. When an older child or adolescent manipulates, fabricates, or steals, using a structured board game allows the therapist to confront such behaviors.

When using structured games with older children in therapy, the following guidelines are suggested:

1. The game has a set of rules which are understood by the child and are agreed on in advance by both therapist and child.
2. The game is at the child's cognitive developmental level.
3. The game is short enough to be finished within the given hour.
4. When possible the toys for younger children are housed in a different room.

Some children who are in therapy wish to move from structured materials to the play therapy setting, to the "talk room," within the same session. The decision about these transitions needs to be flexible and directed by the child. It is reasonable that a middle-year child wants to be "younger" some days and "older" during others.

Stephenson (1973) suggested ways of working with older children in play therapy situations. He said that mutual participation enables the worker to be a model and a catalyst for the child. He suggested that drawings, paintings, and other art work can be used to illustrate and work out feelings. In addition, the overly tidy child can use this as a means of loosening up. He described the use of a playhouse, dolls, and puppets with latency-age children. The therapist can ask children to pretend that they are younger. He described the use of costume play as first discussed by Marcus (1966), the mutual storytelling technique, and games such as checkers as described by Loomis (1957). Loomis suggested that, through the use of checkers, the analyst is able to gain insights into the dynamics of the personality of the child. These are the underlying aggressive needs and competitive drives that ordinarily might be difficult for the child to disclose. This medium will give children an opportunity to see their resistances and character defenses and, when they choose, to retreat into play with the checker game. This medium can be used therapeutically as well as diagnostically. Loomis described the use of checkers in five different case studies. Included among the presented difficulties are one child who had tics and another child who had asthma. Loomis stressed that the value of checker games lies in disclosing the presence of resistances, aiding in analyzing them, and helping to discover their inner meaning. The game becomes much more than a game when used by a skilled therapist.

Meeks (1970) suggested that for the child in the latency period of psychosexual development, games that are competitive and have definite rules are in order. Checkers, chess, and card games are excellent because they are realistic.

MATERIAL USED IN A SCHOOL SETTING

Demaago (1971) described the use of client-centered play therapy for use in an elementary school. Following the concepts of Carl Rogers, she pointed out that play therapy offers the child an opportunity to play out his feelings, explore his thoughts, and describe his experiences. The counselor's role was described as that of a nondirective participant, reflecting, recognizing, and clarifying the child's feelings. She described two types of playrooms that are appropriate to a public school setting, and she suggested that teachers should be trained in the techniques of play therapy. The method of play therapy can be adaptable to the classroom through the use of creative activities and recognition of the child's feelings by the teacher-therapist.

Waterland (1970) described the use of play therapy in an elementary school guidance setting. She followed the philosophy of Axline in reference to rationale, selection of materials, structure, and technique, and used the case study method to illustrate the use of this technique in the elementary school.

In an article on school-centered play therapy, Alexander (1964) stressed the relationship therapy approach as described by Moustakas. He gave a case study to demonstrate the application of relationship therapy to actual situations. As no playroom was available, the counselor carried the toys in a suitcase and used a quiet room for the sessions. He stressed the importance of working very closely with teachers as a necessary part of the total service to the child.

Moustakas (1959a) believed that, in providing play therapy experiences for school children in the school setting, the therapist must project an accepting attitude toward the teacher's experience. The therapeutic relationship between the therapist and child can act as a catalyst in the relationship between the teacher and child. The therapist provides support to the teacher in the struggle to accept and understand the child. The child, he suggested, is helped to make an emotional reorganization in the school environment as a step toward emotional growth at home and in other situations.

A study involving twenty children was reported by Hume (1970). The most effective means of intervention when working with the emotionally handicapped child was twofold. It combined play therapy in combination with in-service consultation for teachers. Play therapy alone was found to be an effective approach, but more gains were observed when this was combined with work with the teachers.

A summary of research about play therapy in a school setting was described by Seeman (1954). He surveyed the approaches to child therapy and also discussed applications of child therapy in practice and research. He concluded that play therapy not only has a place in strictly clinical settings but also has a place in the child's environment, where professionals are finding ways of making a therapeutic approach directly relevant to the educational scene. He cited research by Seeman and Edwards (1954), Bills (1950a,b), and Moustakas (1959a).

Kottman (1995) reported rather intensive work with children in schools as a school counselor who uses play therapy. In her book, she described and recognized the importance of following the child into the school for therapeutic intervention. Kottman stressed the importance of working with teachers and parents in the child's real-life setting so that the therapist will be able to have a more realistic understanding of the child and the child's needs. Using the Adlerian play therapy model, Kottman reported the importance of consulting with teachers about the needs of the child. She gathers information from the teachers, and actually works with the child in the school setting through a school counseling program.

Landreth (1991) suggested that when play therapy is done in schools, the counselor should be careful about the way the program is entitled. He indicated that the term *therapy* may have a connotation that we, as therapists, do not want to introduce into the school. He encourages school counselors to use the model of play therapy and to use the materials described in play therapy to assist children in their growth and development. He recognizes that there are problems involved in taking such a program into a school and suggests that counselors carefully evaluate the limits and the potential of such a program before implementing it.

Knell (1993a,b) suggested that a recent trend in this country has been to use play therapy for preventive purposes. She indicated that a lot of this work has occurred in the school setting and is being utilized by school psychologists and school counselors.

Landreth and colleagues (1995) have referenced dozens of articles recently published in journals dealing with child therapy that are directly related to working with children in schools.

School systems throughout the country are providing elementary school counselors and school psychologists with materials appropriate to use with children in a school setting. The media, the material, and play approach to working with children in schools have become the rule in this country at this time. (This model for working with children represents a significantly positive departure from the old consulting model, wherein school counselors simply consulted with teachers and parents.) Using the concept of play as the child's most natural method of expression, school counselors are reaching children with increased efficacy and understanding. There are problems to be considered when using therapy in a school, but any time we work with children we should be playing with them and using materials so that they can express themselves through their natural language, play. If counselors do this, then they will have a model that works. When a trained adult uses appropriate techniques for working with children (play materials), then therapy occurs. It does not matter whether this is outside on the playground, in the corner of a classroom, or in a privately organized and maintained office designed for play therapy. It is important that we remember that all the conditions for confidentiality and safety must be met and ensured when a caring other involves herself with a child in need.

Basing his philosophy on that of Ginott, Nelson (1966) stressed that the elementary school counselor must utilize play media. Play in a child should be treated as if it is verbalized behavior. Nelson recommended unstructured material because it can be used in a variety of ways. He lists clay, paints, crayons, pipe cleaners, building materials, puppets, telephones, typewriters, finger paints, scissors, paper, soft hand puppets, and dolls. The use of unstructured materials is desirable because they invite a wide range of response and expressiveness by the child.

In an article describing a desirable physical facility for elementary school counseling, Nelson (1967) suggested that it should provide durability. He described a floor covering of vinyl tile or other tough material, a sandbox, a walk-in playhouse, free-form climbing apparatus with gymnasium mats, a large bounce-back toy, and an observation booth with one-way viewing mirror. He added that a counseling office in the elementary school should provide mirrors, a sink, a painting easel, and open shelves with an assortment of small toys suggested by the nondirective therapists.

In another article reporting work in a school setting, Schiffer (1957) described a room set apart in the school building for the exclusive use of the play groups. It was furnished with tables, chairs, work benches, sandbox, and sink. Materials provided for the use of the children included doll families, doll furniture, paints of various types, easels, sand, clay, paper, toys, and games.

An elementary school guidance center in North Dakota was described by Butts (1971). He listed the toys described by the nondirective therapists and, in addition, telephones, portable tape recorders, and toy hand puppets.

This author stated in classroom lectures that her work as a school counselor involved as many as eight elementary schools during the course of one week. This necessitated her developing a bag of toys that she carried from school to school in the back of her car. The system that she developed is described as follows:

When she arrived at a school, a group of children who were designated helpers for the week in that school met her at the car. They carried the materials into the school that were to be used that week. These included the following:

1. Nonstructured media of the week. She would select papier-mâché, egg cartons and paint, wood for bird cages, materials for mutual building projects (for group work), and/or bits of rocks, materials, and found objects.
2. Materials for bibliotherapy.

3. The bag of toys, which included small family members, a folding doll house, small animals, puppets, clay, card games, big crayons, colored chalk, a small sand tray (encased), and small cars and trucks.
4. Two to three board games, which were traded off weekly.
5. "Something special" for a group or a child that would allow the children to know that she remembered their subject matter or color preference.

James's use of materials in the school setting often involved including a specific teacher or groups of children in projects such as stage-building, or "quiet" or "feeling" corners. In these areas would be placed materials that were chosen for their calming effects or their sensory effects. Some materials she would place in the feeling corner would be fabrics of various textures, "magic rocks," and special audio tapes (such as imagery or soothing themes).

MATERIAL USEFUL IN A HOSPITAL SETTING

There has been much written about the value of including a provision for the emotional needs of children in a hospital setting. Davidson (1949) recommended a playroom with a trained counselor for a hospital setting. It should be designed to meet and serve the needs of the child while in the hospital. Davidson contended that the hospital has an obligation to provide for the emotional needs of the child who is under stress in order to lessen the possibility of permanent emotional trauma as a sequel to physical illness. She based her belief on the assumption that unique insecurities develop in a hospital, which should be dealt with at that time. Good nursing care should make provision for adequate experiences in all areas of the child's needs. However, this play program should be directed by a person qualified in child guidance techniques.

It is the responsibility of a hospital to provide for the total needs of the child who comes there, emotional as well as physical, suggested Whitted and Scott (1962). The emotional needs of the child can be provided for through the use of facilities for play and a "play lady." The play lady possesses personal skills that allow her to understand and be helpful to both the child and his parents. She offers fun, relaxation, comfort, and enjoyment. In this particular hospital setting, both indoor and outdoor facilities are provided.

McPherson (1965) and Kimmel (1952) wrote on the value of the play technique in meeting the needs of children in a medical setting. Chalmers (1966) wrote that play is valuable in nursing severely subnormal children. She suggested that nurses working with these children should be trained in play techniques.

The functions of a hospital playroom are described by Despert (1937b):

1. The playroom provides the child an outlet for motor activity under unrestrained, uncensored, nonorganized conditions.
2. It allows the child an opportunity for abreaction of affects of the traumatic experiences often accompanied by separation, the fright involved with illness, and the other uncertainties involved with being in a strange place.
3. It allows the child to gain insight.
4. It allows for sublimation of stress into constructive activities (p. 679).

Richards and Walff (1940) described a play group that functions within a medical clinic setting. The group was open in that the children use the group on the mornings they were scheduled for regular medical services. Play materials were provided for the older children. The playroom was supervised by a trained worker.

Cassell (1965) reported a study investigating the effect of brief puppet therapy upon the emotional responses of children undergoing cardiac catheterization. The study involved forty children between ages 3 and 11 who had been admitted to a children's hospital for cardiac catheterization. Twenty of the subjects were randomly assigned to an experimental group that received puppet therapy before and after the operation. Twenty of the children were placed in a control group that was not given therapy but received the same treatment in other ways. The author reported that children who received therapy were less disturbed during the operation and also expressed to their parents more willingness to return to the hospital for further treatment. The posthospitalization behavioral expectation of the study was not supported. Both groups showed slight improvement in their emotional behavior following hospitalization.

Professionals who use toys that are designed to allow a child to release emotions and to prepare for emotionally painful experiences in hospitals are increasingly being invited to do this in traditional hospital settings where children are ill. A review of work within this type of setting shows that there are issues related to procedures and ethics that have to be carefully considered. Persons who engage in such work generally are of three categories:

1. Those persons hired by the hospital to enhance the treatment of the children in the hospital. These persons might be (a) "play persons" who maintain a room full of toys and do some supervision of play while the child is there; (b) these same "play persons" who go to the child's room or work with her in the playroom to assist her to prepare for such things as surgery or other procedures; (c) nurses who have had experience in the use of toys to assist the child to communicate and remain as calm as possible under the circumstances.
2. Those persons who have admission and treating privileges with the hospital such as a psychiatrist who is invited to consult on a case by the treating physician.
3. Those persons who may have affiliate privileges that allow them to enter the hospital ward at the invitation of the treating physician in order to assist this physician with the emotional needs of an identified child. Psychologists, social workers, and counselors would be included in this category (James 1996).

There are many issues to be considered when taking materials into a hospital setting. The most apparent one is that toys have to be chosen considering the physical limitations of the child. The second consideration is to determine any physical harm that could potentially come to the child with a particular object. For example, when a child is suffering from respiratory distress, the child should not be exposed to chalk. If the child is hyperactive, then calming, constructive activities must be chosen. The physician in charge of the child has to be consulted in advance of planning any activity in a hospital with a child.

It is obvious that when a child is bedridden, soft toys and lightweight materials should be chosen. If the child wishes to paint, then smaller pots and brushes, with plastic material for covering the bed, have to be provided.

When a child has a broken arm or leg, then materials that do not require movement have to be provided. Frequently, the therapist plays at the child's direction. An example of this would be a game involving toy animals or toy people. The child tells the therapist what to do with the objects and the therapist complies.

The concept of nondirective play therapy is not appropriate in a hospital room. However, the concept of a nondirective relationship is appropriate. This entails allowing the child to be the boss, allowing the child to lead while the therapist follows. The therapist does not enter the session with a preconceived plan about what will happen in the relationship or how it will happen. We cannot assume that children wish to deal with their illness, their trauma, their fears, or their anger. They may simply wish to have a break from it all and be a kid for a while.

It is important to remember that sick kids generally tire quickly. Therefore, the therapist should not overwhelm the child with a lot of materials. The therapist should watch for body symptoms of fatigue or pain. When this occurs, it is time to exit.

James (1987) indicated that when she plans a hospital session, she includes the following materials:

1. Small paint pots with brushes and a bed easel.
2. Puppets or dolls to depict significant adults and children. This will always include good and bad guys, nurses, parents, doctors, and sibling dolls.
3. Doctor bag with real items—bandages, band-aids, cotton swabs, and materials for making small casts for doll legs.
4. Clay (when feasible)
5. Small wooden dolls and animals
6. Folding doll house
7. Bed tray for small toy play
8. Sand tray with lid that contains miniature objects.
9. Books

She found that children who are in the hospital feel that their sense of control has been taken away. One of the things James tries to do is allow the child to control the session. She allows the child to control when or if they interact with her. She allows the child to terminate the session when they wish. She allows the child to dictate what she brings for the next session. She does not plan a cathartic session because she believes that structuring the session takes what little control the child has left. She is careful about allowing for catharsis. Allowing violent anger toward the medical treatment to be expressed may reinforce the child's resistance to medical intervention and thus result in physical harm to the child.

Davidson (1949) recommended the establishment of a playroom in a hospital setting. She selected toys according to their facilitative nature as well as their adaptive nature for the hospital child with limited mobility.

She recommended that dolls can be used as doctors, nurses, or patients, and as family members. The doll house should be small enough to fit at a bedside and can be used to duplicate a home or a hospital. Fist puppets can be used in the same way as dolls. She suggested the use of a tray full of clay, crayons, newsprint, and finger paints (provide an apron). She stated that chalk and chalkboard can be used (but not with a respiratory patient). She also recommended the use of games, puzzles, books, and music.

Despert (1937b), in an article describing the use of a playroom in a hospital setting, stated that it should not resemble a regular playground, so that the child will not be affected by past associations of play. It should be equipped with a table, child and adult chairs, and toilet and water basin with running water. The necessary toys include a set of dolls of the different family members, housebuilding equipment, elementary furniture, nursing bottles, water basin, locomotion toys (car, plane), guns, soldiers, plasticine, and drawing materials. With children under 4, she suggested that the most commonly used materials are plasticine, nursing bottles, and containers for filling with water and pouring it out.

Because of many limitations in working in a traditional hospital setting, the therapist may wish to confine the work they do within the structured, cathartic, or release therapy framework. This work is designed for specific purposes, is time-limited, and does not include the concept of regression. It is healing, it is helpful, it is necessary, but it is not long-term traditional play therapy.

PLAY THERAPY IN PSYCHIATRIC HOSPITAL SETTINGS

There are a number of issues that therapists should consider in determining whether or not play therapy is an appropriate modality for the above setting. John Burnside, M.D., (personal communication, March 1996) has wide experience working as a child psychiatrist in psychiatric hospital settings. He suggested that there are a number of considerations that should be taken into account before a decision to use play therapy in such a setting is made.

1. The first thing to determine is whether there is a room equipped for play therapy.
2. The second thing to consider is whether privacy can be assured the child and the family while play therapy is being done.

3. The third consideration is to determine whether the child will be a resident in this setting long enough for the process of play therapy to occur. (Funding issues typically dictate that hospital stays are short.)

4. The fourth consideration for most play therapists is whether the psychiatrist in charge of the case wishes this type of treatment to be done.

5. The fifth consideration is whether the child's rights will be ensured in this setting.

The position of the play therapist may be that it is appropriate for members of the treatment team to use toys as they relate to children in such settings, but the concept of play therapy involves much more than the simple use of toys. For play therapy to occur, the therapist must be assured that they will have time to allow the full treatment process to unfold. The setting must lend itself so that limits and materials can be used appropriately. The relationship between a child and a play therapist is a unique one. When a child is in a hospital setting, frequently the treatment mode is a milieu type of intervention. The child may have one primary therapist, but she does not have the opportunity to develop a relationship such as is required between a play therapist and a child in order for the full range of treatment to occur.

Before a play therapist offers her services in a free-standing psychiatric hospital, it is recommended that she take into account all of the above issues. It is probably more appropriate for a therapist to function as a person who will receive the child after he has been in the hospital, to do the therapy in a private setting. If a play therapist has a child in therapy who needs to be in the hospital, that therapist can maintain a supportive relationship with the child while the child is in the hospital in an effort to augment the hospital treatment program. However, unless the play therapist is a child psychiatrist, in most states she would not be the primary therapist.

MATERIAL USEFUL IN STRUCTURED THERAPY

In describing his technique of structured play therapy as a diagnostic as well as therapeutic procedure, Conn (1939) suggested the use of dolls. They should represent various characters, such as parents, teachers, and siblings. However, in treating fearful children, no attempt should be made to arouse antagonistic or hostile tendencies (Conn 1941a). Guns, pistols, knives, and soldiers are not included in the play materials.

The therapist assumes the role of the friendly, informed adult. This adult allows the child to express his thoughts and feelings through the medium of the dolls, as if they were responsible for all that is said and done. The child is an impartial spectator and can objectively view what is going on as well as participate in an intimate discussion of his own attitudes. The child is able to project fears, anger, jealousy, and hate onto the dolls. Other materials used in this technique involve toy furniture. Situations are structured to provide stimulus for individual cases.

In another article, Conn (1941a) described the play interview technique in working with a timid child. He stressed that this technique allows the child the opportunity to view self objectively while working through the dolls. Conn suggested that this technique allows the child to see "self in action." Random play is eliminated. The child realizes that play and entertainment are not the focus of the session. The child has come to participate as an equal who has something to contribute as well as to learn.

The therapist assumes many roles during the play interview. Sometimes the therapist will speak directly or for one of the dolls in order to inquire why another doll character acted in the way it did. In addition, the therapist may present the voice of experience or even introduce a different direction to the conversation.

Mann (1957) suggested that, in equipping the setting for persuasive doll play, the therapist should provide an adequate and varied set of miniature dolls, representing members of both sexes and of various ages and occupations, complementary materials such as toy furniture scaled to the dolls, a doll house, and various vehicles such as trucks, cars, and fire engines.

Solomon (1938, 1940, 1948) discussed the use of the play technique diagnostically, therapeutically, and in research. The main media discussed by Solomon in all of his work are dolls. These dolls, usually like those described by Levy (1939a) and Conn (1955), are used to symbolize the child and various members of the family. In addition, Solomon has added a doll to represent the therapist in his work with the child (1938, 1948). He suggested that the doll representing the therapist offers the child an opportunity to work out his feelings toward the therapist in a safer way. It is easier for the child to express anger, hostility, and love to the doll than it is directly to the therapist. This is especially true in the beginning stages of treatment and when the feelings are strong.

When introducing the new doll to represent the therapist, Solomon tells the child, "This doll is Dr. Solomon." In this way, children learn that they can express their feelings to the Dr. Solomon doll and finally to Dr. Solomon. Later, the child is able to express feelings onto dolls representing other persons and, finally, to the persons directly (Solomon 1948). The use of dolls and the active role of the therapist in playing with the child aid the therapist in learning about the child. Further, they aid therapeutically, in that the symbolism is clear. At the beginning, the child must be allowed to express self through self-selected medium. Solomon (1938) suggests that clay, finger paints, crayons, or other materials may be the means of entering the child's fantasy world.

According to Levy (1939a), the playroom should have materials that allow the child to get into the structured situation. In addition, he advised the use of certain materials for certain situations. Some of those described are "new baby at mother's breast," in which the child is allowed to work through feelings of sibling rivalry. This involves the use of the mother doll, a baby doll, and a self doll. The child is encouraged to make a breast on the mother doll. The child is then asked to place the baby on the mother. Various dimensions of feeling are explored. Levy devised specific situations to represent specific traumas in the child's life. Each specific situation requires the use of a certain set of materials.

Materials useful for specific problem solving were described by Hambridge (1955). For example, in order to help a child work through genital difference problems, he suggested the use of water, balloons, and baby bottles with nipples. Using these, the child can play out fantasies regarding the function of the organ. Another situation that Hambridge discussed is the invisible boy (or girl) in the parents' bedroom. This type of play requires a mother doll, a father doll, a self doll, and a bed for the parents. Hambridge did not introduce furniture at this time but allowed the child to choose it if he likes. The "birth of a baby" episode calls for a hollow rubber doll with a pelvic opening and a baby doll. Other stressful situations require specific materials that the therapist can structure so that the child is able to express and release his feelings.

MATERIALS USEFUL FOR FORENSIC PURPOSES

When a therapist is using a play therapy room or a room that contains toys for the purpose of evaluation, then specific materials should be placed in that setting. For example, in such a setting, a therapist would have anatomically correct dolls representing more than one ethnic group. There would be doll play materials. The room should include automobiles and any other types of materials that would be representative of the trauma the child experienced. For example, in the event that a child has been involved in a car accident, automobiles that would allow the child representational play to reenact the trauma should be in place. The room should be equipped with audiovisual material for further observation and documentation. The setting would contain a doll house and family toys representative of the members of the child's own family. The design of a setting for forensic work is much like the setting design for structured therapy. The materials necessary for evaluation of the child's world are contained within.

REVIEW OF LITERATURE
ABOUT VARIOUS SPECIFIC MATERIALS

Puppets

Bender (1936) and Woltmann (1940) described their use of puppets in a children's observation ward of the psychiatric division of Bellevue Hospital. The ages of the children ranged from 2 to 16 years. Behavior problems were the chief psychotherapeutic problem presented. The authors suggested that the use of puppets in this situation was ideal in that symbolic characters can give free expression to aggression without causing anxiety and fear in the child. Children can also freely express love through a puppet.

Pinocchio was used by Machler (1965). Children with social and emotional difficulties can easily identify with Pinocchio because of the distressing social, educational, and peer problems he had. Pinocchio was punished, and, in the end, he emerged whole and in better shape than he was before he went through his trials. Machler indicated the Freudian theme of the characters in the Pinocchio play and correlated them with the needs of children in a play setting. This theme allows a child to work through his psychosexual difficulties.

Grant (1950), an Australian psychotherapist, discussed her use of the puppet Kasperl and his sister Greta in her work with children. This character and his sister originated in Vienna and were widely used in Europe after the war for educational purposes.

In her work with puppets, Grant makes up her own stories, which bring out situations with which children generally have to deal. The stories have to do with feelings, difficulties, alternatives, and decisions. The plot is kept flexible, and the children are allowed to interact and redirect the process if they so choose. In this way, they become participants in the life process and not onlookers to the solutions and explorations for alternatives.

Jenkins and Beckh (1942), following the ideas of Bender about puppetry at Bellevue, used rubber balls for the heads of the puppets and allowed the child to paint details on the face. They suggested that these are puppets the child can play with without assistance. The resources of finger puppets lie in the flexibility and dynamic types of dramatization made possible by them. The child can dramatize problems on an impersonal basis, yet at opportune times in the play therapy process the therapist can personalize the problem presented.

Jenkins and Beckh (1942) also used masks in the play therapy setting. The forming of the clay, which is a pliable, flexible material, is therapeutic in itself. The child is able to form, destroy, and make over at will with no fear of failure. The physical experience allows for emotional release. The authors stressed that care must be taken not to place value judgments on the outcome, nor should the product be interpreted. There is wide variation in motor abilities of children. Sometimes they are unable to produce a finished mask that they are pleased with. Because of this, interpretation of the product is likely to be inaccurate.

The use of puppets has been described widely. Marcus (1966), a therapist in Paris, discussed his use of puppets both diagnostically and therapeutically in his work with children. Wall (1950) compiled an entire book on the use of puppets. Hawkey (1951b) described the use of puppets in child psychotherapy. She used them in individual treatment with a child but never used them exclusive of other media. Puppets were kept in the playroom with sand trays, paints, paper, chalk, crayons, water play materials, dolls and doll houses, building blocks, sewing materials, trains, cars, and guns. Hawkey suggested that puppets are valuable because they are suitable for the expression of fantasy and are popular with children of varying ages. Most of the children use the puppets themselves, making up their own dialogue and using the therapist as an audience. At other times, the children request that the therapist make up the story with the puppets, which she does. Hawkey used the case study method in her description of the benefits of the use of puppets with boys 12, 11, and 6 years of age. Her work was not limited to boys, however, because in another article (1951a), she described the use of puppets with a young girl.

Hawkey (1951b) stressed that puppets offer the advantage of allowing children to express fantasy when they feel older. With puppets, children are more able to put feelings into words. They are able to do this without feeling guilt because they are able to project these guilty feelings onto the puppet (who is not permanently harmed by these bad deeds).

Other Materials

Interpretations of the art of children across cultures and time were made by Lowenfeld (1939). She has shown similarities in reference to stages of development and personality characteristics. Bender (1938) wrote on the value of the use of art in the treatment of mental disturbances of children, and Roland (1952) described the use of art, painting, and finger painting in play therapy with children. Cashdon (1967) reported the use of the drawings produced by a child in evaluating process in play therapy. The use of art and play in therapy was described by Gordor (1954). He suggested that if we want to help the child we must first find out what is wrong with the child. Art, he contended, offers the child an unlimited amount of freedom. What children are not permitted to express in words, they can express in drawings. They are able to express experiences and convictions about the drawings that they would be unable to verbalize directly. Gordor suggested that different children behave in different ways in the art experience. The therapist is able to identify many characteristics in the child by observing his use of the material, his freedom, his reluctance to use his own ideas, or his initiative.

Gordor indicated that children will project feelings into their art and, further, will project perceptions of the world into the art experience. As children are able to put the distorted picture down in tangible form, they and the therapist are able to extricate misconceptions. The art experience allows the child to be "magical" or "giant-like" in the world of the pictorial representation. The child has magic power in that the depiction of the feeling can be controlled. This allows the therapist to understand the needs and wishes of the child who is unable to verbalize. The therapist is also able to understand the child's social and family concepts through drawings. The child will draw self in relation to the family. The child will show likes, desires, hidden wishes, and dislikes by placement or omission of the persons in art.

Nickols (1961b) recommended the use of darts, suction-cupped projectiles, air pistols, and appropriate stimulus background materials. This allows children to express feelings about family, peers, and themselves. Nickols felt that this aggressive material allows the child freedom of expression of anger. In another article, Nickols (1961a) described specifications for a multipurpose play therapy and examining table, which is functional and economical in space. The underside can be used for a chalk board. The top has a place for a dollhouse framework and a flat surface for testing. The legs fold, and the table is built to child specifications.

Goldings (1972) has written on the use of books in the playroom. Goldings suggested the use of bibliotherapy as a valuable tool in working with children with emotional difficulties. Books in a library are listed according to the situational difficulties that the child in the book has had to endure. The concept of bibliotherapy involves giving the book to the child to read or, in some cases, reading the book to the child. This gives children a nonpersonal character with whom they can identify.

The use of psychodrama as a technique performed in a playroom setting has been discussed by Marcus (1966) and Drabkova (1966). Marcus discussed the use of costume play in the treatment of an underachieving effeminate boy. He encouraged the child to make up a play with various costumes. Through the use of this technique, the child was able to express conflict and to resolve the feelings generated.

SELECTION OF MATERIAL: RESEARCH

Lebo (1958b) discussed the need for a formula for selecting toys for nondirective play therapy. He stated that toys should be *selected* for the playroom rather than *accumulated* for it. Toys should be selected objectively rather than inferentially.

Lebo (1958b) developed a verbal index formula based on the number of statements made while a particular toy was actually used and the expressive variety of the statements. The rank order of the twenty-eight best toys, based on their obtained verbal index, are: doll house, family furniture, poster paints, brushes, paper, easel, paint jars, sandbox, blackboard and colored chalk, cap guns and caps, coloring books, hand puppets, balloons, nursing bottles, films and viewer, water in basin, pop guns, bubble gum, coffee pot, cord and rope, animals, wood, balls, crayons, baby dolls, bow and arrows, clay, cars, checkers, shovel, masks, toy soldiers, and watercolors.

Lebo (1955a) conducted a study including the recommended toys of the nondirective therapists that are supposed to cause the child to be more creative and release more feeling. He also included a list of nonrecommended toys in this study. These nonrecommended toys were structured in nature and consisted of rubber balls, bubble blowing equipment, checker games, coffee pot, coloring books, comic books, cord, filmstrips, fireman's helmet, ladies' hats, handcuffs, garden tools, marbles, play money, paper pumpkin, ladies' shoes, stand-up-figures of Peter Rabbit and Farmer Brown, man's sweater, thumbtacks, washboard, and a whistle.

Lebo used 4,092 statements made in sixty individual nondirective play therapy sessions by twenty normal children ages 4 to 12. The data indicated that the use of toys suggested by nondirective play therapists did not seem to encourage children to express themselves verbally to a greater extent than did nonrecommended toys or even when toys were not used at all. Lebo also suggested that the nondirective play relationship might not require the creative or dramatic toys of the Freudian diagnostic play relationship. The power is in the relationship, not in the toys. In summarizing, he referenced Hartley (1952), who indicated that children give materials value dependent upon associations with the past and their ability to project meanings and use symbols.

Lebo (1956b) investigated the value of toys in play therapy by examining 166 pages of original play therapy protocols. Six judges were involved in examining the protocols for significant and nonsignificant statements made by children during the play therapy. Twenty-five statements regarded by three or more judges as being significant were randomly selected. In addition, twenty-five statements that none of the judges regarded as significant were randomly selected. The original protocols were reexamined to determine what toys the children were playing with when they made significant or nonsignificant statements. Lebo concluded that the findings suggest that there is no difference in statements made by children when playing with toys or when not playing with toys. He contended, however, that toys do have a place in the therapeutic playroom, as they may serve to make the therapy hour more pleasant from the child's point of view.

In a study describing the use of miniature life toys and puppets, Hartley and colleagues (1952) found differences in the way well-adjusted and troubled children use toys. One hundred eighty-six records were made describing the play sessions of seventy-nine children, ranging in age from 2 to 5 years. The researchers found that the differences between the two groups centered on response to symbols of aggression, to the nursing bottle, to investigation of the dolls' clothing, to creativity in play, to content of play, to use of water, and to the amount of aggression shown.

Homefield (1959) investigated the use of role playing with special reference to the use of masks as therapy for stuttering children. He found this medium to be effective in working with stuttering children. He observed that when children played the authoritarian role, the fluency increased.

The play patterns of three groups of children were investigated by Loomis and colleagues (1957). The children were diagnosed as psychotic, mentally retarded, and nonsymptomatic. Initially, toys were presented one at a time to the children in fixed sequence for a minimum period. Toys were then increased to pairs in order to force choices. Next, the toys were arranged in three corners of the room: a construction-transportation center, a doll corner, and a junk corner. The junk corner contained such small items as clay, a toy telephone, and peg boards. The transcribed protocols of the observer were then subjected to three different scoring approaches. While the results of this study were not conclusive, preliminary indications suggested that play patterns are consistent for any one child or group of children on reexamination. One of the major differentiating features between the severely psychotic child and the normal child was the inability of the severely psychotic child to organize toys into various levels of complexity linked with the construction potential of toys.

The effect of three anthropomorphic models on the social adjustment of children was observed by Schall (1967). She paired eighteen subjects on the basis of social adjustment and overt aggression. One member of each pair was exposed to two different treatment methods for twenty-one sessions. The child was asked to play individually for twenty minutes in a play therapy room. The second group had the same opportunity. Added to this setting, however, were two adult-sized anthropomorphic figures representing male and female and a child-sized figure. Schall concluded that the children who experienced the treatment in the room with the anthropomorphic figures had a significant decrease in overt aggression. Pulaski (1970) investigated the hypothesis that young children would show greater freedom and imagination when engaged in fantasy play with unstructured materials than with highly realistic toys. She used matched groups of boys and girls who ranged in age from 5 to 7. They were selected for high and low predispositions to fantasy. The treatment involved four play sessions in which the children were presented with two related sets of playthings in counterbalanced order (one as structured as possible and one as unstructured as possible). Pulaski found that the less structured toys elicited a greater variety of fantasy themes, but the expected interaction between fantasy predisposition and degree of structure of the playthings did not appear to occur. Children with high predispositions to fantasy showed more creativity regardless of the type of toy.

Kidd and Walton (1966) reported a study in which ten aggressive boys were encouraged to throw darts at photographs of individuals toward whom they had expressed verbal hostility. The dart throwing significantly reduced overt aggression toward nonfamily members but not toward family members.

(The authors noted that they felt that, in order for children to be able to express hostility toward a family member, they would have to have established sound rapport with the therapist. This is an area of high risk for a child.)

In describing the results of a study involving forty children (approximately 150 to 300 drawings per child were collected and organized), Despert (1937a) reported definite patterns. The author explained that the drawings of psychotic children show evidence of regression while the drawings of neurotic and behavior-problem children show no evidence of regression (predominance of characteristics that belong to earlier developmental levels; preservation and automatism are present to a marked degree). In the drawings of the neurotic child, there was evidenced the underlying conflict through the "theme." Despert suggested further studies that would involve comparing drawings of primitives with normal and psychotic adults.

Beiser (1955) described a study involving the controlled use of toys by one hundred children through the use of diagnostic interviews. The children were given free choice of toys from a wide variety that were grouped categorically. The categories included were doll play, motor, pattern, mechanical, and unstructured.

The highest ranking toys in popularity were the doll family, soldiers, guns, knock-out bench, trucks, goose, telephone, animals, and airplane. He indicated that high-ranking toys in fantasy stimulation were the doll family, paper and crayons, clay, blocks, planes, soldiers, animals, trucks, and furniture. The lowest ranking toys in popularity, communicative value, and fantasy stimulation were pencil, paste, scissors, and a ball.

Beiser concluded that the potential for the use of a toy depends far more on the child and his unique use of it than on the toy itself. Beiser offered this information as being helpful in setting up a playroom. He suggested that, for the inexperienced therapist, a simple and standardized play setting is advisable. This standardization allows the therapist to compare with his own experience the behavior of different children in the same setting and in relation to the same toy stimuli. Beiser further suggested that the toys in the study were not necessarily the only toys that could be used but that they have been found to be useful and inexpensive. They are adaptable to any room and could be easily transported to any physical setup.

AGE DIFFERENCES IN USE OF MATERIALS

In a study investigating the preferences of eighty-seven 3-, 4-, and 5-year-old children for block shapes and sizes that were used or unused in building construction, Moyer and Von Haller (1956) found that the preferences of the subjects were not related to age. On the basis of this study, the investigators discounted past assumptions that children pass through stages in their selection and use of blocks. They contended that this is not necessarily related to chronological age. They found that 3-year-old children made their decisions about selection and use of the blocks in essentially the same ways as did the older subjects. Individual differences in the design of structures were just as great within any given group as those between the different age groups. The investigators concluded that the subjects' preferences for block shapes and sizes were made on the basis of their utility.

Robinson (1958) investigated the form and imaginative content of children's block buildings in order to find the range of block building performance characteristic of children between the ages of 3 and 10, to develop methods for ordering block building data so that comparisons can be made, and to determine what differences in block building performance may be related to differences in age, sex, and intellectual level.

Five boys and five girls were used at each of two levels of intelligence (100–115 and 135–160) and in four age groups (3 years, 5 years, 7 years, and 10 years). Each of the eighty subjects built three free-choice buildings and one prescribed construction. Photographs of the constructions and verbatim reports of the verbalizations provided material for the study. The analysis showed that, as children grow older, they tend to use more blocks, to build for longer periods of time, and to build larger and taller constructions. Boys exceed girls in the time spent and in the height of constructions. At every age, the variance among children on these quantitative measures is large. (In my opinion, findings relative to gender issues should be reinvestigated. This study was done in 1958 and much has changed related to gender issues and play.)

It was further found that younger children build simpler structural types such as piles and serial arrangements. Older children no longer build these. Enclosures appear early, and children throughout the age ranges built them. Roofed buildings predominate in the constructions of 5-year-olds. Combinations of roofed buildings and enclosures are popular at ages 7 and 10. Boys more often embellish their constructions with towers and use enclosures as accessories. Girls tend to build simple enclosures, particularly floor plans and furniture. (Again, I think findings relative to gender issues should be reinvestigated.)

Verbal accounts revealed further differences. Younger children most often build a house or a bridge and seldom add many details. The 7- and 10-

year-olds often build public buildings and describe their constructions in vivid detail, frequently placing them in geographical or historical perspective.

Updegraff and Herbst (1933) reported a study that was an attempt to observe experimentally the aspects of social behavior stimulated by certain play materials in young children. The study involved twenty-eight children, seventeen boys and eleven girls ranging in age from 2 years to 4 years and 2 months. Age differences found include the fact that 2-year-old children paid less attention to their partners than did 3-year-old children. The older children made more verbal suggestions to their partners, accepted more suggestions positively, held more conversations, were more sociable, and were more cooperative.

Lebo and Lebo (1957) conducted a study in which they investigated the problem of aggression and age in relation to verbal expression in nondirective play therapy. They hypothesized that children would manifest aggression in their verbal behavior, and also that aggression would be reduced in older children because of the process of socialization. Subjects were selected on the basis of chronological age, intelligence test scores, and aggressiveness. There were ten, twenty-two, twenty-four, and twenty-three children aged 4, 6, 9, and 12 respectively. Twenty-six, twenty-seven, and thirty-six children fell into aggressive, intermediate, and nonaggressive categories, respectively. Ratings of aggressive behavior were obtained. Children found to be chronologically and intellectually suitable for the study were given three one-hour, individual, nondirective play therapy sessions with the same therapist in the same room. Twenty-two of the 644 pages of verbatim records made during the play therapy sessions were categorized by three experienced play therapists using Finke's (1947) revised categories.

Lebo and Lebo concluded that the outstanding findings of this study were that aggression and age exert a marked influence on the amount and variety of speech produced by normal children in nondirective play therapy. The results of a one-criterion variance of the relation between category usage and age revealed significant differences in a majority of categories. Aggressive children made more aggressive statements, threats to playroom rules, expressions of decision, and exclamations than did nonaggressive children. The speech of aggressive children contained more story units than did that of other children. The aggressive children made more favorable statements about themselves, evidenced more interest in the counselor, and made more attempts to establish a relationship with the counselor than did nonaggressive children. Six-year-old children made more aggressive verbalizations than did any other age group. Younger children made more attempts to relate to the therapist and made more favorable comments about themselves than did the older children. Twelve-year-old children employed fewer story units than any other age group. The 6-year-old children employed more story units than any other age group. Lebo and Lebo further concluded that the process of nondirective play therapy, judging from verbalizations, does not seem to be the same for all children. The amount of aggression and the age of the child can predict the way in which children respond to play therapy.

Lebo (1956a) stressed the need for experimental evidence on the matter of age and suitability for nondirective play therapy. He hypothesized that 12-year-old children will make fewer statements while using toys than will children at younger age levels. The experimental data consisted of 4,092 statements made by twenty normal children, ten boys and ten girls aged 4, 6, 8, and 12. Each child was seen for three play sessions. Lebo held constant the toys, room, and therapist, as well as the therapeutic role. After finding that fewer statements were made while playing with toys at the 12-year level than at levels 4 to 10 years of age, Lebo concluded that nondirective play therapy toys seemed to restrict the verbalization of the older children. He further suggested that toys other than those generally recommended by nondirective therapists might make children who are 12 years or older feel more at home in the playroom.

In another study, Lebo (1952) investigated the relationship of response categories in play therapy to age. Using Finke's (*Borke Scale*) categories, he studied the relationship between the age of a child and the type of statements that are made in play therapy. The study involved twenty children who were matched intellectually and in reference to social adjustment. The children were seen in three play therapy sessions by the same therapist in the same room. Five age levels (4, 6, 8, 10, and 12 years) were represented with two boys and two girls at each age level. When fifteen pages of verbatim notes were categorized and analyzed, it was found that maturation, as represented by chronological age, accounted for definite trends in the types of statements made by children in play therapy. Older children discussed their decisions less with the therapist, tested fewer limits, played more independently, and verbalized likes and dislikes more readily.

Lebo (1958c) stated that nondirective play therapists do not deal with the matter of age differences in planning for the playroom. He suggested that this is because nondirective play therapists take the child "where he is." Lebo contended that we must make accommodations for older children in the playroom regardless of their level of emotional development.

II

Theories and Techniques

INTRODUCTION

Play therapy was developed as a technique for treating children when professionals in the field of mental health recognized that interventions they had designed for adults were not viable for use with children. Sigmund Freud (1938) observed children at play in order to gather increased insight about the personality development of adults. In one reported case (Lebo 1958c), Sigmund Freud served as a consultant to a father of the child Little Hans. However, when his daughter, Anna Freud, began her work with children, she determined that the techniques used by Sigmund Freud were not appropriate with children. Frequently, they were not even possible to use with children. For example, one classic technique that Sigmund Freud and his disciples used was "couch therapy." This is a well-recognized and helpful tool often used in analysis with adults. It involves the adult patient's looking at the ceiling and blocking out external stimulation in order to focus on the internal self. Adult patients are requested to lay on the couch, face the ceiling, and free associate. It would be the exception, not the norm, if a child responded to such an instruction from a therapist. Taking the position that children are different and need alternative methods in treatment was considered revolutionary at that time. The need for developing alternative techniques for working with children was clearly stated by Anna

Freud (1928), and she, like the other child therapists who followed, continued to develop techniques that increasingly were more suitable for children. Most of those child therapists devised techniques to use with children by altering existing adult models to include the use of toys.

In the past, child therapists based their theory about personality on the existing adult models and adapted these concepts by using techniques that increased child comfort and communication in the child therapy setting. Most systems that have been reviewed start with concepts about adult personality and work downward. However, there are some systems that are beginning to approach the concept of starting with the child at the child's developmental level.

One example that describes this downward approach from adult psychotherapy to child psychotherapy is seen in analytical therapy. Sigmund Freud described his work in relation to adults. Anna Freud and Melanie Klein took the psychoanalytic theory and tenets described by Sigmund Freud and developed techniques that were more suitable for working with child patients. A second example is seen in the writings of Carl Rogers and Virginia Axline. Carl Rogers, using the phenomenological approach developed the client-centered model for working with adults. Later, Virginia Axline described the client-centered technique for children (Rank 1936). The historical roots of the major theories of personality development and therapy models will be discussed in this section. The technical adaptations of these adult therapy models for work with children will also be offered in this section. There is a growing body of literature that suggests that contemporary therapists are moving away from this "downward" view of child therapy. The movement focuses on the developmental stage of the child and then centers play therapy techniques on developmentally appropriate concepts.

6

The Psychoanalytic Approach

The psychoanalytic method for working with children evolved from the theories of Sigmund Freud. For a thorough discussion of this theory, the reader is referred to Sigmund Freud (1938) *The Basic Writings of Sigmund Freud*, and Hall and Lindzey (1957) *Theories of Personality*.

In 1908, Sigmund Freud referred to child's play and compared it to "poetic creation" (Abraham 1953). He suggested that children create their own world, or rearrange the objects of this world in a new way to please themselves. An example of the way in which Freud adapted his concepts to children is seen in his description of the application of his theory about repetition to childhood. He noted that a child uses repetition in order to master situations. The child repeats the action over and over, using toys to represent the components of the theme to be resolved. Freud stressed that play is used by children (on an individual basis) to give meaning to what they are trying to process. The role of the therapist is to determine what children are communicating as they use toys to symbolize their world. In this way, the toy, or the particular use of the toy, is not symbolic but is an indicator of what the child is attempting to say. Freud stressed that children would be able to develop themes without large amounts of materials. He recognized that children use materials that are available to them and make meaning (in their own way) with what they have (Mannoni 1970).

Freud suggested that childhood memories are important in that, when one relives one's early memories, one is able to bring those memories to the present and then reorganize them so that they make meaning within a context of safety (the therapy setting). Also central to this concept, one can recapture memories and reconstruct that past to one's own wishes. Children use play as a method for bringing up past memories and developing themes around those memories that assist them to resolve conflict. Mannoni (1970) indicates that, in psychoanalysis, the verbal accounts of children are frequently not based on reality, but are based on "views of reality" and desires about how they would like that reality to be or how it should have been. Literature reflects that Freud was interested in children, in that, through observing their behaviors, he was able to further refine and develop concepts about adult personality and therapy.

Anna Freud and Melanie Klein interpreted Freud's theories differently, each having her own view of the development of the ego and the superego. They also developed separate analytical techniques (Kessler 1966, Murphy and Fitzsimmons 1960). Anna Freud began her work in Vienna in the 1920s and moved to London in 1938 to continue her practice and teaching. Her approach has developed among her followers into the Vienna School of Child Psychoanalysis. Melanie Klein began her work in Berlin, and in 1926 went to London to continue her study and therapy with children. The psychoanalytic play technique that she developed is referred to as the English School of Psychoanalysis (Murphy and Fitzsimmons 1960).

ANNA FREUD

Anna Freud stressed the relevance of child analysis. However, she appeared to recognize that it is costly, intensive, and time-consuming. Anna Freud (1928) emphasized that, where children are concerned, analytic methods require special modifications and adjustments and should be undertaken only subject to precautions. Furthermore, new decisions about modifications to the basic theory and techniques should be approached with care and should be based on clinical successes and failures of similar cases. In other words, Anna Freud stressed that a therapist must assess and modify the approach as various cases provide increased knowledge. Thus, Anna Freud seemed to be providing therapists with permission to use knowledge gained through personal clinical cases, but to incorporate this theory and technical change with caution.

The analyst who works with adults wants, in the beginning, clients to ally themselves with the analyst against a part of their ineffective inner being. However, in the case of children, the decision for treatment rarely comes from the child. Since children are usually not the sufferers, they generally do not recognize that they have trouble. Therefore, this alignment with the analyst is not easily accomplished. Also, children generally do not have insight about the causes of these troubles. Anna Freud (1928, 1951) stressed that children rarely come to therapy with either the pain or the insight that the adult will likely bring. Because children do not recognize their need for therapy, they must be induced into therapy by "wooing."

Since children do not come to analysis with the mindset on which an analytical model is based, Anna Freud used the first stage of therapy in order to get the child ready for the analysis. This period is often referred to as the "wooing" period. During this period, the child is assisted to develop personal awareness of the trouble, to develop trust in the therapist, and to develop a personal desire to be involved in therapy. This first stage of the relationship has nothing to do with real analytical work. The purpose of this stage is to prepare the child so that analysis can occur in the traditional sense. In this way, Anna Freud appeared to mold the child to fit the requirements of the analytical model rather than to mold the analytical model in order to fit the needs of the child.

To "woo" the child, Anna Freud used every technique at her disposal. She reported that, if the child showed her rope tricks, she made better ones; if the child made faces, she made funnier ones; she wrote the child letters and made things for the child during the earlier sessions (Dorfman 1965). The establishment of rapport was crucial to the success of the work to follow with the child. During this preanalytic period Anna Freud stressed that the use of toys and play materials were essential in developing readiness to work (Freud 1928). She indicated that initially children were frightened, and that the therapist should use personal resources to provide the child with security. A child in the presence of a stranger cannot be expected to "follow an unknown path." Anna Freud (1951) suggested offering herself as an ally to the child while giving the child the promise of cure in order to wrap the child in safety.

Anna Freud (1951) indicated that she purposefully enabled the child to establish a strong attachment and come into a relationship of real dependence. She wrote that analysis could be accomplished only in the presence of a strong transference, and therefore her behaviors were justified. She indicated that a child requires more safety than an adult, thus there will be more attachment. Her writing indicates that the potential for growth in the child is enhanced when the child forms an attachment to the therapist. This is consistent with the concept of attachment and constancy. Within the therapeutic relationship, Anna Freud indicated that the analyst should put herself in the position of the child's "ego ideal." To achieve this, the analyst must exhibit greater strength and authority than the other adults in the child's life.

Because the therapist is not a shadow, children do not displace their feelings about significant other adults onto the analyst. Children are forced to see the analyst as a separate and strong person in their lives. In Anna Freud's view, these techniques disallowed the formation of a transference neurosis. Consequently, children continue to display their reactions to the parents because the original relationship that existed between parents and children is never transferred to the analyst (Freud 1928, 1951, 1954, Murphy and Fitzsimmons 1960).

Anna Freud used many techniques that were first developed for adult psychoanalysis and adapted those techniques to her work with children. She used the techniques of history-taking, dream interpretation, free association, and drawings.

One technique used in adult analysis is history-gathering through accessing the patient's unconscious memory. Children do not bring the same quality or quantity of memory to therapy that adults do, for obvious reasons. Most theorists agree that very early events are not remembered by children (such as those that occur during infancy) and also the history of children is short because of their age. Further, children tend to live in the present and generally do not place as much relevance on their past as do many adults. In addition, children are rarely able to compare their own inner self with those of others. Recognizing these factors, Anna Freud (1928, 1954) recommended that the child's case history be taken from the parents.

Two other analytical techniques, dream interpretation and free association, were adapted by Anna Freud for use with children. Anna Freud theorized that a child dreams about the same amount as an adult. Dreams of children (like adult dreams) contain resistance, distortions, and wish fulfillment. Anna Freud (1954) gave a description of how she assisted a small child to learn to interpret dreams. She explained to the child that they (the therapist and the child) would be able to understand what the dream meant by discussing it. She argued that the child can easily get into the interpretation because the child stands "nearer" to dreams than does the adult. She wrote that even unintelligent children can be successful at dream interpretation.

The technique of free association was used by Anna Freud (1954) as she encouraged the child to verbalize daydreams or fantasies. When she felt that the child was having difficulty discussing feelings and attitudes, she encouraged the child to sit quietly and "see pictures." By using this technique, the child was able to learn to verbalize innermost thoughts and, using the interpretations of the analyst, to discover the meaning of these thoughts.

In addition to using toys during the initial "wooing" period, Anna Freud (1954) saw toys as valuable in working with the very young child. By using toys, the child who has not yet developed to full verbal strength is able to explain a personal environment. By using toys, the child is able to replicate fantasies and bring them into the world that exists between the therapist and the child.

Anna Freud modified her father's work as she developed her own approach for working with children. She used dream analysis and interpretation but with modification so that, as it became relevant to the child, dream material took on a different meaning than it did when used by Sigmund Freud with adults. Her approach to free association also offered the child a vehicle for expressing feelings. Her use of storytelling in the therapeutic setting has provided future therapists with viable vehicles into the unconscious processes as well as the future dreams of the child. The "let's see a picture" technique is widely used in therapy when the therapist uses imagery in order to assist the child to remember stored material or when the therapist wishes the child to plan a brighter future. Anna Freud, in her approach, engaged the child through these techniques to bring up memories, understand the magic of dreams, and develop insight into unconscious processes.

In reviewing the work of Anna Freud, it seems apparent that her understanding of the world of the child was clear. Her work allowed therapists to use the analytical model with children. The flexibility of her adaptation supports this writer's opinion that major contributions in the field of child therapy have been made by people with courage and insight enough to use themselves and their own intuitions in their work.

MELANIE KLEIN

Melanie Klein's theory and techniques are modeled after those developed by Karl Abraham and Sigmund Freud. Klein (1932) wrote that the child internalized and projected Oedipal fear onto the outside "threatening" world. She disregarded the effect of reality in a child's life and focused on biological, innate factors. She attributed complicated psychological conflicts to the infant and stressed that the Oedipus complex exists in the first year of life (Lebo 1958a). Because she stressed that the conflicts arising from the oedipal fear develop so early, and because of her focus on biological factors, she indicated in her writing that all children can profit from analysis.

Sigmund Freud (1938) stated that guilt is aroused by the conscience or superego. In 1923, Freud coined the term "superego." He suggested that, before the final internalization of socialization, the child does not feel guilt, but has only the fear of discovery (Kessler 1966). Klein theorized that the superego develops in infancy, between the ages of 3 and 6 months. She described this superego as punishing. Klein stressed that because of the early development of the punitive superego, the young child engages in fantasies that are intricate and sophisticated. The child, having this early psychic development, is susceptible to troubles that also supported Klein's view that all children would profit from analysis at an early age.

Klein (1932, 1955) disagreed with Anna Freud's guidelines of adjustment and educability. Following another premise of Sigmund Freud's theory, she argued that the problem area in children was their fantasy about the mother–child relationship. The intensity of this love drive created tension that necessitated resolution.

Klein observed play to discover ambivalence in the conception of the object relationship. Children divide the world into good and bad objects, while attributing to these objects protective and aggressive roles against the danger that can be either internally or externally centered (Mannoni 1970). Klein (1932) contended that this presence of aggressive intention in all love drives unconsciously impels children in states of crisis to attempt to repair an imaginary injury that they think they have inflicted on their mother.

Klein believed that free association provided accurate access to the unconscious part of children. She used transference in order to access and analyze the unconscious. Klein equated child play to adult free association. She interpreted child play as symbolic. She recognized that play is more natural for children than is language. Klein used both toys and drama as vehicles to bring out the fantasy world of the child. During Klein's early years as a therapist, she saw children in their own homes, and allowed them to use their own toys. Later, Klein said that children may evidence inhibitions in their own homes and indicated that they needed to be protected. Klein then moved her work to an office setting. She indicated that moving children to a setting that was not home enhanced the development of transference (Murphy and Fitzsimmons 1960).

For Rita, a child patient, Klein (1932) gathered a few toys and put them into a cardboard box. This box became the prototype for her later playroom closet of materials. Each child patient had a box of specifically chosen toys. This box and the toys in it became an individual experience for the child. It was taken from the cabinet before each session and locked up after each session. The child was able to use this private collection of toys to enhance the development of awareness of the unique nature of self. No other child had access to these toys and the box of toys became representational of the ego of the child. This box was explored only in the context of the psychoanalytic session. The child had personalized toys that had been selected by Klein, which frequently were representational of objects and persons in the child's real world. Klein felt that this allowed the child to act out his feelings using play. The use of toys took the place of adult conversation for a child. Thus, Klein interpreted this play just as analysts do with adult verbal offerings.

Klein refrained from becoming educative or imposing moral ideas. She used traditional psychoanalytic techniques. These procedures were designed so that the therapist would better understand the child's unconscious and be able to assist the child to develop insight. Klein (1932) described the value of interpretation in her work with a specific child. When the child selected a few toy figures and surrounded them with bricks, the analyst interpreted the figures to symbolize people who were in a room. This represented the connection between the child and the unconscious. Through the interpretation, children realized that the toys stood in their minds for people and, therefore, that the feelings they expressed toward the toys related to people.

Klein (1932) stressed the importance that a child be aware of the existence of the unconscious part of self. She did not suggest that the child will be able to verbally express the insight gained through exploring and recognizing the unconscious. However, the child would show by "telling looks" that insight has occurred. This then indicates to the therapist that the child has understood something, or developed a new awareness.

Klein stressed that the focus of analysis is on anxieties and on the defenses against them. She observed the play of the child and interpreted the content. She felt that this assisted the child to reduce anxiety. She used the language of symbolism which she felt was similar to the child's method of expression when the child used play (Klein 1932). Klein also stressed that each child assigns and uses unique meaning to the individual use of toys. The use of toys is individual and representational of the private world of each child.

Anna Freud and Melanie Klein disagreed about how to use interpretation with children. Klein (1932) stressed that young children are able to benefit from this technique when toys are used as representational symbolisms of their real world.

Anna Freud also disagreed with Melanie Klein on Klein's position about the use of transference. Klein (1955) wrote that the child transferred early experiences, and feelings first to his parents and, later to people in the extended environment. Later, within analysis, the child transferred those feelings and emotions to the therapist. Klein analyzed the nature of this transference, and used it to understand the unconscious part of the mind. She wrote that anxieties and fears started in infancy, in relation to the first love objects. After the therapist understood the nature of the primal relationship, then the therapist would be able to assist the child to re-experience these early emotions. After that, the therapist would be able to assist the child to reconnect with their primal relationships. However, Klein, like Anna Freud, felt that the parents of the child would have to develop personal insights before a healthy relationship could be developed.

7

The Structured Approach

Structured therapy was an offshoot of the psychoanalytic school. The structured therapists adhered to the basic tenets of psychoanalytic theory in reference to the development of personality; the difference was in the approach used. They set up situations so that the client would have the opportunity for catharsis and abreaction of specific feelings. The structuralists stressed that after cathartic experiences surrounding a specific issue, the child would be able to reconstruct and continue with development. Like the psychoanalyst, the structured therapist assumed the major responsibility for the therapeutic experience. Therapists using the structured approach assume that the therapist is more aware of the needs of the child than is the child. Because of this assumed knowledge of the child's difficulties, the structured play therapist justified controlling the direction of the therapeutic hour. During specific stages in the therapy, this technique was used to provide a controlled setting that would encourage a specific abreaction.

Structured play therapy was described by Hambridge (1955) as a technique used within the playroom setting wherein the therapist designed a series of specific stimulus situations that the child plays out. This type of therapy has been referred to by David Levy (1939a,b) as "release therapy," by J. C. Solomon (1938, 1940, 1948, 1955) as "active play therapy," and by Jacob Conn (1939, 1941a, 1955) as "the play interview." The major theorists using this particular orientation differed in approach. However, they shared the attitude that structured therapy offers economy of effort and close approximation to the desired result.

Conn (1939, 1941a, 1955) and Levy (1939a,b) suggest that there is no need for the development of a strong relationship between the therapist and the child. Solomon (1938, 1940, 1948, 1955), however, stressed that the development of a relationship between the therapist and the child is crucial to the total treatment. Hambridge (1955) contended that the play experience should not be structured until the relationship has been firmly established and the child is completely comfortable in the therapeutic setting.

Hambridge (1955), Solomon (1938, 1940, 1948, 1955), and Conn (1939, 1941a, 1955) concurred that structuring the play situation was a technique which was appropriately used in an "already" established play therapy relationship. These therapists agreed that the structured technique should be used selectively with different patients and at different times during the treatment of one patient. Hambridge cautioned that structured therapy was not indicated for use with every patient.

HAMBRIDGE

Hambridge (1955) used the structured technique only in an already established relationship. He gathered a thorough history from the parents of the child and by observing the child at play. He then developed hypotheses about those situations in the child's life that were the sources of stress. The therapist would then recreate the stressful situation using dramatic play. This, Hambridge proposed, allowed the child to abreact the pain. Hambridge indicated that it was important not to frighten the child. He disapproved of the practice of flooding (which he described as a massive and uncontrolled release of all kinds of uncompleted acts from the past). He insisted that this could lead to regression in the child.

Hambridge (1955) suggested that the types of play should be introduced based on a gradient of potential threats to the child. The structured play should start with less threatening material, and move slowly to material that would be more threatening to the child. Hambridge also stressed that the therapist has an obligation to assist the parents to learn to structure their child during the changes that would be expected to occur.

LEVY

David Levy (1939a,b) based his theory of release therapy on the rationale that the individual never outgrows the need for the relief afforded by primary process thinking. For example, after a child experiences a traumatic event, the simple reenactment of it allows the child to "release" the pain and tension it caused because abreaction has therapeutic value. The role of the child changes from passive to active as the theme is replayed. There is total control experienced during the structured play because the child determines when it will be started, stopped, or replayed. The repetition of the event, which the child controls, leads to a feeling of mastery over the original pain. Release therapy was designed for use with children who had experienced an acute trauma.

Levy (1939a,b) advocated that when a child experiences trauma and suppresses the feelings surrounding that trauma, then the pain of the event will stay in the unconscious. In order to resolve the conflict caused by the trauma, Levy suggested the use of release therapy. He described two types of release therapy, specific and general. Specific release therapy is used when the symptom has been present for a short time, occurs in a young child, and where there are no apparent family problems. The child in this situation is permitted to engage in free play initially in order to gain comfort in the setting. The therapist introduces the structured situation at the appropriate time by asking questions and by introducing specific play materials designed to allow the child to replicate the event. General release therapy is used when the problems are a result of excessive demands made on the child too early in life. Using this approach, no specific experiences are relived. This strategy is designed to assist the child to change social attitudes, to release aggression, to release infantile pleasure, and (as discussed by Levy) to release masculine striving in girls. (Again, I think that in light of current attitudes about gender bias, this material is now dated and should be considered prejudiced.)

Levy defined play situations according to events in the child's life that the therapist perceived to be causing the trauma. These situations were designed around certain themes, such as new baby at mother's breast (sibling rivalry play), balloon bursting (for release of aggressions), peer attack, punishment or control by elders, separation, or genital differences. Each scene involved specifically selected and designed toys. For example, in the "new baby at mother's breast" scene, Levy used a mother doll, a baby doll, and a self doll. The therapist used modeling clay to mold a mother's breast and encouraged the child to act out feelings about the new baby being succored at this breast.

SOLOMON

J. C. Solomon (1955) developed a theory that stressed the importance of the integration of the ego as primary in the development of self. He used the play technique as a means of direct therapy for the child, and also as a diagnostic tool and as a research device.

In Solomon's view, the child who comes to therapy is suffering from a confusion or conflict of motivations. In the child, the therapist is concerned mainly with conflicts involving the primary motivations or instincts, either with each other or with the secondary motivations represented by the superego. The conflict involves an "internalization" of the problem. In order to experience release from the conflict, the child must develop an internal way of viewing the pressures of his life.

According to Solomon, it is important to know when the traumatic event occurred related to the integration of the ego. If ego integration occurred before the onset of symptoms, then the prognosis for reduction of the symptoms is positive. However, if the child was traumatized before ego development occurred, then the prognosis is poor.

The first stage of integration occurs through the use of play. Play within this model is useful because it allows pleasures (ego) to be enjoyed while the child is also releasing the "rage" that results from the frustrations of pleasure (brought about by conflict caused by the superego). Solomon (1955) further suggested that

> through play the child is able to express his own regressive tendencies, thereby lessening the need to act out such forms of behavior in his real life situation. Instead, he is afforded the opportunity to move forward toward more realistic solutions for his problems. [p. 394]

The use of play with a child allows a means of expression and also provides a way the therapist can talk with the child since "the world of the child is extremely distant to the adult and play is useful in narrowing this gap" (Solomon 1955, p. 403). Change within the therapeutic relationship is seen as "movement from the indefinite to the definite, from the unreal to the real, and from the magical to the reasonable" (Solomon 1940, p. 594).

In his use of the structured play technique, Solomon (1948) used dolls to represent significant persons in the life of the child, including a doll to represent the therapist. He contended that there are many issues in the relationship that the child needs to work out. He stressed that it is easier for the child to work through these feelings through the use of a doll than to have to talk with the therapist face to face. Later, after the child practices talking to the doll, then the child will be able to talk to the therapist. In this way, the child learns to use dolls to practice conversations with other significant persons.

CONN

Conn (1939, 1941a) contended that his goal as a therapist was not to "make over" the child but to restore what was there originally. He developed his method of "play interview" to supplement, not replace, basic child guidance procedures. This technique provides a wealth of information quickly, and allows for immediate insights into the child. The structured nature of the session guides the child away from random play. The child has not come to play or to be entertained but to participate as an equal who has something to contribute as well as to learn (Conn 1941b). The therapist may play many different roles during the play interview, including giving advice, playing character roles, or even introducing the topic of play.

8

The Jungian Approach

JUNG

The theory of Carl Jung combined thermodynamic principles with Freudian methods of observation. Jung believed the personality of an individual to be a complex combination of the persona, male and female attributes, archetypes, and the self. Unlike Freud, however, Jung did not believe that the unconscious was static or the individual's alone, but rather a collective process constantly evolving toward self-realization. Jung's observations also led to his conclusion that a human being is a composite of forces and systems, both physical and psychical in nature. With regard to these systems, Jung (1966) proposed the principles of equivalence and entropy.

The law of equivalence assumed that if some event caused a change in the physical or mental state of the individual, the energy displaced would not be lost, but would reappear in another part of the system to the same degree. Repression, for example, would manifest itself in dreams or motivation. Similarly, the law of entropy dealt with energy, but its focus was on the manner in which the energy was displaced. Values fluctuate equally so that the whole would maintain an even distribution. The ideal state of *stasis* was referred to by Jung as the healthy "self," but because he believed it would lead to entropy, this theoretical state could never be attained (Hall and Lindzey 1957).

To Jung, the individual is on a continually evolving journey that includes not only the self's past and future, but also a collective past and future, with some amount of interference from genetic and environmental influences. The healthy self naturally integrates the various systems while reaching actualization. If, however, the self is unable to reach that goal, intervention is required to unite opposing systems. Jung (1966) suggested that the essence of healing is not what the therapist does directly to the client, but how the therapist sets the conditions in the therapeutic setting. Further, under the right conditions, individuals have within themselves the power for self-growth and healing. The function of transference in the relationship is to assist individuals to realize their own power so that it will assist them in the healing process. In the presence of a safe relationship, when the client has transferred memories and feelings about others onto the therapist, then the client can use the safe conditions—containing both the therapist and the setting—to begin the integrative process.

Jung (1965) recalled his own childhood experiences and began to describe his blocked memories through his writing and through the use of symbolic reconstruction of those memories. Because of his own experiences he began to recognize that children could benefit early from symbolic play as a method for working through pain and fears. He recognized that it would be of therapeutic value to use these methods with children by allowing them to work through painful memories and issues before they were stored and forgotten. He became supportive of the notion that specific strategies designed for children would enhance this process.

LOWENFELD

Margaret Lowenfeld (1935) described her ideas about play in childhood. Within the section on the toys that she described as necessary to allow children to express their feelings is a discussion of her model of The World and how she used those materials. She stressed that therapists should recognize the understandings a child has formed about the outside world. This is accomplished by providing a cabinet in the playroom that stores miniatures of objects representational of the child's world. These objects are then used by the child to symbolically express this world. The cabinet contains several trays in which small objects are placed according to classifications. This tray is used generally in conjunction with the sand tray. She elaborated her techniques using the World Technique in further teaching and writing (1939, 1950, 1979). Gradually the material expanded to include the technique of sand play using sand tray materials.

KALFF

Kalff (1971), who has taken theories of Jungian analysis and developed techniques for working with children, has described the use of sand play. Her work follows Lowenfeld's techniques, but she has elaborated those methods into more descriptive, stylized uses of the techniques and materials. The therapist selects small objects for the use of each individual client. The child is allowed to present personal feelings and memories by using the objects to represent the different parts of fantasy that they carry within themselves. Through the representation of scenes in this way, the child begins to develop insights into self.

BRADWAY

Bradway (1979), a contemporary therapist using these strategies, indicates that she uses very little verbal interaction with the child, and just allows the theme to unfold. However, for clarification she does ask questions. Pictures are taken of each scene and the scenes are studied for the development of themes. Carey (1990) emphasizes that through the utilization of sand play one is able to observe the unfolding of the imagery and archetypes of the collective unconscious. She observes the choice of materials and the use of them interpretatively in order to understand the unconscious contents of the child. She stresses the balance of the use of verbal and nonverbal interaction with the child.

ALLAN

John A. B. Allan (1976, 1977, 1978, 1988) has made a major impact as professor, writer, and therapist. His model for Jungian play therapy includes the principles and constructs of the writings of Jung as the theoretical basis of his work. However, his work has provided current therapists with tools necessary to relate the theory described by Jung to a comprehensive treatment model for children. In the many articles and lectures that Allan has provided the field over the past twenty years, he has incorporated the concepts of using the sand play techniques that were first described by Lowenfeld and elaborated by Kalff. He has also described techniques and concepts that allow the child a broader use of media.

Allan uses a playroom setting that contains many different materials. He also stresses that therapists should allow the child more freedom of choice in the use of materials than do the therapists who use only sand tray methods. Allan is clear about how Jung's theory is tied to the play therapy technique. The basic premises Jung described are the psyche that is developed around the ego (the unconscious mind), the parts of one's self that one has personally experienced (which are not available to one's self because of repression, lack of awareness, or denial), and the collective unconscious, which contains the various universal archetypes (Allan and Brown 1993). The focus of Jungian play psychotherapy in this model includes providing a safe environment (*temenos*), so that the psyche of the child will be free to utilize innate self-healing power in order to integrate the opposing parts of the self and thus resolve the tension that prevents these conflicting parts from becoming integrated.

In this model, the therapist is nondirective. The child provides direction, and the therapist follows. Allan and Lawton-Speert (1993) describe the concepts of *acting-out* and *acting-in*. They suggest that *acting-in* occurs when the child engages in fantasy play or purposeful play that may not be considered socially acceptable (but occurs within the context of the therapeutic theme). They describe *acting-out* as behavior that is an "angry act" designed to test the limits of the playroom or of the relationship. They indicate that the therapist has to make the decision about distinguishing the two by using personal knowledge of each particular case. This includes the therapist's knowledge of the transference and countertransference that has occurred within the relationship.

Allan stresses that in the context of the playroom, the child will be able to freely express unconscious processes by projecting these feelings onto the media. Since the child has control over choice of expression, the child will be able to correlate mastery over media with mastery of the self. This leads to increased strength, which will ultimately result in the child's being able to integrate the opposing parts of the self. The repetitive nature of the process of play is described by Allan and Berry (1987). They suggest that children often repeat toy and play themes over and over in an attempt to resolve the conflicts of the major issues that they are working through.

Allan and Levin (1993) have described the use of techniques in the Jungian theoretical model in the case of Miko. In this case study, the components of therapist variables, the safety of the play therapeutic setting, the issue of "acting-in," the concepts surrounding the necessity for repetition of themes so that a final resolution or integration can occur, and the nature of following the lead of the child are all seen. This writer was impressed that Allen and Levin had the courage to allow the analysis of this child to occur in its purest form. Considering that therapists are controlled and influenced strongly by societal norms and professional ethical guidelines, it is refreshing to see therapists who will take risks so that wholeness can occur.

Han (1994) studied sand play therapy from the content-oriented approach, which examines the placement of toys and the composition of the sand tray for diagnostic purposes in differentiating normal children from abnormal, psychotic, or retarded children. He then examined a second approach, which was process-oriented. He outlined a model that integrates process and content approaches. He used the case study method of three cases and analyzed the play in depth to describe an integrated approach to sand play that is based upon both content and the ongoing dynamics of process.

9

The Adlerian Approach

ADLER

Alfred Adler and his contemporaries added a social component to personality theories, because they believed that style and quality of life have bearing on how the individual personality functions and how an individual views his or her surroundings. This world view, as Adler (1927) defined it, is developed early in life and remains constant even when modes of expression are altered. Adler's position on fulfillment was centered in power, aggression, and a desire for superiority.

According to Hall and Lindzey (1957), Adler later combined his belief that basic personalities were fashioned from nature and social input, but were influenced by birth order, situational causes such as neglect, and memories of significant others. Through his studies of childhood memories, Adler discovered that failure was the result of inferior feelings and weaknesses that were not addressed, leading to pathological lifestyles.

Dreikurs and Soltz (1964) used Adlerian principles to describe their position on parenting. This material and the later work with which Dreikurs has been involved has served as consultative material about how adults can manage children (Dreikurs 1967, Dreikurs and Cassell 1972). The focus of this material, in this writer's opinion, is not play therapy but parent education. Later, Dinkmeyer and Dinkmeyer (1977, 1983) and Dinkmeyer and colleagues (1987a), Dinkmeyer and McKay (1989), and Dinkmeyer and colleagues (1987b) used Adlerian theory as the basis for developing models for teachers and parents to use in managing children. Dinkmeyer and various associates have written and talked about how to use these principles in the school and in the home in order for children to have better understanding of themselves. These materials have provided application of Adlerian theory to child concepts and acknowledgment of the person of the child, but do not fit into the model of play therapy.

KOTTMAN

A contemporary writer, Kottman has taken Adlerian theory and the interpretations of Dreikurs and the Dinkmeyers and has developed a model for working with children in play therapy. Kottman has strong current influence on the field of play therapy because of her prolific writings, workshops, and lectures. Her book on the subject of Adlerian play therapy (Kottman 1995) is the first material that this writer has reviewed that actually takes Adlerian theory and describes rationale and methodology for working with children in the context of play therapy. Kottman indicates that "child's play and child verbalizations are metaphors representing the child's lifestyle and life situation" (p. 22). Kottman (1995) stresses the importance of building an egalitarian relationship with the child, which leads to a cooperative, growth-producing relationship between the child and therapist. This allows the child the use of the safety of the relationship in order to grow and understand the self so that this knowledge can be used in the real world outside of the playroom. Kottman starts the equal power concept with the child from the beginning in which she uses the phrase, "This is our playroom" (p. 52). Later in the relationship Kottman explores the child's lifestyle by asking direct questions. She is mindful of attempts at manipulations and uses these attempts as opportunities to assist the child to learn about the self. Kottman (1995) suggests that many children who come to therapy are discouraged. She encourages children to develop a sense of strength by giving unconditional acceptance, acknowledging the emerging abilities of the child, recognizing that the child is putting effort into the playroom work, and focusing on the strengths of the child.

Following Dinkmeyer's discussion of the discouraged child (Dreikurs and Soltz 1964) Kottman stresses that if one can identify the goals (or compensatory strategies) of the discouraged child, one can lead this child from

dysfunctional coping techniques to functional strategies of living and relating. She incorporates components of Adlerian theory in her treatment
planning and implementation, such as the erroneous need for power and
the dysfunctional striving for control. She includes concepts that accommodate the notions that people who feel inferior are discouraged and
manipulate in order to gain a greater sense of control over their lives and
their environment. By using the equalitarian relationship, Kottman describes healing within this model.

Statton (1990) used the Adlerian counseling model and studied
whether the technique of inquiring into early recollections of children was
a viable one for the play therapy setting. The study addressed seven research
questions regarding changes in early recollections for children in Adlerian
counseling as compared with children not in Adlerian counseling. The
treatment group was engaged in Adlerian counseling for ten weeks. The
investigator conducted precounseling and postcounseling interviews to
collect a total of six early recollections from nine subjects. The comparison
group was not engaged in treatment for counseling. The investigator conducted interviews at an interval of ten weeks. The investigator summarized
that the treatment group manifested greater change in early recollection
content as compared to the comparison group on six of the seven research
questions. On the basis of these findings, she concluded that the early recollections of children are a valid source in measuring therapeutic progress
and are a reliable measure of the thematic apperception of children. This
study provides a foundation that endorses using early recollections with
children.

10

The Existential Approach

Fundamental beliefs about dualism and personal responsibility are central to the Existential philosophy. Further, this theory declares that humans and the world in which they live cannot be mutually exclusive (Hall and Lindzey 1957). The individual's perceptions and the coming to terms with the self and the world became the focus of psychologists such as Boss (1958, 1977) and Binswanger (1958).

For existential psychologists, all theories related to basic concepts begin with the mind/body connection and the individual's world design. Individuals are believed to have freedom of choice, including the freedom to choose authenticity. If authenticity is rejected as an option, the result is anxiety and guilt. Other areas of concern are man's alienation, overwhelming feelings of nothingness and the fragility of the human condition (Hall and Lindzey 1957). Medard Boss (1958, 1977) described inherent characteristics as "existentials." These characteristics included existential spatiality, temporality of existence, bodyhood, human existence and individual characteristics. He recommended that the combination of a supportive relationship in tune with the individual's true nature would lead to a positive experience.

The existential philosophy provides roots for child therapists. As most theories function in the actual practice of technique, these roots have grown in many directions. At times they are isolated in form and structure, and at times the roots are enmeshed. However, they all have a common thread that moves them back through the mother trunk of the "here and now" and the "I, thou" concepts.

Included in this chapter is a discussion of the theorists who described the relationship views of therapy. Relationship therapy evolved from the philosophy of Otto Rank. It has been described for use with children by Frederick Allen (1942), Jessie Taft (1933), and C. E. Moustakas (1959b).

The premise that every person shares the common trauma of birth, leaving this person with a permanent fear of "individuation," was stressed by Rank (1936). Rank did not emphasize the importance of unconscious and historical roots of personality development. He focused on the current conscious processes that the patient was able to bring to the relationship. He felt that transference was not relevant to treatment. He described as relevant the way in which a person was able to creatively conceptualize the use of time. Rank used the limit of time both for the length of total treatment and for the length of each session to give meaning to the relationship.

TAFT

Taft (1933) followed the existentialist view, and emphasized the meaning of time to an individual as being central to anxiety and/or growth. He suggested that the human dilemma is the existential question, "If one cannot live forever, is it worthwhile to live at all?" (p. 13.) The existential orientation emphasizes the present while looking neither to the past (birth) nor to the future (death). In describing views on the existential dilemma, Taft (1933) stated,

> the reaction of each individual to limited or unlimited time betrays his deepest and most fundamental life pattern, his relation to the growth process itself, to beginnings and endings, to being born and to dying. [p. 13]

Therapy is defined as "a process in which the individual finally learns to utilize the allotted hour from beginning to end without undue fear, resistance, resentment, or greediness" (p. 17).

The power of the relationship between therapist and patient is described as the essence of existential therapy in that it represents "a depth of union never risked since birth or weaning" (p. 291). Taft stressed that the quality of the relationship is based first on the extent that the therapist has developed personally within the existential philosophy.

The process of separation at the end of each hour and at the end of treatment is a major focus of the process. They are reenactments of the original trauma, birth. When therapy has a favorable outcome, the patient "takes over the birth fear and transforms it into an ego achievement" (p. 282). Termination is viewed as an integral part of the process itself, and the time limit is set on the calendar before the beginning of the therapy relationship. When the termination of the relationship is accomplished within this context, it "diminishes the fear of individuation, since to leave convincingly is to find that one can bear both the pain and the fear of withdrawal and to discover within the self a substitute for the lost wholeness" (p. 291).

ALLEN

Allen, like Taft, discussed differentiation and individuation. However, Allen focused on the actual physiological separation that occurs as a result of the birth process. He felt that this explained the etiology of the existential trauma. Allen (1942) considered the birth process to be traumatic because of the extreme physical and biological changes that the newborn child experiences at the moment of birth. In referring to this experience, he states, "Birth ushers in a new and final phase of differentiation" (p. 22).

Allen (1942) stressed the importance of the relationship between the therapist and the client as the crucial factor in the successful outcome of the treatment, saying, "Therapy begins when the therapist is brought into a relationship as a supporting and clarifying influence around the patient's need and desire to gain or regain a sense of his own worth" (p. 22).

Emphasis is placed on the present rather than on the genetic development of problems and conflicts. Allen did not use the time limit as did Taft. He stressed that a child needs to self-affirm in a changing, unpredictable world. In order that this happen, the child needs therapeutic assistance. This therapy teaches the child how to live the experience of life in a day-to-day manner. This teaches the child to focus on the possibilities of the future without being held by the "shackles of the outlived past" (Allen 1942, p. 306).

Allen (1942) wrote that it is important to be involved with the child, yet this involvement is not to be confused with being friendly. The child is allowed freedom of expression, but the therapist sets limits as needed. Allen indicated that the child has a strong capacity for recreating the self through growth. This growth is child-directed and starts with the child's stage of development. The child has the internal capacity to decide what should change. This change is not to be planned or directed by the therapist.

MOUSTAKAS

Clark Moustakas should be credited with framing the major portion of theory and technique that is used in many of the current approaches to play therapy. He described therapy as a unique growth experience that happens because of the relationship between the child and the play therapist. This relationship is alive, vital, potent, and ever-changing. Central to the relationship is integrity.

In the therapeutic relationship, this mutual growth is continuous and centered in the present. The therapist holds the responsibility for self-awareness of personal strengths and weaknesses and recognizes that the child can grow no further nor experience no more deeply than does the therapist. The integrity in the relationship is vital to the life of the relationship, because a child cannot grow where dishonesty exists (Moustakas 1959b). The relationship that Moustakas describes is one of mutual participation between the therapist and child. The child brings resources, as does the therapist, to the "living relationship." Moustakas did not acknowledge neurosis or illness. He did not deal with the issue of dependency with child patients. Because the child feels free to accept the self within the relationship, the child grows.

According to Moustakas, the therapist holds the responsibility for self-awareness and continuous growth and development. The therapist is nondirective and allows the child to determine the way in which the relationship will develop. Moustakas stresses that growth occurs in the presence of a relationship that conveys acceptance, respect, and faith. The role of the therapist involves self-awareness and continued openness for growth. It is important to begin with the child where the child is and to convey unqualified acceptance, respect, and faith. The therapist conveys respect for the child and faith in the process by allowing the child to lead, while the therapist follows. The play is unstructured and the therapist is non-directive. The concept of listening for what the child is feeling is central to the idea of respect. Moustakas does not interpret, yet he describes the therapist as an active participant in the process. However, he is clear that the child makes the plan. If the child requests, then Moustakas will become so active as to play with the child.

11

The Gestalt Approach

OAKLANDER

Violet Oaklander is a contemporary author, lecturer, and therapist. Her concepts have impacted the field of play therapy in a profound manner. Her book, *Windows to Our Children* (1988), described the way in which she has used gestalt therapy in the playroom. More recently, she has written a case study that further describes her approach using gestalt theory (1993). Oaklander stressed the need for children to develop a sense of their contained selves that occurs when children are able to differentiate themselves from others. Oaklander follows the gestalt philosophy, which stresses that, in the emerging human, the child is unable to understand where the separation or boundary between self and world begins. Because of this lack of differentiation, children are unable to understand their own selves. Until a child develops a sense of separateness, then the child will not be able to define a separate self. Until this occurs, the child will not be able to develop the potential strength that hides within. While the boundary disturbances exist, the child is forced to use coping strategies that are oftentimes not functional in order to fit in with those with whom the child is in contact. One purpose of therapy is to assist the child to develop a sense of boundary between self and others (which Oaklander describes as *point of contact*). The therapist teaches the child how to set those boundaries, and further how to define and develop what is contained within the boundary. Oaklander (1993) indicated that the prime goal of the gestalt therapist is to assist children to identify their own processes. Oaklander (1988, 1993) stressed that her role is to provide a relationship of safety and respect for the child so that the delineation of the boundary between child and therapist will be established. At times, Oaklander uses a nondirective approach, allowing the child to select the media to be used. At other times, she preselects the media to be used. Her nondirective techniques surface when she allows children to describe the use they have made of the media. Other times, she directs the children to make certain objects or representations using the media she has chosen.

These media include paper, paint, fabric, natural fibers, pipe cleaners, modeling materials, or anything that will serve the purpose of allowing children the expressive possibilities they need. She may direct the production that is to be made, but she allows the child to explain the production. In other sessions, she may ask questions about the production and then assist the child to relate the production to symbolize a part of the process that is relevant to his own life. She stresses the importance of assisting children to get in touch with their internal processing and to connect the internal with their own body or external boundaries. She does this by utilizing various materials and allowing children to experience the media through various modalities. This may be through the tactile, the kinesthetic, the auditory, or the visual. She encourages the children to continuously connect their internal feelings with the body experiences which they are having with the media.

12

The Phenomenological Approach

Existential theory and phenomenological theory have much in common. However, there are differences in philosophy that should be addressed. The major difference is in the view of how pathology and dysfunction develop. The existentialist view stresses that dysfunction develops because of the inability of the individual to differentiate and separate. The phenomenologist stresses that dysfunction occurs because an individual views the world from the inside to the outside. Also, this inside/outside evolution of personality is interactive. When an infant is developing, early experiences influence the way in which the perceptual field is formed. As the developing person attempts to make sense of the environment, information is continuously formed and recreated. In order to accommodate certain information from the environment, children develop strategies to accept this information. Every time an accommodation is implemented, distortions in the perceptual field occur. Eventually, the perceptual field is so fraught with distortions that messages are not received with accuracy. Since this is occurring continuously, children are unable to develop accurate views of themselves, others, or the environment. Therefore, children act on the perceptions that they have developed based on their own distorted perceptual field. The therapist working with a child within this framework views the purpose of therapy as giving the child a clear mirror so that reflections coming back to the child move through the perceptual field without distortions. The theory is then expanded to acknowledge that if the child can self-correct, then the power of the creative self can begin to develop a perceptual field that moves toward clarity and accuracy. Out of this philosophy grew the theory and techniques of the client-centered school of thought.

ROGERS

Carl Rogers described personality based on the experiences he had as a therapist. Rogers (1959) stressed that an infant perceives that experiences are real within the framework of personal experience. The infant accepts what has already been incorporated by self- definition, and rejects what does not fit. Later, because of the interaction between the inner world of the child, the child's personalized filtering system, and the environment, the child develops a self-concept that is personally created through perception of the self in the environment.

When a child experiences an environment that is harsh, conditional, and rejecting, then the child develops a negative self-concept. The child begins to develop defenses that disallow any information that does not fit the defined sense of self. To accept information that does not fit the established concept of self would create incongruence. In order to recognize and accept the information, the person has to distort the information so that it will be accepted into the (already existing) perception of the self. Otherwise, the incongruence will lead to anxiety. The defenses that disallow the entrance of the incongruent information are rigidity, distortion, and denial. In the event that the child is not able to balance the perception of self with the environmental implosions, the defenses will not serve as a "safety net." When this happens, disorganization occurs.

Therapy provides the individual an opportunity to reformulate the perception of self within the environment so that the defenses will no longer be needed. At that time, the individual will be able to value self within the environment with increased clarity.

Rogers (1959) stressed that the responsibility of the therapist is to provide an environment that contains only components conducive to the person's seeing himself as worthwhile. The therapist views the person with positive regard, unconditional acceptance, and empathy. Using these components as a mirror, the person will be able to develop a sense of self-worth.

Virginia Axline (1947, 1955b, 1964) and Elaine Dorfman (1965) both made early contributions in the adaptation of the client-centered approach to child therapy. Landreth (1982, 1991) originally worked within the client-centered framework as described by Virginia Axline. However, he has gone beyond Axline's work and has developed a model that uses phenomenological ideas as well as components of existential theory. This model is now described in the literature as the child-centered model of play therapy.

AXLINE

Axline (1947), like Rogers (1959, 1965), adhering to phenomenological philosophy, saw the child as having a reciprocal relationship with the environment. A child develops self-perception based on the information reflected by significant others. This is a dynamic experience, because both the child and the environment are constantly changing. Axline suggested that the child strives toward growth in order to satisfy basic needs. She explained the basic drive of the individual as that of "complete realization" (1947, p. 12). Axline (1955a) described the difference between the adjusted child and the maladjusted child as being the way in which the child deals with the environment. According to Axline's theory, the adjusted child directs behavior in order to achieve complete self-realization. However, the maladjusted child has not learned how to achieve self-realization without using "devious methods." The maladjusted child continues to unsuccessfully struggle until the self must distort in order to regain a balance between the unmet needs and the harsh environment. This striving toward regaining congruence requires that the child use the defenses of rigidity and distortion. When these defenses no longer protect the sense of self, the child becomes completely disorganized. In order to be restored to a state of congruence, the child needs therapy.

Reorganization of the the self will occur when the conditions of the therapeutic environment are established. These conditions consist of allowing children to see themselves as being worthy in an atmosphere of unconditional acceptance. Axline contended that children have all of the components necessary for growth and change, and can utilize these when in the therapeutic environment with the nondirective, accepting therapist. Children will grow when they are in a state of readiness within the right conditions. The role of the therapist is to assure the children that the conditions of safety are in place (Axline, 1947, 1955a, 1964). In order that these conditions be met, the therapist creates conditions that are different from the ones that caused the original disorganization. The playroom and the therapist are special and different and like no other place the child has been. The process occurs because the therapist has incorporated a certain set of values, which are carried into the therapy, and has set the right conditions (Rogers 1965).

Children describe their world and express their feelings through their play. When the children are in an environment where they control the language and the content, they are able to experience their feelings and to reorganize those feelings. Within this understanding of the unique needs of childhood, Axline developed techniques for working with children using the approach of nondirective play therapy. This setting and nondirective conditions provide children with the option of allowing needs to surface so that these needs can be reevaluated in a safe setting. When this occurs, the child corrects distortions, gives up dysfunctional strategies and defenses, and moves to a state of congruence.

Axline suggested that the relationship is structured within the framework established by eight basic principles. From the beginning, the therapist works toward developing a relationship with children that will be different from any other relationship they have experienced. Axline stressed that this relationship has no room for shame, bribery, or compliments. The therapist continuously recognizes the child's feelings and reflects those feelings back to the child in a way that adds to the child's sense of individuality. "The therapist accepts the child exactly as he is" (1947, p. 87).

Acceptance of children at their own rate of growth is necessary to successful therapy. As children develop they must be able to discern different types of reflections from others. Since the person most able to provide this clear reflection is the therapist, then acceptance of the child is critical, otherwise the child will, again, realize that a significant other is not authentic. The therapist shows children acceptance by allowing them to move at an individually defined rate of speed. The therapist allows children to make personal choices in the playroom (Axline 1947). Axline (1947) indicated that "the therapy hour is the child's hour" (p. 43). This implies that the therapist follows the child's plan in a nondirective manner. Axline does indicate that the use of limits are necessary so that the relationship can develop in an authentic way.

Axline (1947) made a distinction between reflection and interpretation. Interpretation, according to Axline, implies explaining the symbolism that children express in play. Reflection of toy play is done so that the child will know that the play has been understood. Children gain insight because the therapist uses clear words to describe feelings. When this occurs, children can experience feelings in a different way, and thus develop new perceptions about themselves because these feelings have been validated by a significant other. When the feelings are placed in a context of safety and reality, they are no longer diffuse. They are clear, and children have the ability to recreate perceptions so that those perceptions reflect reality. Children have a natural propensity for growth that will surface when they are allowed to use meaningful language and play in a therapeutic relationship, on a self-directed time line.

LANDRETH

Gary Landreth (1978, 1982, 1987, 1991) began his work with children by following the theory of personality described by Carl Rogers and using many of the approaches described by Virginia Axline. Landreth has contributed actively in the field of play therapy for over twenty-five years. He has been actively involved in therapy, writing, research, and training master's and doctoral level students. During this span of time, Landreth's work has evolved markedly from what was described by Virginia Axline. Landreth's work has resulted in an approach that is uniquely his own, to such a degree that his model should now be recognized as separate and apart from Axline's model. The model that Landreth (1991) describes provides the foundation for the development of a different theory in the field. However, the full conditions for theory development have not yet been met in his model.

Landreth draws from both phenomenological and existential theoretical premises to define his views of personality growth and development. He has incorporated information from Ginott and Moustakas as well as Axline in the development of his techniques. The unique and theoretical nature of his work begins to unfold in his 1991 book and in the work he produced after this.

Landreth describes statements that can be measured. Using those concepts that were researched by Carkhuff and Berenson (1969) and Carkhuff (1973), it is now possible to teach students measurable statements. Once students are able to measure each statement that occurs in the process, then they can be taught to alter statements in order to increase the therapeutic nature of a statement. This is a major contribution to the field of play therapy. Landreth has formulated many statements that serve as guidelines for students as they evaluate each session.

When a model of therapy describes methods for research, it stands on the threshold of exponential growth. It can be replicated with accuracy by others, and it will stand the criticism of the scientific community. In my opinion, the development of these vehicles of research will allow Landreth's model to surpass his clinical work.

Landreth describes the actual clinical treatment of a child as taking place in a relationship and within a physical context that is different from any other the child has experienced. The relationship contains the components described by Axline, Ginott, and Moustakas. It is a living, developing relationship in which growth occurs in the child as well as the therapist. Limits are set on actions but not on feelings. Landreth has described specifically the types of materials to be included in the play therapy room (see Chapter 5).

In summary, the client centered view is best described in the works of Carl Rogers, Virginia Axline, and Garry Landreth. Rogers' philosophy grew out of his work with people in therapeutic and teaching relationships. His philosophy has been a living one. It has grown and changed as a result of his life experiences and of his integration of these experiences. These experiences have affected his perceptions, attitudes, values, and, finally, his sense of self. His is not a stagnant philosophy but a living one.

And so, the client-centered philosophy which was first described by Rogers and interpreted for work with children by Virginia Axline focused on the philosophy that a human has the components for growth when the conditions are "right." Following these concepts, Landreth further interpreted the approach in his writings on child-centered play therapy. The concept that the client is the center of the theory is basic to the concepts of these authors. Additionally, the theoretical conditions for growth are used simply to "set the stage" so that the client will be in a safe environment (which includes the therapist) as the client draws on their innate propensity for growth.

13

The Developmental Approach

PIAGET

Piaget (1951), in his intensive study of knowledge and how it was acquired, found that children and adults reason differently and have different perspectives. This led him to interview children of different ages, during which period he developed his theory of the stages of cognitive development. The first stage is termed the *sensorimotor* stage, because children receive their impressions through the senses and motor activity. The second stage, *preoperational*, deals with language acquisition and imitation. Until the child reaches the age of 7, he is incapable of forming operational thought, or of understanding concepts such as object constancy or reversibility. The child views the world solely from his own perspective. The third stage, *concrete operational*, deals with the child's learning to distinguish laws of conservation and mentally reversing actions. However, it is not until the fourth stage of *formal operations* that the individual is capable of forming hypotheses and structuring abstract concepts.

The implications for using the cognitive developmental stage of the child was discussed by Belter and Grisso (1984) and Grisso and Vierling (1978), in stressing that therapists clarify our ethics when working with children (see Chapter 4).

Jeffrey (1984) stressed that children naturally play in a way that is correlated with their stage of development. When a child is left alone to play, in the absence of developmental delays, the child will play in accordance with his developmental needs. Jeffrey described Hellersberg's (1955) psychophysical stages of development, Anna Freud's (1951) analytical stages of development, Peller's (1955) psychosexual stages of development, Erikson's (1950) social stages of development, and Piaget's (1951) cognitive stages of development. Using the developmental stages that cross emotional, social, physical, and cognitive domains, Jeffrey developed a model that consists of four phases of therapy. Jeffrey stressed that it is critical that a therapist know and understand the level of development at which a child is in order to understand the meaning of the play during the session and across the course of therapy.

BRODY

Viola Brody (1978, 1992,) and Brody and colleagues (1976) describe a model of therapy that treats children using developmental concepts in play therapy. Central to the concept surrounding this model is the primary stage of development that should occur between the mother and child, which when accomplished results in bonding. The model describes the way in which Brody approaches the child at the presented stage of development and proceeds onward. She focuses on the need for touch as basic to human growth and development, and suggests that frequently children in our society present with an emotional deficiency that can only be healed by using the power of touch. Brody holds, touches, rocks, and cradles the child. This model stresses that as therapy progresses, the child gradually moves away physically from the therapist. However, just like the developing 2-year-old child, independence is often seen as transitory. The child in therapy will frequently leave the safety of the lap to explore, and then return to this safety for a bit of strength.

Brody describes the critical need for *bonding* between a mother and a child. When this bonding does not occur at the critical early period of development (described in Part I of this book) then the child is unable to move on to the next levels of development. Developmentally correct play allows the child to bond with the therapist. When the child has appropriately bonded with the therapist, then the child is able to move to the separation stage of development and to symbolically leave the therapist. Hopefully, the child will be able to use this bonding in a relationship with his own parents that will involve increased intimacy.

The models employed by the developmentalists are exciting because these models start with the child and move forward. They are not "boiled-down" versions of adult therapy models. Based on all empirical evidence about cognitive, emotional, social, and physical growth in children, the promises of these models make absolute sense. However, the techniques employed by these models still lack empirical evidence.

When a therapist thoroughly understands developmental stages, then it is possible to measure the level of regression when the child enters therapy. Using regression as one benchmark for the need for psychotherapy, one can measure progress in play therapy by watching for movement past the stage of development (across domains) where the child presented. This makes a sequential prediction of process possible.

The concept of sequential development is so primary to understanding children and their needs that it should serve as a basis for assessment of a child regardless of the philosophical model one uses. Central to this concept is the fact that children cannot read until they can talk. They do not ride a tricycle until their motor and cognitive processes have reached that stage of readiness. In therapy, they do not develop insight until they have developed language. And their level of insight is tied developmentally to their level of cognitive growth and development. For example, they may be able to play out aggression within the family, but they may not develop insight about the influence of this aggression until they have reached cognitive stages that allow abstract reasoning. The beauty of play therapy is that children are allowed to use their language "play" to express their world. They play at the stage of development that encompasses social, cognitive, emotional, and neurosensory descriptors. Unless forced, they do not play in advance of those stages. Children progress through the stages (unless growth is interrupted) sequentially and naturally. However, when growth is interrupted or when regression occurs, play therapy assists the child to develop.

14

The Cognitive–Developmental Approach

Harter (1977, 1983) focuses on the necessity of understanding the development of cognition as we attempt to understand a child. She uses cognitive-developmental concepts to describe why a child is unable to progress in therapy past his or her developmental cognitive stage. For example, when a child is at the preoperational period, he would be unable to free associate. This is tied to what the child is able to cognitively employ at this stage of development. Free association requires higher-level abstract cognitive skills than the child possesses at the preoperational stage of development. Harter stresses that we must understand a child's cognitive developmental level in order to assess his understanding of certain emotions. An example given is that a child can understand "sad" or "mad" but can't at a certain stage of development go beyond those statements to elaborate feelings. Harter studied and reported the child's ability to maintain and report two feelings at one time and to describe different feelings that were experienced simultaneously. Harter (1983) explains (based on Piaget's model) that a child has to reach a certain level of development before he is able to accommodate many of the abstract concepts used in therapy. The applications of these concepts to play therapy are described in her work on the phases in the therapy process. Play allows the child to use symbolism in the resolution of emotional conflicts. The therapist's role involves gradually moving

155

from passivity to increased involvement and to verbally interpreting the meaning of the play scenario. Later, as development occurs, the child is able to use increased levels of emotional understanding, which the therapist raises as the child is cognitively and emotionally ready. Harter stresses that this process of growth is not sequential and is not consistent across domains (social, cognitive, and emotional).

15

The Cognitive–Behavioral Approach

The cognitive-behavioral school developed from the work of Anna Freud and Melanie Klein and their adaptations of psychoanalytic theory for children. Beck and Emery (1985) and Beck and colleagues (1979) furthered knowledge about cognition and its effects on the behavior of adults through studies of depression and neuroses. Cognitive theory was later expanded to include its use with certain personality disorders and with persons suffering from somatic disorders. Later, techniques for working with children were added to this model. Because children function at different cognitive levels than do adults, many modifications were required to allow the techniques to be effective for use with children. Knell (1993a,b), wrote, "Rather than assuming young children lack the cognitive abilities to engage in cognitive therapy, we must consider ways to make cognitive interventions more developmentally appropriate, and therefore, accessible" (p. 42).

The behavioral model took into account the earlier work of the developmentalists, which included Erikson and Piaget. However, the cognitive-behavioral therapists supported the belief that treatments such as systematic desensitization, positive and negative reinforcement, and behavioral modeling could be effective methods to cause changes in behavior. None of the early adherents, however, stressed the need to involve the child in the behavior change, but instead gave the therapist or the parent the authority. This frequently led to resistance on the part of the child (Knell

1993a,b). Behavior therapy per se has little implication as a method of play therapy, although Knell admits that behavioral techniques are used in the context of play therapy. When behavioral techniques become combined with cognitive therapy, behavioral techniques will be a more effective tool for preparing the child in therapy for change.

Cognitive-behavioral play therapy (CBPT), as defined by Knell (1993a,b), became more than the use of cognitive or behavioral techniques. It provides a theoretical framework based on cognitive-behavioral principles and integrates these within a developmental framework.

The following are the six basic tenets of CBPT:

1. CBPT involves the child in treatment via play.
2. CBPT focuses on the child's thoughts, feelings, fantasies, and environment.
3. CBPT provides a strategy (or strategies) for developing more adaptive thoughts and behaviors.
4. CBPT is structured, directive, and goal-oriented rather than open-ended.
5. CBPT incorporates empirically demonstrated techniques.
6. CBPT allows for an empirical examination of treatment.

Knell (1993a,b) used behavioral techniques on a limited basis, including them to establish rapport, to encourage self-monitoring (beginning with clients as young as age 4), and to devise schedules of activities to be used as reinforcers. The therapist involves parents in these activities while encouraging children to make decisions and choices in their struggle for autonomy.

Dysfunctional behaviors in children are linked with dysfunctional thinking. Treatment that was designed for use with adults is not appropriate for children. For example, adults might be requested to maintain a journal or log to establish a record of thoughts. In CBPT, the parents are asked to be the record keepers of statements made by the child.

Another tool employed with adults is bibliotherapy. This method must obviously be altered to work with young children. Knell suggested that reading stories to the child and showing videos was effective with this age group. Further, she wrote stories specifically aimed to target the problem area so that the child in therapy could identify with a scenario with which the child could interact.

Knell and Moore (1990) describe their work with an encopretic child using cognitive-behavioral play therapy. The subject described was a 5-year-old boy who presented with functional nonretentive encopresis. The authors collected baseline data for twelve days and then proceeded with their treatment strategy of cognitive-behavioral play therapy. They incorporated the structured, directive behavioral intervention into a nondirective play therapy setting and approach. The therapists used the techniques of shaping, exposure to the feared object (which was the toilet), positive reinforcement, and shaping of socially appropriate feelings. The authors identified irrational beliefs, assisted the child to change those irrational beliefs, and assisted the child to use increased positive self-statements. The therapeutic intervention involved having the therapists close by, reflecting the child's feelings, and using toys to assist in the desensitization process. These authors suggest that the benefits of cognitive play therapy are that a child is able to use play to focus on thoughts, feelings, and fantasies. Within this context the child learns strategies to change behaviors, and cognitive play therapy has an empirical base that allows for accurate treatment assessment. Knell (1993a,b) further elaborated on the use of cognitive behavior play therapy as she described how she works with the child in the playroom. One of the techniques she describes are role playing, which she says allows the child to practice skills that the child will need in the outside world. The therapist typically uses herself, puppets, and other toys. The therapist uses behavioral contingencies, which generally involves reinforcing the child as he acquires new skills. These are typically positive reinforcers, shaping, fading, extinction, and other types of reinforcers. Knell describes some of the materials that she would use for social reinforcers, such as stickers and praise. Knell suggests the use of a combination of reinforcement and extinction simultaneously. Knell describes the incorporation of Bandura's (1977) work on modeling. In summary, Knell uses the play therapy setting as was discussed before. She advocates the use of toys and other materials. Additionally, she incorporates traditional behavioral strategies in the development of behaviors which she wishes to occur in classic desensitization and extinction of behaviors which she wishes to extinguish. She also reinforces new skills by using role playing, modeling, behavioral contingencies, and positive reinforcement.

16

The Ecosystemic Approach

O'Connor (1991) described a theoretical model that he has developed and worked with, which he calls Ecosystemic Play Therapy. O'Connor (1993) described his work with a group of children using this model. O'Connor rightfully takes the philosophical position that when working with a child the therapist must take into account the fact that this client is embedded in a number of small systems that, when taken together, form a larger system. It is impossible to correctly treat a child without assessing these small "subsystems" and the impact they have on the life of the child. Further, at times the play therapist will directly intervene in one or many of these "nested" systems.

  The first system that O'Connor described is the family. His philosophy takes into account the interactive effect of the child within the family system. The second system is the school and the peer group of which the child is a part. These entities will not only mold the child but can be utilized to assist the child to grow and develop. Certainly, the legal system could have a direct impact on the child. This is seen when the child becomes a ward of the court, or when the family system is either controlled or supported by the legal system. The biological issues unique to the child patient are also taken into account in the planning of interventions. O'Connor indicated that understanding the components of the child's ecosystem is the first step in the therapeutic process. Assisting the child to interact with the various components of this larger system in more productive and efficient ways is also a goal of therapy. Using an example from the 1993 article, O'Connor describes how the quality of the child's peer social interactions can be altered through the use of group ecosystemic play therapy. O'Connor makes use of relaxation and guided imagery in the group therapy. He establishes a behavioral system that includes reinforcers, both negative and positive. He includes cognitive strategies to assist the group members to connect behaviors to emotions. O'Connor structures the group around selected activities such as games, art, and other developmentally appropriate activities. The concept of developmental appropriateness is stressed within this model. The group is carefully structured around intelligence, age, socioeconomic status, and size of the group. The therapist is directive and structured.

17

The Eclectic Approach

Dr. Charles Schaefer is a psychologist, author, eclectic theorist, editor, and organizational leader in the field of play therapy . Schaefer has been a practicing psychologist using play therapy for over thirty years. Schaefer (personal communication, 1996) indicated that he regards himself as an eclectic play therapist. By eclecticism in play therapy, Schaefer means that a therapist who works with children has an obligation to know many theoretical approaches. Schaefer then uses his own judgment in selecting theory and techniques that are appropriate for each individual child patient. Schaefer utilizes a broad array of theories and techniques, and respects those that have empirical foundations. Using eclecticism in play therapy, Schaefer provides a prescriptive approach to treating children.

Schaefer is the co-editor or author of numerous books that have enlightened persons in the field of play therapy (Kottman and Schaefer 1993, Schaefer et al. 1991, Schaefer and Millman 1977, Schaefer and O'Connor 1983, Schaefer and Reid 1986). He describes his motivation for pulling together articles in an edited form as growing from his dedication to present multiple well-formulated theories and techniques. Persons in the field will have access to a broad base of knowledge.

His book on game play in play therapy (Schaefer and Reid 1986) has addressed the issue of ways in which children who are past the fantasy stage can be worked with in the play therapy setting. When children move into stages of development where they wish to engage in material that has relevance and meaning, then the concepts described by Schaefer are necessary. The concept of game play resembles activity therapy in that issues such as limits, rules, competency, and increased development of ego can be addressed. Schaefer has also stressed the importance of using the play therapy setting for assessment.

18

Summary

The work of the psychoanalytic child therapists was presented through a summary of the writings of Anna Freud and Melanie Klein. The similarities and differences in their theoretical and technical base were explored. The structured theory and techniques of Gove Hambridge, J. C. Solomon, Jacob Conn, and David Levy were presented. In addition, the work of the relationship theorists, Frederick Allen, Jessie Taft, and Clark E. Moustakas was summarized. Finally, the client-centered philosophy was explained. The adaptation of this theory to work with children was explored through a discussion of the writings of Virginia Axline. The child-centered therapy described by Landreth was summarized, and Kottman's work on Adlerian play therapy was summarized. The Jungian model described by John Allan was presented. Other contemporary writers and theorists, such as Oaklander and the developmentalists, were covered. The cognitive-behavioral model, which is organized and presented by Knell, was included. Finally, the ecosystemic model being developed by O'Connor and the eclectic concepts of Schaefer are presented.

There are strong similarities among the psychodynamic theories. These models are based on the assumption that what has been done to the child can be undone. In addition, the psychodynamic theories stress that the relationship between the therapist and the child is crucial. They all provide opportunity for abreaction and reeducation.

It was found that theoretical commonalities tended to exist among all of the psychodynamic theories presented. More commonality is evidenced in theory than in technique. There is a strong theoretical relationship between the psychoanalytic orientation and the structured orientation. There is also a strong relationship between the orientation of the relationship theorists and that of the nondirective theorists.

The psychoanalytic and structured theories assume that the therapist is cognizant enough of the needs and dynamics of the personality of the client that the therapist is able to define the deficiencies as well as the supplements. They assume that the plan for the therapy lies with the therapist and not with the client. In this situation, the client is the recipient while the therapist does something that causes cure.

The client-centered, child-centered, and relationship theories stressed that the power for growth and development is within the client. The client has the potential for growth and development. The therapist or counselor provides an atmosphere (client-centered, child-centered) or a relationship that allows the client to feel safe, so that the unfolding process can occur. Unlike structured theories, the client-centered relationship group does not see the therapist as teacher. The latter group feels that the answer lies with the child rather than with the therapist.

Therapists using the Adlerian model of play therapy expect the child to develop the concept of equal responsibility with the therapist in the playroom. The therapist is a "knowing more" person, in that the therapist has an understanding of the psychological needs of the child. However, technically, the child is expected to function as an equal partner in cognitively digging for concepts, as well as at the basic level of operation, such as in assuming joint responsibility in cleaning the playroom.

Cognitive behaviorism shares common positions with the Adlerian approach in that they both exhibit a directness and a structured orientation toward the child. The therapist using CBPT begins with techniques used by the relationship and child-centered therapists to assist the child to have a vehicle for communication. However, the work of the therapist is planned and implemented by preconceived design, just as is that of the Adlerian play therapist. The ecosystemic model of play therapy incorporates a plan that is developed in the initial stages of therapy based on the systems in the child's life that seem to be in conflict with the child's growth and development. Like the cognitive-behavioral play therapist and the Adlerian therapist, this therapist determines that things have to change, and develops a plan for doing so. All of the three theories share common assumptions that the child is a part of the real world and the child has to continuously be prepared to interact with this larger system. The focus of therapy from the very beginning, in all three of these models, appears to be to assist the child to function in the outside environment more effectively. Although the stated goal of all play therapists is that the child function more effectively in the outside environment, the analysts, the child-centered therapists, and the Jungians would work with the child for a long period of time before expecting the child to interact efficiently. The cognitive behaviorists, the Adlerians, and therapists using the ecosystemic model would likely expect this interaction to occur more rapidly. The playroom experiences would include more emphasis on what is happening outside and bring this outside "in" so that practice could occur.

The Jungian model, like the Freudian psychoanalytic model, allows for regression, analysis, and then reintegration. The child-centered therapists, the relationship therapists, the structured therapists, and the cognitive therapists do not incorporate these concepts in the body of the theory.

Developmental therapists start with the assessed developmental level of the child. Some of the components of the developmental theory are similar to the analytic model in that the basic level of relationship between mother and infant is often assessed. The Jernbergs (using theraplay) and Brody would assess the mother–infant relationship. All of the developmentalists believe that child therapy has to start at the child's level of development. They do not include the concept of regression as do the Jungian and Freudian models of analysis.

All theorists discussed work with the child in a setting that allows the use of media. The therapists make different use of the play media. The psychoanalytic approach of Anna Freud involved media only as it allowed the therapist and the child to establish a strong rapport. Melanie Klein used media so that she was able to interpret clearly the unconscious processes of the child. The structured therapists stressed that each article of play material was valuable if the therapist structured the scene for specific abreactive effects. The relationship and nondirective therapists use media so that the child will have a comfortable, natural means of expression. The Adlerian therapist uses the playroom in much the same way as the nondirective therapists; however, the Adlerian therapist is more involved with the child and sets limits in a different sort of way. The cognitive-behavioral therapist uses toys and materials. However, the toys may be used more specifically to assist in change or acquisition of targeted behaviors. The developmentalists, Adlerians, or cognitive-behaviorists do not address the "magic" of the playroom in the same way as the child-centered and the relationship therapists. The materials and setting appear to serve the function of providing a haven for the interactions between the therapist and child to occur.

Different uses were made of the therapist–client relationship among the theorists described within the psychodynamic therapies. Anna Freud stressed the need for strong ties to be developed between the therapist and the child. She saw these as going from the child to the therapist and not being reciprocated by the therapist. She described these ties more in terms of respect and idealization rather than transference. Melanie Klein felt that in order for therapy to occur, the transference neurosis had to develop. She saw these ties as making the child very dependent on the therapist during the course of treatment.

Conn and Levy both suggested that there is no need for the development of a strong relationship between the therapist and the child. Conn indicated that there should not be "ties of gratitude." Solomon, however, stressed the development of a relationship between the therapist and the child as being crucial to the total treatment. Hambridge contended that the play experience should not be structured until the relationship has been firmly established and the child is completely comfortable in the therapeutic setting.

Moustakas stressed that the therapeutic relationship is crucial to the progress of the child and the progress during each hour. He saw this relationship as being one in which both the child and the therapist are involved in a mutually growing, developing experience. Axline indicated that the relationship is used to provide a setting of safety. She did not focus on the mutual growth of the relationship as did Moustakas but indicated that, by the responses and attitudes of the therapist, children become aware of acceptance and so begin to accept themselves. In the context of this different relationship, children are able to reestablish congruence, which had been lost as a result of the experience of other types of relationships with significant others.

The developmentalists would stress that the relationship between the therapist and the child is the most central part of the entire therapy. Brody begins with the concept of attachment with the child and works with the child until the child is able to differentiate and separate. The Jungian therapist focuses strongly on the relationship that develops as being central to the safety in the setting. This safety allows the child to surface repressed parts of the self and to reintegrate them within a new, safe situation.

The Adlerian therapist relies heavily on the development of a strong relationship with the child before implementing some of the more cognitive components of the model. The Adlerian therapist does not appear to assume the strong role of "caretaker" as do the analysts, the relationship therapists, or the developmentalists.

The Adlerian therapist and those doing theraplay, as well as the cognitive-behavioral therapist, rely heavily on the parents as a part of the therapeutic model. Other therapists may take the position that parents need to be informed, or may need personal or family therapy, but therapists would not be so actively involved in the actual therapy as with the Adlerians, those doing theraplay, or the cognitive behavioral therapists.

Regardless of the model chosen by the therapist it is important to remember that there are more similarities than differences in their stated beliefs about the needs of children. The needs of the child, rather than the system or the family, are the central focus of therapy in all models.

III

Phases and Stages

INTRODUCTION

The steps in play therapy are not as definable as are the steps in baking a cake. And with that concept as a given, therapists know why a cookbook orientation does not work. Therapy is an art (with some empirical evidence as a base). Part of the skill of a good therapist lies in planning the procedure of play therapy so that the child is able to move, without hindrance from the therapist or setting, from one stage to the next. The therapist does not direct the child from step to step, but the therapist continuously assesses the child in order to anticipate and plan for the essential elements that occur within the context of therapy.

19

Stage I—Parental Involvement and Collection of Information

The play therapist should conduct the first session with the parents or legal guardian, excluding the child. This session should be well structured and the points covered should be thoroughly documented.

The second session should involve both the parents and the child. Much of the same material is covered in both sessions. However, the second session is unique in that the contents are tailored to meet the developmental level of the child.

During the first session with the parents, an overview of ethics, confidentiality, boundary issues, techniques of play therapy, process of play therapy, termination, communication, and fee arrangements are discussed. The therapist offers information about personal bias, philosophical position, and prognostic limitations. The parents offer history, clarification of their goals, treatment needs, and expectations. Historical and current information is gathered through a structured interview format. The parents are asked about medical history, family background, family values, school history, and their concerns about their child. An historical timeline is developed for the family and the child that contains the critical developmental issues of each. Essential ethical considerations should be covered in the introductory session. Those are described below (see Appendix).

At the time of the initial contact between the parents and therapist, it is important to clarify the following: the general concerns the parents have about the child; who has custody of the child in the case of a divorce; the reason that the first session is for parents only; the materials they are to bring, such as school records, medical records, and developmental records; the fee for the first session; the referral source; the emergent nature of the service; and the credentials of the therapist.

The first stage begins when the parents call the therapist for an appointment. Since the first contact is with the parents, they are instructed to come to the session without the child and at a time when both parents can be there. Even when parents are divorced, it is important to insist that they both be seen at the same time. There will be many unexpected happenings during the course of therapy with a child, and it is necessary to control as many of the external variables as possible. One such external variable is the communication with the parents. When parents are seen together, they both receive the same information and have the opportunity to ask questions and hear the responses of the therapist. When a therapist sees the parents individually (as is often necessary) then the therapist can potentially fall into conscious or unconscious manipulative entrapments by the parents, which may eventually result in the failure of the intervention to the child. Often, the therapist will unknowingly become a part of parental triangulation that results in undue pressure for the child. As was discussed in the section on ethics, it is important to determine who is the custodial parent (in accordance with state law). It is illegal to treat a minor child without the consent of the custodial parent. However, when both parents are involved in the treatment of the child, movement is more powerful, regardless where the child resides.

During the first stage of the therapy a careful explanation of the nature of play therapy is given to the parents through discussion and often through additional written material. Parents are given information about costs, and about the proper dress for the child. Stages and process are explained. The nature of play therapy and the potential therapeutic effects are discussed. The parents are informed how toys, limits, and privacy add to the power of the relationship. Parents are informed about how they can assist the child, other siblings, and the therapist in the intervention that is to begin. Beginning and termination are outlined. The therapist and the parents develop a schedule for parent conferences (which are scheduled on a separate day from the child's session.) The therapist requests proper authorization, release of information, and history forms from the parents. The first session with the parents sets the tone and contractual relationship that is to follow. The health of the relationship among parents, child, and therapist is usually directly correlated with the quality of the first session with the parents.

ORIENTATION TO THE PARENTS ABOUT PLAY THERAPY

During the first session with the parents it is critical that they develop an understanding about play therapy. Frequently, parents have read about counseling or therapy, but they do not have information about the unique nature of play therapy. If they are not well informed, communication problems can develop that could have been avoided. For example, it is not unusual for the uninformed parents to bring their child to the first session dressed in the child's best clothing, and feel demoralized when the therapist informs them at that point that the child will be playing with "messy" media. Frequently, parents bring their child in anticipation that the therapist will talk to the child, then consult with the parents and fix the problem. They may also remember descriptions of the very early models of child therapy, in which the parents "deposit" the child, and after a number of months and a lot of money, the therapist calls the parents in to inform them that the problem has been resolved.

In order to prevent any misconceptions from interfering with the work that is to be done, the concepts, process, techniques, and other issues unique to play therapy have to be explained. The parents need to understand the concept of messiness and the probability that messiness will occur. It is, therefore, a part of the discussion that the therapist request that the child be brought in washable play clothes. The parents are shown the playroom, the toys in it, and the potential therapeutic value of each of the materials to be utilized. If not given appropriate information, parents may be confused about why they are charged when all the child does is play.

The parents are informed about the stages the child will move through during the process of play therapy and how this might influence behaviors at home. The parents are told that they will be kept informed about the stage of process that the therapist feels the child is progressing through at each step of the therapy. Regular parenting conferences will be scheduled as well as informal telephone conferences.

Depending on the philosophical view of the therapist, it is frequently necessary to explain to the parents that the therapist will not "visit" or confer with the parent immediately after the session. Parent conferences are scheduled in advance on a regular basis and are put on the calendar during the first session. These times are separate from days in which the child therapy is scheduled.

The therapist's position on limits should be clarified with the parents. When a therapist has to employ the strongest of all limits (removing the child from the playroom before a session is over), many parents become confused about why they have to pay for a session that did not last the entire time. In order to ensure confidence in the therapist continues, this possibility should be discussed in advance.

Discussion of time is critical in issues related to fee for service. One hour of therapy will include working with the child, taking notes, and cleaning the playroom. It is sometimes hard for parents to understand why they pay for an hour of service and the therapist only maintains personal contact with the child for 40–50 minutes. In an effort to avoid conflict later in the relationship, these concepts should be explained to the parents in specific terms. For example, the therapist can indicate that there will be 40 minutes of direct contact with the child (assuming the child does not break limits to the degree of having to leave the playroom). There will be 10 minutes of clean-up time, which is necessary considering the medium that is being worked with. There will be 10 minutes for taking notes. The parents are advised that this all constitutes a therapeutic hour.

The parents are informed that the therapist does not take the child to the toilet. Therefore, the parent has to be present in the waiting room in order to assume the responsibility for toileting, for any emergencies, and to be able to receive the child if the session is terminated early.

COLLECTION OF HISTORY AND INFORMATION

A careful history is taken. The history that was developed by James and James in 1995 (see Appendix) is being used here, with full rights for the reader to copy and use in a practice setting. Certainly, the therapist would need to alter the material to suit his or her own needs. It would not be helpful to the parents, child, or therapist for information to be gathered in areas in which the therapist does not have training to the degree that he or she would be an informed consumer. The history that is offered (see Appendix) is being offered only as a guideline and each therapist will want to develop his or her own history form.

OTHER NECESSARY INFORMATION

Following the acquisition of the parental written history, and the interview that is used for clarification of the material, the therapist also gathers information from the other adults who work with the child, if the parents give permission. Teachers and school personnel need to be contacted at this point. There are many questionnaires available that can be used. The following is the necessary information:

1. What is the child's general emotional and physical state during the day?
2. How do the emotional states vary from day to day, week to week, or hour to hour?
3. What are the times and conditions during which the child has the most trouble?
4. What types of troubles does the child have?
5. What types of interventions have been tried?
6. Does the child have friends? Is the child highly chosen, moderately chosen, isolated, or rejected by peers? When possible request this sociometric information from the school counselor (see Appendix).
7. What is the nature and type of any educational problem, whether formally diagnosed or not?

The therapist needs to review copies of school records. This includes attendance, grades, achievement testing, individual psychological testing, and special education records and/or services.

The therapist should also confer with the child's physician. Additionally, when the child has been seen by other therapists or specialists it is helpful to have access to the insights from these professionals.

As a part of the collection of history and information, the therapist also collects the family and social history. The following areas should be included:

1. Marital issues
2. Discussion of the family constellation of both parents and grandparents of the child.
3. Discussion of the current dynamics of the extended families.
4. Description of the family constellation of the child's siblings to include birth order, and cognitive, emotional, physical, and social descriptors.

5. Assessment of dynamics within the child's family.
6. Relevant information about parental careers.

HISTORICAL TIMELINE

Once all the material is gathered, the therapist develops a formal timeline of critical events in the child's life. This includes birth, family history, school history, emotional and social history, illnesses, or other critical events in the child's life (see Appendix).

20

Stage II—The Initial Session

The parent(s) and the child are invited into the private office of the therapist. At this time, introductions are made. The therapist asks the child if he or she has been informed about the purpose of the meeting. If the child indicates that he has this knowledge about coming to the playroom, the therapist says "We will go into the playroom for our time together, and Mom and Dad will wait here." If the child has not been properly informed about the visit, then the therapist, the child, and the parents will have a conversation about what the therapist and the child will be doing together. Many therapists explain to the child that they are a person who children often visit when they want to talk about feelings. The therapist may indicate the following: "We do a lot of things here: sometimes we play, sometimes we talk, sometimes we just sit." The therapist may continue with, "I will be with you in a special room and at a special time that is all your own. You will not have to share your time or place with anyone." The therapist then suggests that the child and the therapist go to the playroom and proceed with the first session.

THE RESISTANT CHILD

If the child hesitates, or seems fearful about separating from the parents, the therapist may wish to sit with the child and the family while there is an additional discussion about how the child might be feeling and how the adults can support the child at the time. Other times, the therapist may wish to engage the child in toys and materials that are kept in the private office for that purpose. At this time puppets, toy animals, and even card games can be used. Later, during the first session, the child and the parents can go with the therapist to look at the playroom. Hopefully, by the second session the child will leave the parents and go into the playroom with the therapist alone. Should the child be unwilling to do so, the therapist can suggest that the child go into the playroom and select a special toy to bring back to the private office. It is rare that the child will not separate by the third session. However, should this be the case, then the therapist brings the parents back in for additional private work before reintroducing the child to therapy. Sometimes the attachment issues are so severe that the parents need to work through many of their own anxieties before the child senses a state of family readiness for separation. During this time the therapist instructs the parents how to work with the child at home, using filial therapy techniques, which were described by Guerney (1964). The therapist uses this step to assist the parents to get started in working on an enriched relationship with the child. Often a component of the filial therapy involves the therapist sending specific toys or materials home with the parents to use with their child. It is made clear to the child that the toy came from the therapist's office. The toy provides a powerful message to the child that the shared toys will be used as a vehicle to start our relationship. With other parents, the therapist may suggest that they seek marital therapy or individual therapy from a professional colleague before entering the child into formal therapy. When the timing seems appropriate the child is brought back into the office and the process of the initial session is started again. The child symbolically brings the toys that have been used during the home play time back to the playroom.

ONCE IN THE PLAYROOM

The therapist walks around the playroom with the child step by step. They start at the door. The therapist indicates that the parents are right next door in the private office. The door is closed because "this is our special time together." Each toy area is presented. The child is shown the location of the toys, how the water faucet works, and the other mechanical issues in the playroom by saying, "Here we have the easel and here we have the paints and here we have the blocks and here we have the toy animals." The tour of the playroom ends at the playroom clock. The therapist may wish to say "And here we have the clock. We are here until the big hand gets to (with a young child two twenty-minute sessions per week seem to offer the most opportunity for change. However, one forty-minute session per week would be the next choice. This depends on the child's age and the family conditions)." There is much to be gained by seeing the child two to three times per week, however, many families cannot commit to that amount of time. In any event, that has already been decided in advance with the parents.

The therapist then sits and says, "You and I will be here together until the big hand on the clock gets to eight. This is our special time together. You may spend your time here with me anyway you wish to. This is our special time." The therapist then gives the time and the session to the child. During the first session a number of things can happen. It is never possible to predict in advance how any child will react so the therapist must have control of his or her own needs for predictability. The following are some of the types of symptoms that may be seen in the initial session.

THE DESTRUCTIVE CHILD

Many children will stand for a moment and then proceed to explore and attempt to destroy every object in the playroom , test every limit possible, and push the therapist's psyche to the edge of the cliff. With these children, the therapist immediately begins setting limits within the framework described below in the section on limits. This should be done immediately so that the child will understand that this is a safe place for the child, the therapist, and the relationship.

THE RELUCTANT CHILD

Frequently children will simply sit and stare at the therapist with a variety of emotions on their faces. The therapist states that this is their time in the playroom and that they can use it any way they wish. When the therapist observes identifiable emotions on the child's face, the therapist attempts to reflect what the child might be feeling without moving in too fast or with interpretations that are too strong. The therapist continues to emotionally stay in contact with the child and to reflect the feelings that might be happening. One such reflection might be, "Sometimes it is hard to know how to spend your time here," or "You're wondering about this place."

THE FEARFUL CHILD

When the child immediately indicates that they wish to go back to the parents, the therapist reflects the feelings and sets the limit time. In some extreme cases the child will show symptoms of decompensation. Should this happen, the therapist takes the child back to the parents and attempts to work back to a place of safety with the child.

THE BATHROOM BREAKER

The parents take the child to the toilet before a session begins. This has been discussed in advance so that a discussion with the parents about this issue does not take place in front of the child. This prior toileting should allow the child to complete the session without having to go again. However, children seem to be fascinated with toilets, and have learned that they can escape almost any situation by showing body signals that a urination or defecation is imminent—regardless of where they are. The therapist should not take chances that the body signals and the verbalizations of "I have to—right now" are not accurate and real. The therapist takes the child to the parent next door and the child is taken to the toilet by the parent. Once it has been determined that the child is not ill, or is not voiding at the toilet, the therapist will deal with the need to leave the playroom as a therapeutic issue. The therapist and the child have a discussion about feelings the child may be having that cause their wanting to leave the playroom. The issues might be about anxiety or control. Later in therapy sessions, the therapist sets the limit that when the child leaves for an unwarranted toilet break, the session is finished until "our" next time together.

THE CHILD WITH A MILLION QUESTIONS

Children ask questions for many reasons. It is the role of the therapist to determine why this child is choosing this way of relating. These strategies are seen during the first session in the following types of children:

1. The bright, curious child who truly wants more information about the setting or the relationship
2. The verbal child who has learned to relate to the world verbally, rather than through exploration
3. The "adult-oriented" child who has learned that many adults like verbal kids
4. The "manipulative" child who is attempting to control the setting
5. The avoidant child who wishes to develop distracting strategies away from the self
6. The insecure child who wishes the therapist to define the world of the playroom
7. The fearful child who is asking, "Am I really safe here?"

In all of these situations the therapist must remember that this type of behavior represents a learned coping technique, which may evidence maladjustments that have to be observed, analyzed, and dealt with.

THE HELPLESS CHILD

Frequently the child will approach the toys as if he simply doesn't have the skill or the strength to use them. The therapist must be certain that the child is not impaired or ill. If this is determined, then the helpless behavior reveals either (a) the child has learned to manipulate and control adults by acting helpless, or (b) the child is paralyzed by feelings of inadequacy, anxiety, depression, or fear. The therapist does not assume that a child is being manipulative. First the therapist determines that the toys are appropriately accessible to the child or that the stool for "making us taller" is available. The therapist may take the child around the room again to demonstrate how things work. (It is important to note here that everything the child can see in the playroom is hers to play with. Also, all these materials should be within her reach.) Once this is done, the therapist will sit and determine what the child might be feeling and attempt to reflect those feelings back to the child. The therapist does not "rescue the child" by assisting with the task of playing with the toys. However, the therapist will frequently make statements such as, "The doll is so big, you wish you could rock it. It is disappointing when you cannot hold the big doll." At this time, the therapist may suggest other alternatives, such as, "I know you would like me to help you hold the doll, but this is your time in the playroom with the toys. I am here to be with you. You can rock the bear, or you can rock the other doll, but I cannot do it for you. I will be here with you."

THE WITHHOLDING CHILD

Frequently children will enter the playroom , move silently into toy play, and never make eye contact or verbal contact, or attempt any engagement. The therapist may find that this is a difficult situation because of his or her own needs to be helpful to the child. In these types of sessions the therapist must continuously monitor her own feelings and focus on what the child might be internally processing. The therapist will find that when his own needs are known, acknowledged, and managed, the issues within the child will surface. At this time the therapist moves into the position of verbal following. The therapist makes statements that reflect what the toys are actually doing. Such statements might be: "You put the doll to bed," or "The boy is in the car."

The therapist must remember that all behaviors are descriptive of the inner child in this little person. The question that the therapist continuously asks throughout the first session is, "What is the child trying to tell me with this behavior? How has it worked in the past? What does the child expect or hope that I will or will not do?"

The initial session with the child is fashioned to allow some of the central elements of the therapy to occur. First, hopefully, there will be interactions that will allow the clarification of limits to surface. Sometimes, simple issues such as the limit of time will communicate to the child that there is structure and safety in the playroom. Frequently, boundary issues surface that will allow the therapist to communicate to the child the limits involving the issue of separateness. The therapist and the child will not be extensions of each other. For example, it is not unusual that the child requests that the therapist "hold" something, or "fix" something. At that point, the therapist has an opportunity to describe boundaries and set appropriate limits. Regardless of the issues that surface during the beginning, the therapist is well advised to recognize that this session sets the stage for the sessions that follow.

21

Material from Other Sources about the Initial Session

Many of the writers in the field, both past and present have described their views about the essence of the initial session. For example, Anna Freud (1951) used the initial session as the start of the "wooing" period of the child. Kottman (1995) stressed that this is the time when the therapist begins to communicate the nature of the egalitarian relationship that the counselor and child are beginning. She states to the child, "We are equals in this world of play, and I do not want to look as though I am starting out with a size or power advantage" (p. 50).

Kottman employs a number of techniques during this initial time that communicate to the child the future nature of the relationship. Kottman uses her first name. She communicates to the child that "we are here to have fun." She states, "This is our playroom. In here you can do many of the things you want to do" (p. 52). Kottman makes it clear that the child is not given total permission, but limits are set as the need arises. Structured therapists or release therapists will typically use the first session for relationship building and for introducing the materials that will be used for catharsis.

Axline (1947), Ginott (1961a,b), and Moustakas (1959b) explained their approaches to the success of the first session in the play therapy process. They generally refer to the process that occurs during this initial session as *structuring* the relationship. However, it is not structuring in the strictest sense of the word, in that these therapists are all nondirective in approach. Their use of the term structuring means providing a framework.

Axline (1947), Ginott (1961a,b), and Moustakas (1959b) all wrote about structuring the relationship, which begins during the initial session. Ginott dealt specifically with some of the technical problems that are likely to arise and possible solutions to them. For example, he suggested that the decision to receive or reject therapy should not be left up to the child. In the event that the child comes to the clinic and refuses to come to the playroom, the therapist takes a firm hand. He does not plead with the child, but extends his hand to the child. The therapist may either take the child himself or allow the mother to take the child into the playroom. Mothers should be given all of the information possible about the playroom so that they can help children through the initial session. Ginott stressed that the mother should be prepared by the therapist in advance to deal with fear, crying, and clinging of the child should it occur. He further suggested that the parents should be aware that the playroom is not a place where the child is coming to "have fun." It is a place where the child learns to make decisions, to gain independence, and to express his thoughts and feelings in a constructive way.

The therapist should be prepared for the tricks that the child is likely to try, such as the bathroom need, temper tantrums, coughing, and other escape mechanisms. Once the child is in the playroom, the therapist can reflect the child's feelings and empathize with the child.

Ginott (1961a, b) stressed that children will try behaviors that are akin to their previous relationship patterns. He suggested that the therapeutic relationship should offer from the beginning the fact that it will be different from any other relationship in which the child has engaged. He cited in particular the withdrawn child, who is likely to present special problems. The therapist has to be careful not to be "rapport chasing." The child should initiate therapeutic movement. The therapist can empathize with the child's feelings of being fearful and accept the child. He should exhibit a faith in the child's capacity to move forward under his own steam.

The therapist structures the relationship by his initial responses. Essentially, he conveys to the child his respect and acceptance. The therapist conveys this by a simple statement, such as, "You can play with these toys any way you want to" (Ginott 1961a).

Not only does the therapist interview the child during the first session, but the child also interviews the therapist. The child is finding out about limits, attitudes, and how he will be treated by the therapist. It is important to look beyond the verbalized words to the feeling that the child is stating.

Moustakas (1959b) suggested that during the initial session the child is introduced to the playroom and the permissive nature of the situation is conveyed to him. Through the statements of the therapist, the child gains an understanding of the therapeutic relationship and the nature of the freedom and responsibility of the setting. Structuring statements such as, "This is your time and place" are suggested by Moustakas (1959b) as being helpful in aiding children to become aware of themselves, to face inner conflicts, and to work through painful, negative self-attitudes. These statements give recognition to the internal selves of children and assist them to come to terms with themselves. They also allow children to express their own feelings, thoughts, choices, and wishes.

Initial session play therapy behaviors of maladjusted and adjusted children were compared, to investigate the value of children's play for diagnostic purposes by Oe (1989). The Play Behaviors Adjustment Ratings Scale (P.B.A.R.S.) was used to rate each child's play behaviors in the initial session. Children were rated for the following behaviors: exploratory, incidental, creative or coping, dramatic or role, relationship building, relationship testing, self-accepting, self-rejecting, acceptance of environment, nonacceptance of environment, positive attitudinal, ambivalent attitudinal, and negative attitudinal. The results of the analysis indicated that maladjusted children exhibited significantly more self-accepting and nonacceptance of environment behaviors as well as more intense dramatic or role behaviors and acceptance of environment behaviors than did adjusted children.

22

Setting Limits

My 7-year-old son, Hunt, had invited a young friend for the regular Friday night sleepover. When it was dark outside and the tree started to scratch against the window, the young friend became frightened and started to cry. Hunt explained, "In our house, you don't ever have to be afraid." When asked, "Why?" Hunt replied, "Even if a lion comes to the door, my mom would stop it."

The function of limits is to protect the sanctity of the play therapy experience from harmful outside influences and to deal with the "big scaries" that surface within it. The essence of the play therapy experience is centered on the way in which the child views the safety of the room and the therapist. The way in which limits are set and imagined by the therapist allows this safety to occur.

Limits are set that allow the child to feel safe from the outside world and from personal internal fears. The limits are set as the need arises, using words in a typical conversational tone. "You know, in our city we worry about wasting water. In here, we use one pailful of water in the sand pile." Limits are specific. They are related to the experience that is happening at the moment. Limits are designed to:

1. Enhance the child's own self-respect
2. Enhance the child's trust in the therapist because of the honesty of the encounters

3. Enhance the child's feeling of safety
4. Enhance the child's development of mastery over the self.

In the playroom, a child does not:

1. Destroy expensive toys
2. Exhibit destructive behaviors toward the building or room
3. Engage in behaviors that would cause shame and embarrassment to themselves or undermine the respect they have for the therapist. This includes defecating or urinating in the playroom, disrobing, or making overt sexual contact toward the therapist. (Respect for the therapist is viewed not in the sense of expecting the child to treat the therapist in the way he or she would treat an elder or authority figure. Respect in this context is central to the concept that a strong relationship allows the child to know that this relationship will be different from any others. Within this type of relationship, the child can grow. Without it, the child has only encountered another person who does not have the courage to go through the "tunnel of pain" with him.)
4. Cause self-harm
5. Leave the playroom at will. When a child shows evidence of decompensation, the therapist does not force a child to stay in the playroom for the full hour because this would be viewed as a violation of child rights. However, it is made clear that once the child leaves the playroom, the therapy session is over for that day.
6. Violate the limit of time. The therapist sets the limit of time (using the playroom clock). The therapist gives the child a five-minute reminder and a one-minute reminder. The child then leaves the playroom . If the child does not leave willingly, the therapist or the parent physically removes the child (face away from the therapist/or parent).
7. Take his or her own created works of art and/or toys from the playroom.

Limits that the therapist must self-impose in order to maintain safety include:

1. The therapist maintains psychological and social boundaries, confidentiality, and continuing self-awareness through continuing personal analysis or therapy.

2. The therapist can tell the difference between a "lion" and a "puppy dog." The purpose of play therapy is that a child will have the opportunity to bring up and "primary process" material. At times, this material may be so strong in content and symbolism that the therapist may become overly concerned. At this point the therapist has to observe the material being presented, continue to follow the child in the content they are presenting, reflect feelings, and be very careful about interpretation. Only when the actual meaning behind the symbolism is clear to the therapist would the therapist interpret. The therapist must be cognizant of his own processing in order to understand the nature of the content the child is presenting. The therapist must be careful to not overpathologize or underpathologize the symbolism presented by the child. The therapist must remember that when material surfaces from the primary process it is frequently disorganized and distorted at the outset. Only after the child has worked with the concept through play for a period of time does it start to have meaning for the child and the therapist. It is critical that therapists maintain their own emotional boundaries as the child presents and works through these symbols.

3. The therapist stays current with knowledge and research in the field through continuing study.

The play therapy process allows emotions to surface quickly. The child learns that these strong emotions can surface within the context of the safety of the playroom. There will be power in the safety of the room that allows both the therapist and the child to deal with these emotions. Children can bring their fears, their worries, and the contaminants of their environment, and they will be contained in the playroom. The therapist and the safety of the playroom provide the strength to endure the fears. Because limits set the stage for safety, the magic that happens in the playroom can come forth and become an entity itself. The child can play out or symbolize any memory or current emotion and the safety of the environment will surround the meaning and keep it within the playroom. Because of the safety that develops as a result of the limits, the "dragons" will stay in the playroom when the child leaves. The child can symbolically hide them, bury them, destroy them, or just leave them out there on the floor. The child knows that the limits that are established will hold the dragons.

At the end of the session, all of the material is restored to its original place and the room is cleaned. When the child returns, the work from previous sessions can be recreated, or the child can start anew. The limit of confidentiality assures the child that none of the material they have raised will be let out of the playroom. It is his or her own. The therapist protects these products and material. This protects the child. The therapist protects the room and materials. And the therapist protects the mutual respect that the child and the therapist develop between them.

23

Limits in the Literature

The limits described above are not unique. They have been described by past and contemporary theorists in the field. Most child therapists agree that reasonable and consistent limits are necessary in play therapy with disturbed children. However, there are differences of opinion about the specific limits required in therapy. Therapists such as Bixler (1949), Ginott (1959, 1961c), and Ginott and Lebo (1963) stressed that limits are an integral part of the process. Axline (1947, 1964) and Moustakas (1959b) insisted that setting limits allows the process to occur and adds unique dimensions to the play therapy relationship. Others such as Dorfman (1965) and Schiffer (1952), who did activity therapy, set very few limits in their work with children.

Klein (1955) took a strong position on the importance of establishing limits in the play therapy setting. In this context, Klein (1955) stated:

> It is an essential part of the interpretative work that it should keep in step with fluctuations between love and hatred; between happiness and satisfaction on the one hand and persecutory anxiety and depression on the other. This implies that the psychoanalyst should not show disapproval of the child's having broken a toy; he should not, however, encourage the child to express his aggressiveness, nor suggest to him that the toy should be mended. In other words, he should enable the child

to experience his emotions and fantasies as they come up. It was not part of my technique to use moral influence. [pp. 228–229]

Klein (1955) stressed that she would not tolerate attacks on herself by the child because such attacks are likely to arouse guilt within the child. In addition, such measures protect the analyst. Klein contended that because she was careful not to inhibit the child's aggressive fantasies, the child did not need to act out in an aggressive manner.

Solomon (1948) suggested that the therapist set some carefully defined limits. If the child destroys property or attacks the person of the therapist, the therapist must make every effort to curtail such activity, but without anger or vindictiveness. Solomon suggested telling the child that the child "can do anything one wants to the rubber doll representing me [therapist] but that the child must not attack me actually" (p. 408). In working with an anxiety-phobic case, care should be taken not to repress the child further by setting repressive limits. In other words, Solomon suggested that limits should be set for each child according to unique needs.

Maisner (1950) described appropriate limits for the retarded child in a training school setting. She stressed that the child must "clean up the mess at the end of the hour, and the child is not allowed to hurt another child, nor to destroy irreplaceable property" (p. 242).

Taft (1933) stressed the limit of time in therapy. Following the work of Rank, Taft suggested that if the child can learn to live within the framework of one minute and one therapeutic session, the child has within his grasp the ability to live all minutes to the fullest. In addition, with the separation of the therapist at the end of each hour, the child has the opportunity to reexperience the separation from the womb at birth. The child learns that future separations are safe.

Moustakas (1959b) contended that one of the most important aspects of a relationship is limit setting. The designated limits for a child define boundaries within the relationship and tie the relationship to reality. Limits remind a child of responsibility to self, to the therapist, and to the playroom. This offers the child security and, at the same time, permits free and safe movement within the playroom. Limits are important to the child in that limits offer reality and allow the child to function freely without risking the stimulation of anxiety and guilt. Moustakas stressed the importance of setting time limits. He did not allow children to take toys home or break expensive and irreplaceable toys. Moustakas did not allow the child to abuse the therapist or to do himself harm. Moustakas did not allow the child to reenter the playroom once the child chose to leave. Moustakas recommended that health and safety standards be maintained.

Dorfman (1965) differentiated between playroom limits and those outside the playroom by suggesting that the playroom limits are fewer, and that there is an acceptance of the child's need to break the limits. She concurred with Axline and Ginott in stressing that the child is not allowed to attack the therapist. This, she suggested, would do the child harm and would interfere with the relationship between the child and the therapist. Dorfman stressed that limits lend structure to the situation and this reduces anxiety. Limits also add security for the child and therapist because limits serve to provide predictability.

Axline (1947) expressed that the purpose of setting limits is to bring about structure to the relationship and the situation. She believed that a nondirective therapy relationship requires only a few limits and those limits should be set as needed. Axline emphasized the importance of establishing only those limits that protect the child's sense of reality, the child's understanding of the relationship, the materials, the room, and the therapist. She stressed that the limit of time is critical in the relationship. Axline (1947) allowed the child to express all feelings. However, she set limits on the way in which the child could express those feelings. For example, she did not allow the child to attack the therapist (this would cause the child emotional harm because it would damage the therapeutic relationship). She encouraged the child to redirect feelings to appropriate objects, such as the "punching bag" or other toys.

Ginott (1959, 1961c), like Axline, stressed that time was a limit to be established. Since the relationship between the therapist and child was deeper than the materials in the playroom, the child was not allowed to take materials home. Limits were set to protect the child, the expensive toys, and the playroom. Ginott also stressed that to allow the child to attack the therapist would cause the child emotional harm, therefore this was a firm limit. Ginott (1959, 1961c) indicated that setting limits was nonpunitive and should be set in a way that leaves no room for ambiguity in the relationship.

Ginott (1959) described a four-step sequence for setting limits. He suggested that (1) the therapist recognizes the child's feelings or wishes and helps the child to verbalize them as they are, (2) the therapist states clearly the limit to a specific act, (3) the therapist points out other ways in which the child can express feelings, and (4) the therapist helps the child express feelings of resentment when limits are set.

According to Ginott (1959, 1961c), limits allow the child to translate feelings to symbols and to release them safely. These limits protect the child and also allow the therapist to continue to maintain the necessary positive attitudes toward the child. He stressed that therapists are human and have to stay in touch with personal feelings or boundaries that would negate a healthy relationship. Ginott further indicated that the therapist has a responsibility to maintain health and safety standards within the playroom. This included not allowing the child to ingest harmful or contaminated materials.

Bixler (1949) wrote that, in general, the limits that therapists set are individually based on the therapist's comfort level. Limits are imposed in order to provide safety to the persons, property, and rights of those involved in the setting. These limits allow the therapist and the child to have a relationship based on integrity, which is essential to progress. They should protect the rights, property, and physical well-being of others. They allow the therapist to maintain an accepting attitude toward the child. Provision of limits also helps to differentiate this relationship from others that the child has known, and so allow the relationship to develop on a level of integrity.

Bixler (1949) stressed that there should be few limits imposed and that those limits ensure the safety of the child and the therapist, protect the materials of the playroom and the building, protect the essence of time, and protect confidentiality via the materials produced within the therapy session. When these limits are clear and timely, they provide security for the child. Bixler listed four steps for setting the limits:

1. Reflect the desire or attitude of the child
2. Verbally express the limit
3. Provide an acceptable alternative
4. Control by physical means if necessary.

Those who have written about the use and value of limits in the play therapy process have also discussed the actions that the therapist should engage when the child refuses to accept the limit. Axline (1947) stressed the need to remain accepting of the child even when the limit is broken. The therapist should "stay right there with her reflection of feelings" (p. 132). The therapist should try to prevent the child's breaking a limit "if she can do so without engaging in a physical battle" (p. 133).

According to Bixler (1949), in the event that a child breaks a limit and the therapist is unable to enforce it without a physical battle, the therapist should terminate the session. He contended that an initial warning should be given before the termination and removal from the playroom.

Ginott (1959, 1961c) suggested that to put a child out of the playroom in order to enforce a limit may encourage the child to learn to manipulate the therapist in order to gain control of the adult. He took a firm stand on this issue and suggested that removing the child from the playroom does not add to the process the therapist is attempting to establish. He stressed that it is important that the therapist not argue or talk too much because it encourages the child to manipulate. Limit breaking often causes fear in the child. Because of this, it is important that the therapist not emotionally lose control, but stay consistent. It is important that the therapist and child not engage in a battle of wills. This frequently results in the demoralization of the child.

Moustakas (1959b) indicated that when a child breaks a limit, it gives the relationship more opportunity to develop. The therapist sets the limit and enforces it. The therapist may even put the toy away or stand next to the child so that the child will not repeat the behavior. During this process of enforcement, Moustakas stressed that the child should continue to be accepted. Like Ginott (1959, 1961c), Moustakas (1959b) emphasized that the therapist should not terminate the session when a limit is broken. This is based on the belief that the material presented through the limit breaking should be dealt with while it is still current. This gives the therapist and child a chance to work through the situation.

Landreth (1991) stressed that just because child-centered play therapy is permissive it does not mean that the therapist should "accept all of the behaviors a child uses" (p. 209). Setting limits are important, according to Landreth, in that they allow the child an opportunity to grow and to learn. He does suggest that limits should be minimal and enforceable. They should be well planned by the therapist and stated when the therapist is calm. One of the purposes of setting limits is that it assists the child in understanding where the responsibility for a behavior lies. He suggests that limits are not set until the need arises. Landreth stresses that limits are set for seven reasons in the playroom. They are:

1. Limits help assure the physical and emotional security of children.
2. Limits protect the physical well-being of the therapist and facilitate acceptance of the child.
3. Limits facilitate the development of decision making, self-control, and self-responsibility of children.

4. Limits anchor the session to reality and emphasize the here and now.
5. Limits promote consistency in the playroom environment.
6. Limits preserve the professional, ethical, and socially acceptable relationship.
7. Limits protect the play therapy materials and room.

Landreth (1991) further suggests that the function of limits is not to stop the behavior but to change the behavior by giving children a framework of alternatives to the behaviors. He suggests that the steps in the therapeutic limit setting process are threefold. "Step one is acknowledge the child's feelings, wishes, and wants. Step two, communicate the limit. Step three, target acceptable alternatives" (pp. 222–223). His most extreme limit occurs in an additional stage, which he describes as the final choice. Landreth suggests that as a final choice he would remove the child from the playroom after all else has failed. Allan and Levin (1993) suggested that limits should not be set until they are deemed necessary. Allan stated that the limits he employs follow those described by Axline. Additionally, he stressed that relaxed limits tend to allow behaviors to surface in the playroom, and causes them to decrease in the "regular world." The current survey of the literature indicates that even though hundreds of writers have contributed material to the field, in the area of setting limits the material that was written by Ginott, Moustakas, Bixler, and Axline continues to provide the major formulation for the way contemporary practitioners set limits.

24

Process

Process refers to the interactions that occur during the course of treatment that describe movement or change. This movement can describe the changes in the relationship between the child and the therapist, either that of growth or regression, or it can describe the changes that occur within the child or within the therapist as a result of the play therapy experience. Play therapists generally agree that this process occurs during the course of planned treatment. However, researchers have also found that change can occur within the child even before the original appointment is kept—just because the adults in the child's life-space have perceived that the child needs help. There is something about having one's own uniqueness validated that apparently causes healing. Other information suggests that change occurs within children when their environmental milieu is adjusted in order to attend to their needs. There is a possibility that when a therapist is open to his or her own intuition, internal processing may even begin to occur in preparation for the new child who is to become a part of the therapist's growth experience. The gestalt therapists consistently report that growth occurs within the relationship, within the child, and within the therapist as a result of the healing power of the therapeutic relationship.

During the first stage of therapy, observable changes in the child and in the interaction between the therapist and the child become apparent. There is a general consensus that this process is not linear but fluid, in that it moves back and forth. This fluctuation of movement has been reported to occur within sessions, over the duration of time of the total treatment, or after the actual treatment sessions are formally terminated.

The direction and fluctuations of movement can be measured. For instance, the changes observed in the interaction between child and therapist can be a movement from nonrelationship to relationship, from nonrapport to rapport, or from a superficial relationship to a risk-taking relationship. The child or the relationship either grows as a result of the therapeutic hour, or else they do not. This movement is defined as process.

Play therapy has a direction. Most therapists report that they have a conceptual framework that allows them to see and predict movement within the relationship.

The therapists who describe their work within the psychoanalytic philosophy vary in describing process. However, the writers in this field do indicate that growth within the child client follows a progressive mode through various stages. Anna Freud (1928) insisted that there must be a preparatory stage in the relationship. During this stage, Anna Freud established herself as a person with whom the child would feel safe as they started on an unknown journey. According to Anna Freud, she and the child stay in the preparatory stage until they develop a "working alliance." She provides the child with toys that they can use together. The toys during this stage are not used for interpretation, but rather are used for the development of the relationship between the therapist and the child. Later, the play therapy mode is used by analysts for observing the child, in order to develop a more comprehensive diagnostic assessment for the present and ongoing treatment.

Klein (1929, 1939) saw play as being equivalent to free association, which is seen in adults. Thus the play allowed the therapist an opportunity for interpretation of the child's internal processing. Play is also used by some analysts as a medium through which they observe the child's material, which can be used for interpretation. Play does provide the analyst with a modality so that a therapist and a child can communicate. Within the analytical model the communication of fantasies, conflicts, and transference allows the therapist to observe and understand what the child needs in order to resolve conflicts in a more functional manner. It would be erroneous to describe stages of the play therapy process within the analytical model past the first stage, which is described as a preparatory phase.

John Allan (Allan and Brown 1993) described process as it occurs within the Jungian model with several stages. The first step of the process is that the therapist has the obligation to become aware of his own conscious and unconscious processing. Allan emphasizes that extensive personal analysis is a requirement before the Jungian therapist enters into a relationship with the child. The next stage of the Jungian process centers on a comprehensive historical understanding of the child and the child's family. This includes providing the parents an assurance that their child will be cared for during the process of the therapy. The second issue that seems to be of utmost importance within this framework is the concept that the play therapy room becomes a sanctuary, or *temenos*, for the child. Within the context of this safe place, with a therapist who has self-awareness of his or her own processing, the child is able to regress. As the regression occurs, the child is able to bring up the components of unconscious processes. Through the symbolism of play, the child reveals the material that has been repressed. With the assistance of the therapist, the child then begins to align with the self-healing part of the self. The therapist functions to assist the child in identifying those parts so that they will able to move together as an integrated whole in the present. In summary, the stages of process as described by Jungian therapists could be outlined as follows:

1. The development of a sense of safety
2. Providing the freedom to the child to regress
3. Allowing the child to express stored memories and instincts through symbolic play
4. The integration of the stored material with the current feelings and environment of the child.

Kottman (1993, 1995) described the stages of development that she conceptualizes in play therapy. She indicated that within the Adlerian framework, play therapy progresses through four stages. She stressed that these stages are overlapping and stressed that these overlaps are fluid and tend to occur rather continuously throughout the treatment period. The beginning stage is described as one in which the therapist builds a relationship with the child that is described within the egalitarian model. This includes working with the parents and assisting them to develop a sense of trust. During this stage, Kottman focuses on developing the egalitarian concept with the child by communicating to the child that his feelings are understood and that the therapist and child will work out a relationship that will assist the child to solve problems. She also sets forth limits as the need for them occurs, to assist in the development of the egalitarian nature of the relationship. She describes the second stage as the "informa-tion gathering" phase (Kottman 1993, p. 139). During this stage, she gathers information from a variety of techniques. After she understands the child's logic, she begins to assist the parents and the child to recognize current strategies the child is using. Finally, Kottman supports the child and fam-ily as they try new ways of conceptualizing and behaving.

My understanding of the way in which Kottman assesses growth in her child clients is that she looks for behaviors that reflect alternative ways of understanding their options, their goals, and ways of getting their needs met. The steps that the Adlerian play therapist goes through are well de-scribed and fit clearly within the Adlerian model.

Harter (1983) indicated that within the cognitive-behavioral model she uses, the process involves a transition from the indirect expression of needs and conflicts in play to the more direct verbal expression of these issues. She proposes that after thoughts, feelings, and conflicts surface at the conscious level, then there is the opportunity for the view of reality to change. The two phases that she stresses involve first the diagnostic phase, in which the therapist is described as a participant-observer following the child's lead. Later the therapist becomes more directive and guides the child toward a more cognitive awareness of the meaning of their play. The next phase Harter describes is the interpretive phase or phases. Harter indicates that after she has developed hypotheses about the nature of the child's prob-lems she begins the first subphase of interpretation. Harter would use toys to represent different characters in the child's life, to assist in the interpre-tation of feelings and thoughts, so that the child would be able to raise these into her own perceptual awareness. During the interpretive phase the thera-pist also uses indirect interpretations, which might involve stories or dis-guised information about other children. At this time Harter suggested the use of metaphors to assist the child to incorporate the interpretation. She suggested that the final subphase involves interpretive comments that she would make directly to the child. Because the child is stronger, and the relationship is stronger, the child is able to accept and accommodate the direct information that the therapist is giving.

The issue of emotional adjustment and the play therapy process was described by Moustakas (1955a). He stressed that there is a parallel be-tween normal emotional development in the early years of life in a family relationship and the emotional growth seen in a play therapy relationship. He reported that an analysis of the case studies of disturbed children in play therapy showed the following levels of the therapeutic process:

1. Diffuse, negative feelings, expressed everywhere in the child's play
2. Ambivalent feelings, generally anxious or hostile
3. Direct, negative feelings, expressed toward parents, siblings, and others
4. Ambivalent feelings, positive and negative, toward parents, siblings, and others
5. Clear, distinct, separate, and usually realistic positive and negative attitudes, with positive attitudes predominating in the children's play.

Moustakas (1955b) described the difference between the attitudes of well-adjusted children and those of disturbed children. He suggested that they differ only in frequency and intensity, not in type. He contended that because the growth process is impaired at some level of development and the degree of the disturbance is a reflection of the intensity of anxiety and hostility attitudes in the family, this process must be reversed. The unique interpersonal relationship provided in the play therapy process affords the disturbed child an opportunity to achieve emotional maturity and to grow through the expression and exploration of the various levels of the emotional process. The child's problems and symptoms are reflections of attitudes. As these attitudes are modified, the child's problems and symptoms disappear. In play therapy, exploration and growth move from pervasive, generalized, and negative attitudes that immobilize the disturbed child to clear attitudes, both positive and negative, that enable the child to feel adequate and to express real potential and abilities.

In the same work, Moustakas (1955b) suggested that, the movement from stage to stage does not occur automatically. One will see levels overlap at many points, as do the attitudes of the child. The process does not go step by step but will vary in movement according to the individuality of the child. The power of the new relationship in the child's life causes change to occur because this relationship is the opposite of the one that originally caused the disturbance. The therapist responds with constant sensitivity to the child's feelings, accepts the child's attitudes, and maintains a sincere belief in the child.

Axline (1950a) described the stages that a child goes through during the first sessions of play therapy as follows:

1. Feelings for which the child does not assume responsibility, but rather has a doll or another toy express his feelings;

2. feelings directed against a toy or an unseen recipient placed in the playroom by the child's imagination;
3. feelings directed at a person who is part of the child's real world; and
4. feelings for which the child assumes responsibility.

Her descriptions of this process suggest that there are various observable patterns of play. She indicates that a child will first have the toys relate to another toy. Next, the child may have a toy relate to an invisible person. The child will then relate to an imaginary person. The child may relate the toy situation to a real person. Finally, the child will relate the toy to the real object of feeling. Axline (1950b) suggests that one way of assessing the successful conclusion of therapy is to see the child's own feelings and to express these feelings openly and honestly.

Cashdon (1967) divided the process of play therapy into five stages. He identified these stages through the use of the child's drawings. Cashdon suggested that these stages progress through the problem statement, relationship defining, emotional learning, separation, and adaptation and adjustment.

Miyamoto (1965) indicated that silence in the play therapy relationship goes through qualitative stages. Miyamoto suggested that in the beginning stages of therapy, a child may need to be left alone, and thus use silence as a defense. The child may also use silence to indicate regression to a more simple, less demanding level of development. Silence in this situation is seen as blocking because it provides the child with a usable barrier for the next action period. Silence during the first stage of play therapy is seen as evidence of negative process. A positive silence is described during the second stage of therapy, when the child may be attempting to move closer to the therapist in order to strengthen and clarify the relationship. The last stage involves the child's expressing ambivalent feelings. These are positive and negative feelings toward parents, siblings, and others. During this stage, the child gains insight in silence.

Rosenzweig and Shakow (1937a,b) described the levels of play normally found working with children as falling within four categories. The first category described spontaneous constructive play wherein the experience is happy and creative. Clinically, these children could be described as well adjusted and as having socially acceptable aggressiveness. The second category was described as compulsive constructive play, characterized by rigidity and a lack of fantasy. The child playing in this way is often found to be moderately well adjusted, timid, and fearful, and he has deeply inhibited aggressiveness. The third category of play is characterized by pretense, dawdling at constructing, and it usually ends in failure. This type of child often has psychopathic symptoms and is passive-aggressive. The final category described a child with aggressive impulses who is sublimating these by verbalizing a destructive tendency and at the same time is overtly being creative.

Maisner (1950) described the reeducative process in two steps: (1) the development of acceptance and rapport, and (2) the clarification of feelings and desensitization. During the first stage, the therapist is nondirective. However, during the second stage, the therapist becomes more directive. He involves himself in the child's play, clarifies feelings and, at the same time, maintains the reassurance of a calm acceptance.

Leland and Smith (1962) suggested the use of unstructured media within the play therapy setting, contending that the first goal is the process of conditioning children to the idea that their behavior, their ideas, and their reactions to stimuli are theirs and that they have originated in themselves and they are responsible for them. This occurs in an unstructured play therapy setting where acceptance is unconditional. The second phase is based on conditioning the children to organize their behavior around their cognitive associations. This implies that impulse control is closely related to development of communication between the therapist and children. Once children have, in the first phase, been conditioned to know that their behavior is theirs, it then becomes a necessity for them to learn that by increasing acceptable behavior, cognitive associations are clearer. Leland and Smith described the third phase as the process of conditioning children to organize their behavior around mutual cognitive associations. The behavior of the therapist falls into three categories: cognitive stimulation, reward, and punishment. In the playroom, this can be seen as the permission the therapist gives children to be themselves, to be active. At times, the therapist will block activity, and will set limits. The children begin to see this as punishment.

The importance of unstructured materials for this type of therapy lies in the patient's greater ability to control, create, change, and develop play activity with them. Thus, children can learn that they are persons capable of creating and controlling materials and things. This paves the way for learning that they can control themselves and interact with others. Children learn that they are not necessarily dangerously destructive persons, and they see that their impulses, which have been destructive, are primarily destructive to themselves. Children learn that their ideas and efforts can produce tangible differences in reality. They learn that they can destroy and construct. In this way, children gain control over their environment and themselves.

Myrick and Haldin (1971) described three stages through which the therapy progresses. These were described within the nondirective approach with a case that lasted over a seven-week time frame. The authors discussed the three stages that described movement. The first stage describes the establishment of a relationship. They indicated that the unique quality of this stage is that this relationship is different from any other relationship the child has experienced. It is unconditional and client-centered. During the second stage the therapist is more assertive. During the third stage the therapist becomes directive, in that the purpose of therapy at this time is to prepare the child to become more ready to make changes in his environment.

Landreth (1991) indicated that stages do occur within the play therapy process when the conditions of growth are met. His model for providing those conditions is described in Chapter 12. One remarkable contribution Landreth has made to defining the stages of process using the child-centered model is the development of a laboratory for the study of play therapy. The laboratory he designed contains well-equipped play therapy rooms, audiovisual equipment, and intensive supervision so that the process and other components of play therapy can be studied. He has supervised a number of doctoral level studies that were designed to investigate the process that occurs during the course of the child-centered play therapy experience.

Landreth (1991) described his own insights into process in play therapy. He suggested that the changes within children are often slow to develop and are subtle in presentation. Further, play which evidences change, may occur over time. He indicated that frequently therapists will become discouraged when they observe the same behaviors over and over. However, he stresses that the therapist has to be aware that this discomfort is due to the therapist's needs for adequacy and not because of what the child needs to do in therapy. He stressed that children are on their own growth schedule and that the therapist has to follow the child's lead. He reminds us that growth is a slow process. One rule of thumb Landreth suggests we use in determining process is to watch for "firsts." If something happens for the first time in the playroom, the therapist should take note of it and see it as a sign of movement in the relationship or within the child. Landreth suggested that the therapist must watch for the development of themes in the child's play. He indicated that repetitive toy themes may indicate emotional issues the child is playing out. He suggested that when the theme is no longer used it may indicate to the therapist that the child has grown past this level of need.

Moustakas (1955b) studied the frequency and intensity of expression of negative attitudes of nine well-adjusted and nine disturbed 4-year-old children. They were matched on intelligence and sociometric background. Each child had four play therapy sessions with the same therapist. Verbatim recordings of the children's statements were kept. From the protocols of the first and third sessions, a total of 241 negative attitudes were selected and rated in terms of intensity of feelings expressed. Both groups of children expressed approximately the same types of negative attitudes. The disturbed group expressed a significantly greater number of negative attitudes in a more diffuse, persuasive manner. Moustakas concluded that intensity of attitudes differentiated disturbed children from well-adjusted children more clearly than did frequency of such responses. This study suggested that, as therapy progresses, the negative attitudes of the disturbed children become similar to those of well-adjusted children. In addition, the negative attitudes are expressed more clearly and less frequently. This is also true with mild or moderate intensity of feeling.

Because it was not feasible to force children's statements into adult categories, Finke (1947) developed new categories based on an analysis of children's statements made during nondirective play therapy. She used complete protocols from six therapists who worked with six children ranging in age from 5 to 11 years. The number of contacts varied from eight to fourteen. Expressions of feelings were emphasized. Finke felt that these would mirror the children's changing emotional reactions resulting from play therapy. She found that the protocols revealed similar trends for the different children, which seemed to divide the process of play therapy into three stages. She found that during the first stage, the child can be either shy or highly verbal. When an aggressive child is seen, he or she generally shows that aggression during the first stage. She found that aggression (if demonstrated during the first session) does not decrease. The child continues to test the limits of the therapy into the second stage. During the second stage, she indicated that children frequently indulge in imaginative play. During the third stage the child tries to develop a relationship with the therapist, and wishes to engage in direct play with the therapist.

Lebo (1955b) presented a revision of Finke's categories, referred to here as the "Helen Borke" (from Finke's married name) categories for quantifying play therapy process. Lebo used Borke's scales A through U and added to these scales V and W. He suggested that these two additional scales are needed to differentiate types of verbalizations in older and younger children. These were sound effects (such as sirens, guns, explosions) commonly used by younger children, and mumbling or talking to oneself commonly seen in older children.

Hendricks (1971) reported a descriptive analysis of the process of play therapy. She analyzed and described the patterns of play activities, nonverbal expressions, and verbal comments made during the process of play therapy. In addition, she sought to determine whether phases of emotional and/or social development exist during the process of client-centered play therapy, and to describe these phases.

Hendricks reported some distinctive patterns of play activities in the process of client-centered play therapy. In addition, she determined distinct phases of emotional and/or social development. She found that, initially, the children engage in exploratory, noncommittal, and creative play, express curiosity, and make simple descriptive and informative comments. Behaviors such as curiosity about the playroom and its contents, as illustrated by exploratory play, are expressed during the beginning sessions. As the process continues, Hendricks found, curiosity decreased. The first sessions are characterized by noncommittal play, which gradually changes to more definite activities as the child becomes more familiar with the setting. Another characteristic that tends to separate the stages of process is the testing of limits. Hendricks found that limits are not tested so much during the exploratory stage as they are during later stages.

The second stage observed by Hendricks is characterized by more creative play and more aggression. The children test more limits. The aggression tends to move from generalized aggression in the beginning sessions, to being directed to specific people or situations, to final disappearance from the play activities. During the third stage, creative play yields to dramatic and role play. In the beginning sessions, the children tend to role play impersonal matters. Gradually, they begin to verbalize specific fears, anxieties, or hostilities.

During the middle sessions, the children increase the amount of time they spend in checking the counselor's reactions, seeking approval, confirmation, and suggestions. There is a noticeable increase in the children's overtures to establish a relationship with the counselor as the play therapy progresses.

Hendricks's study tended to be in agreement with Moustakas's (1955b) conclusion that the levels of the emotional process and the changes in the "feeling tones" are not always identifiable as a child goes through the play therapy experience. Changes occur, according to Moustakas, in the child's play and the emotional content of the play therapy session in no specific sequence but in individually varying sequences. He concluded that the levels of the play therapy process overlap at many points, as do the child's feelings and attitudes.

Levin (1992) studied process in nondirective play therapy in an attempt to identify and describe the principal verbal and play themes and the transformations that emerged over a course of play therapy. Levin studied four preschoolers who each received twenty weekly play therapy sessions, which were videotaped and transcribed. She found that the arrays of play and verbal themes and their patterns of transformations were highly individualized. However, a number of themes emerged in common to all cases: exploration, aggression, messing, distress, and caregiving. Based on her research, she described three phases of therapy. The first phase is typified by exploratory play. The middle phase is typified by intensive involvement in play and by experiences of disinhibition. The last phase is characterized by the introduction in the child of a sense of hopefulness, confidence, and integration.

Withee (1975) found that during the first stage of therapy children acknowledge the counselor more, exhibit high levels of anxiety, and engage in more exploratory activities. During sessions four through six, Withee found that exploration drops off while aggressive play and verbal sound effects increase. During sessions seven through nine Withee found even less aggressive play while creative play, expressions of happiness, and information about their outside lives increase. The relationship between therapist and child seems to be strongest at about session twelve. At session thirteen through fifteen, anxiety and anger resurface and control of the therapist appears to be at the highest level. Her study clearly shows evidence of identifiable movement from stage to stage.

Landisberg and Snyder (1946) examined the protocols of four children, aged 5 and 6, who were seen by three nondirective therapists. Three of the cases were considered to be successful, and one was incomplete.

Every speech and every action were categorized using Snyder's categories, which were derived from adult statements. The authors reported that within this context the children made more responses than did the therapist. There is power in nondirective statements, in that these types of statements preceded 84.5 percent of all child responses. They also indicated that within this nondirective context, the children tend to increase the amount of emotional material expressed. Negative emotions increase as the process evolves, whereas positive expression of feelings remains the same. The children tend to express more feelings toward others outside (in the outside world) than they do toward the therapist or themselves. They found no verbalizations that indicate an increase in insight. They indicated an assumption that the amount of insight achieved in play therapy is related to the cognitive developmental level of the child. They also concluded that the value of a nondirective play therapy process is cathartic, not insightful nor educative.

Daly and Carr (1967) explored the development of trust as a result of therapy. They measured the changes in the tactile contacts made by the child toward the therapist. Their premise was that a characteristic of the disturbed child is that the child withdraws from human contact. This is evidenced through the amount and quality of his touch. Further, they described this child to show more gross body contact and less meaningful hand-touching contact. The purpose of their study was to explore the role of tactile contact in relation to the development of trust the disturbed child shows toward the therapist. They contended that, as trust develops, the relationship is stronger. This results in freedom in the child.

An observer recorded the number and type of all verbalizations and tactile contacts. The researchers found that significant differences in the nature and frequency of the tactile contacts were observed during the course of the therapy. In addition, the child changed the method of contact from gross body contacts to hand contacts.

As a result of working with children in a monitored playroom, discussed in the literature by three researchers, L'Abate (1968), Golden (1969), and Rogers (1969), they identified three stages in the process of play therapy: exploratory, aggressive, and constructive. Rogers contended that, on the basis of these stages, it was possible to chart the process of play therapy from session to session.

IV

Outcome and Follow-up Research

25

Outcome Research

An investigation to determine the significance of client-centered play therapy on a short-term basis was reported by West (1969). He used twenty-six children from grades one through five. The children had normal intelligence and were diagnosed as having emotional problems, learning difficulties, and behavior problems. The children were randomly assigned to three groups, experimental, placebo, and control. Individual play therapy sessions were conducted for one hour each week for ten weeks. Five hypotheses were formed in references to the effect of the play therapy group. The variables examined were intelligence scores, self-concept, social adjustment, and perception of school adjustment. All hypotheses were rejected. This was an indication that the experimental group, which was exposed to play therapy, did not benefit significantly from the experience.

Paul (1993) hypothesized that their overall functioning would increase as a result of play therapy when children were placed under the protection of the government. He used the functioning index for children for assessment and showed that after the completion of the sessions all the children had improved.

In reporting a study investigating the personality outcomes of client-centered child therapy, Dorfman (1958) hypothesized: (1) personality changes occurred during a therapy period, (2) they did not occur in the same child during a no-therapy period, and (3) they did not occur in the control group. She used psychological tests, therapist judgments, and follow-up letters in order to investigate the outcome. The basic experimental design consisted of the pretest and posttest variety. The design involved observation during three time periods for the therapy group of twelve boys and five girls. (These children were aged 9 to 12, had average intelligence, and were considered to be maladjusted by their teachers.) They were tested over three time periods, which were pretherapy or control period, therapy period, and follow up period. The experimental group was tested four times: thirteen weeks before therapy, immediately prior to therapy, immediately after therapy, and a year to a year and a half after therapy. Dorfman found that reliable test improvements occurred concomitantly with a series of therapy sessions. She also found that time alone did not produce reliable improvement on tests.

Two secondary hypotheses were also supported: effective therapy can be done in a school setting, and therapy improvements occur without parent counseling in spite of the emotional dependence of children upon parents.

Cox (1953) investigated the nature of interpersonal relationships and individual adjustment before and after play therapy in a study involving two groups of orphanage children. There were nine children in each group, matched individually for age, sex, residential placement, adjustment, Thematic Apperception Test scores, and sociometric measures. Both groups were chosen so that they would be a representative sample of the orphanage population. The experimental group was given ten weeks of play therapy. The control group received no therapy. At the end of therapy, and again fifteen weeks later, both groups were retested. The adjustment scores and peer ratings of about half of the children in the experimental group showed improvement. The control group showed no gains.

The effectiveness of nondirective therapy with maladjusted fifth-grade pupils was investigated by Quattlebaum (1970). The purpose of the study was to determine if the self-concept of these students could be improved through the use of play therapy or counseling. The study involved three groups of maladjusted fifth-grade pupils. One group received no therapy, a second group received individual counseling, and a third group received play therapy. This was done in order to assess the effectiveness of play therapy and counseling in contrast to no treatment. Nine students were involved in four months of treatment.

Based on the results, Quattlebaum surmised that there were a substantial number of maladjusted elementary students, and, from all indications, teachers were quite reliable in categorizing them. Even though overall significant differences were not found in the three treatment effects, individual children did improve as a result of treatment.

Pelham (1971) investigated the use of group and individual play therapy in increasing the social maturity of kindergarten students who had been identified as socially immature. The study involved seventeen children in the experimental group, nine of whom received group therapy and eight of whom received individual therapy. The control group consisted of eighteen other children. All of these children had been identified by their teachers as being socially immature in terms of classroom behavior. Each child in the experimental group received six to eight forty-five-minute therapy sessions held at the university. One investigator conducted all of the sessions.

Based on the results of the pre- and posttest evaluations, which included the Missouri Children's Picture Series, the Children's Self-Social Constructs Tests, and the Behavior Problem Checklist, it was concluded that few significant differences in social maturity could be found between the experimental and control groups. The experimental group was shown, however, to have developed more complex self-concepts, but it decreased in maturity as measured by the Missouri Children's Picture Series. No differences could be found between the children who had received group therapy and those who had received individual therapy.

Cowden (1992) studied the effects of client-centered group play therapy on self-concept. Cowden attempted to show that group play therapy would increase the self-concept in seven children using eight sessions of play therapy group. Her findings were statistically inconclusive; however, she indicated that the progress based on clinical notes indicated a progression toward increased self-concept.

The effects of play therapy and behavior modification approaches with conduct problem boys were compared by Perkins (1967). Twenty-seven subjects were randomly assigned to one of three conditions. These conditions were the control group, the play therapy group, and the reinforcement therapy group. They were assigned to one of three therapists. The subjects were seen over a three-week period for nine twenty-minute sessions. The therapists were found to be significantly more effective in increasing responsiveness to social reinforcement in a reinforcement therapy condition than in the play therapy or the no-treatment control condition. Perkins contended that the play therapy condition did not differ from the no-treatment controls in its effect on responsiveness. Social reinforcement therapy procedures produced greater behavioral improvements than did play therapy.

Herd (1969) investigated the relationship of play therapy to behavioral changes in interpersonal relationships, mature and desirable behavior patterns, more adequate use of intellectual capacities, and improved adjustment. Subjects ranged in age from 6 to 11, were of at least average intelligence, and were identified by their schools as having behavior problems. The subjects were randomly placed into three groups: an experimental play therapy group, a play group, and a control group. Little statistical significance was found in the measuring data to support the hypothesis that positive behavioral changes would occur as a result of play therapy. There was evidence, however, that did support the hypothesis. These were interviews with parents and teachers, letters, and statements, and observations made by the therapist.

Wolaver (1992) used five cases involving girls aged 7 to 9 from middle-class white families with at least average intelligence and no sign of neurological problems. Wolaver used books and oral stories to assist the children as they explored metaphors. The children created stories along with the therapist. The qualitative findings from the stories and metaphors created collaboratively by the child and the therapist indicate that the process begins with projection and externalization, and is followed by the process of identification, catharsis, and resolution. The story creation process is supported by communication through the child's primary sensory language and applied to therapeutic metaphors. The themes in the stories created reveal an Adlerian adaptive process of changing beliefs about how to get basic social needs met.

Levitt (1957) surveyed thirty-five reports of child therapy outcomes. Two-thirds of the children examined at termination of therapy and three-fourths of those seen in follow-up showed improvement. Approximately the same percentages of improvement were found in groups of untreated children. Levitt concluded that the published figures "fail to support the view that psychotherapy with 'neurotic' children is effective" (p. 195).

In a later study, Levitt (1963) combined the results of a number of studies to include nearly ten thousand child patients. Of those who received treatment, between two-thirds and three-quarters were improved, but a similar improvement rate occurred in those who were not treated.

Oppenheimer (1988) studied the appropriateness of existential play therapy for children in middle childhood. He derived variables from four major approaches to play therapy (psychoanalytic, client-centered, behavioral, and existential). He stated that a consensus of child development experts agreed that existential play therapy consists of methods that are cognitively and affectively appropriate for children in middle childhood. He also indicated that clinicians who are aligned to different theoretical prospectives could recognize the content of neutrally worded interventions as emerging from the theoretical and philosophical foundations of existentialism.

Reams (1987) studied thirty-six preschoolers attending a therapeutic nursery who were given individual play therapy to supplement their ongoing milieu therapy or were given only milieu therapy. The children in the treatment group were superior to control children at posttest on amount of isolated play only. The implications of this might be that when an emotionally disturbed child is involved in play therapy the affect of play therapy might allow this child to play more independently. Reams offered a number of explanations for the lack of statistical results in his findings.

Trostle (1984) studied the effects of child-centered group play therapy on sociometric, self-control, and free play ratings of three 6-year-old bilingual Puerto Rican boys and girls. The purpose of the investigation was to examine the facilitative effects of child-centered group play therapy upon these children's social peer preferences, self-control ratings by teachers, and play behaviors in free settings. The study included forty-eight subjects equally divided in terms of gender, who were randomly assigned to either an experimental or a control group. The twenty-four children in the experimental group participated in a minimum of ten child-centered play therapy sessions over a period of five weeks. The twenty-four control children received no treatment. The results of the investigation showed that the child-centered group play therapy sessions facilitated the boys' positive ratings of other peers, the children's self-control ratings, and the children's make-believe and reality play behaviors. The children who received the ten sessions of group play therapy showed higher scores on the measures that were given to show progress.

In a study conducted in Great Britain, Barbour and Beedell (1955) reported that they found no difference in outcome between treated and untreated children. They also reported no difference between short-term therapy outcome and long-term therapy outcome.

Flint (1969) reported a program designed to rehabilitate infants and preschool institutionalized children who were emotionally and culturally deprived. An experiment was conducted in the children's homes, which involved using volunteer mothers in addition to daily provision of play therapy for the children. The children gradually showed emotional, social, and speech development and became more competent in self-help skills. After fifteen months, forty-four children were returned to their parents or placed in foster or adopted homes. Results indicated that an institution could promote healthy development by recognizing the individuality of the children, providing close relationships with other people, encouraging initiative, and being consistent in care and discipline. Flint included five case histories to show the trend of development as a result of the provision of increased services.

Stockburger (1983) studied twenty-four students who were identified by their teachers as needing assistance but who were not described as being emotionally disturbed. Twelve of the students were assigned to the treatment group and twelve to the nontreatment group. The treatment group received four twenty-minute play therapy sessions over a four-week period while the nontreatment group received four twenty-minute periods out of their classrooms listening to tapes of children's stories. The researcher found that the I.Q. scores of the treatment group increased; however, the children in the treatment group also showed an increase in the number of negative behaviors that they exhibited as compared to the nontreatment group. This study would indicate that short-term play therapy generally will increase overt acting out at first. Only with increased numbers of sessions will the play therapy have positive effects.

Variables affecting child therapy outcome were investigated by Levi (1961). The variables were: type of parent, identity of therapist, length of treatment, age, sex, and symptoms of the child. Of these variables, only the identity of the therapist and the length of treatment were found to be related to outcome. The children who were seen by one particular therapist had a much higher level of success more quickly. Other therapists, less able, achieved success, but it took them a longer length of treatment.

Rogers's (1937) survey indicated treatment should be selective. It pointed to the fact that, in treating children, the use of social, educational, and medical therapy as well as psychotherapy should be employed. He suggested using specific types of therapy for specific types of children. He further suggested that we should welcome all methods that promise help for children, but therapists should recognize that some of the techniques are applicable only in certain cases.

The level of experience in a child as a predictor of short-term play therapy outcome was used by Eme (1972). Twenty-four boys between the ages of 8 and 12 participated in twelve one-hour individual play sessions. Eme attempted to predict therapeutic outcome by using pretherapy measures of level of experiencing and level of adjustment. Level of experiencing was assessed by the Rotter Incomplete Sentence Blank Test using Dorfman's modified criteria. The level of adjustment was assessed by the subject's responses on the Incomplete Sentence Blank Test. In addition, parental reports and target complaints were used. None of the statistical tests used after treatment showed the significance necessary to indicate that the level of experiencing is a favorable predictor of play therapy outcome.

Henderson-Dickson (1991) studied how children communicate their inner stories through creative work in treatment. The central premise is that there is a relationship between storytelling in therapy and healing and changes in the self. The connection between themes of fantasies in children's therapeutic and fictional stories was also studied. Henderson-Dickson studied two children in long-term play therapy. Results of the cases suggest that the children communicated their sense of self and the world to others through creative play and expression. They used metaphorical messages that were received and brought into consciousness, resulting in an opportunity for healing. The author related that children seem to be empowered to make changes in their stories that reflect the transformation of self. They also utilize fictional stories to project fantasy and to re-work their own stories.

Stiber (1991) studied a 7-year-old boy who was having temper tantrums as he went through a therapeutic time in play therapy. As a result of play therapy, the author stated that the child made clinical progress in decreasing his temper tantrums, decreasing his aggression at school, and in verbalizing his feelings more clearly. Her findings support the use of play therapy with children who display temper tantrums.

Crow (1989) studied the effect of play therapy on children who were having reading difficulties. This research showed that participants in play therapy scored significantly higher in self-concept than did those who were not exposed to the treatment. There were no statistically different findings between the two groups of children in terms of reading achievement. However, since low achievers in reading tend to have low self-concepts, it is reasonable to assume that improved self-concept could be related to improved reading scores. The author recommended further study in this area.

Subotnik and Callahan (1959) investigated the outcome of play therapy for institutionalized, educable, mentally retarded boys. Based on the data gained from their study, they posed such questions as (1) Who needs treatment? (2) How can the need for treatment be quantified? and (3) What is treatment? They saw a need for assessing psychotherapy and for a better formulation of the goals of psychotherapy, reflected in the selection of subjects for treatment, and a need for a more holistic method of evaluation compatible with the complexities of personality. There should also be more sophisticated expectations of change to allow for individual variations.

Eisenberg and Gruenberg (1961) found short-term treatment as intensive as long-term psychotherapy. Phillips and Johnston (1954) reported an attempt to evaluate the effectiveness of short-term therapy as compared with conventional treatment. Short-term therapy consisted of a stated number of interviews in which treatment was directed "not at retrospective self-examination, but at the child's pattern of interaction in current situations" (p. 267). Of sixteen short-term cases, two were considered successful, and the rest improved. Of fourteen conventionally treated cases, one was considered successful, eight improved, and five failed. Of the thirty control cases, four were considered successful, nineteen improved, and seven failed. The authors conclude that the similarity in outcome between short-term and conventional methods was great enough to warrant further study.

Phillips (1960) did a follow-up study comparing short-term and conventional therapy. To do this, he obtained ratings from the parents of thirty children seen in conventional therapy and from the parents of twenty-seven children treated in short-term therapy in a guidance clinic. He also obtained information from fifty-two children seen in short-term therapy in private practice. The criteria involved assessing growth in the areas of: improvement in original complaint, parental ability to handle the child, and the child's behavior at home, school, and with peers. As a result of the information gathered, Phillips suggested that the short-term therapy was more effective than the depth therapy. He suggested that, for some cases, it is possible to evolve procedures that shorten therapy without jeopardizing results.

Hare (1966) reported a study designed to evaluate a shortened method of treatment at a child guidance clinic, in order to compare the results obtained with other similar studies. The study involved 119 consecutive cases carried out by one psychiatrist in the clinic. The average number of attendances per case was 6.3, and the median number of months under treatment was 3.8. A follow-up assessment was made approximately two years after discharge. Adequate information was obtained on 95 percent of the cases. At discharge, 49 percent of the cases were recovered, and 23 percent improved. At follow-up, 75 percent were recovered, and 24 percent improved. Outcome was better in girls than in boys, and in older than in younger children. Outcome was best in neurotic cases and poorest in conduct disorders. The improvement rates compare favorably with those of other studies. They add to the evidence that short methods of treatment are as effective as longer conventional methods.

26

Follow-up Research Studies

The research discussed in this section was done to assess the long-range effects of the play therapy experience. There was a wide range in type of study and effectiveness of study included.

In a follow-up study involving a group of fifty children who had been exposed to only diagnostic study, Witmer and Keller (1942) found there was little difference between the later adjustment of the successfully treated children and the untreated children. The children were chosen to constitute a control group for the children described in the study by Shirley and colleagues (1940).

The adjustment found in the follow-up of the "diagnostic" group was as follows: 48 percent made successful adjustment, 30 percent had improved but still were somewhat maladjusted, 22 percent remained unimproved. They found that by late adolescence or young adulthood a majority of maladjusted children outgrew their problems. Those who missed therapy in childhood did about as well as those who were successfully treated.

Shirley and colleagues (1940), in a follow-up study of child guidance patients, assessed children twelve years after termination of treatment. Of the thirty-five treated subjects considered successfully treatment, 60 percent remained well adjusted, 23 percent displayed some problems, and 17 percent were definitely maladjusted. Of fifty children considered unsuccessfully treated, 56 percent remained unimproved, 20 percent had improved, and 16 percent were well adjusted. In other words, when treatment was successful, the chances were six out of ten that the patient would still be well adjusted years later. When treatment was unsuccessful, the chances were only two out of ten that the patient would be found well adjusted.

Axline (1950b) reported the follow-up of twenty-two children whose therapy was deemed successful and whose parents did not receive treatment. She used the following interview procedures: the therapist met the child and asked an introductory question, "Do you remember me?" There were no probing questions or suggestions. Those who could not be contacted personally were reached by mail. Axline found that the twenty-two children were still successfully adjusted a year after termination of treatment. She did not discuss her criteria for adjustment.

Axline (1947) reported a sharp gain of functioning in the case of Billy in a follow-up assessment. Upon entering play therapy, his intelligence quotient was measured at 65, and upon retest, it was 68. He was tested again in six months and was evaluated at 96. A year later, he scored 105. Axline used this as an example to attest to the lasting effects of play therapy.

Phillips (1985) reviewed a number of articles that described process and outcome research in the field of play therapy. He reports a continued dearth of research in both areas. He indicates that some of the problems with research in this area continue to be methodological inadequacies. Another problem he suggests is our lack of a conceptual model of how children are helped or changed by play therapy. Models for play therapy vary considerably, as well as the techniques that professionals in the field use. Because of this, it is difficult to target those things that need to be tested. He suggested another issue is that therapists tend to be more focused on the emotional needs of their child patients and on treatment than they are on research. In addition, researchers have not clearly looked at the daily clinical needs of the therapist when they are designing experimental projects. Another issue he described is that play therapy may not be taken seriously by the academic community. Because of this, academicians have not yet developed an understanding that their research respectability would be enhanced by evaluating such a thing as what happens in play therapy. Phillips did indicate that with the emergence of cognitive behavioral techniques the field will be able to observe more specifically for growth. He suggested that play therapy needs a systematic program of research that clearly sets out its hypotheses and designs well-controlled studies.

27

Methods Used in Research

This chapter includes information and material related to play therapy that are not considered to affect the play therapy procedure. Also included in this chapter is a discussion of the methods used in evaluating the process and outcome of studies in play therapy. The material found in this area consists of pre- and posttest measures. It includes methodology of research. In addition, mechanical devices for recording process are described and discussed.

TESTING PROCEDURES

Mehlman (1953) reported the use of the Stanford-Binet and the Haggerty-Olson-Wickman Behavior Rating Scale in an effort to show growth in group play therapy with retarded children. He stressed that both scores would show improvement and that there would be a correlation between raised intelligence and better behavior.

Pelham (1971) used three instruments in his investigation of the outcome of play therapy on socially immature kindergarten students. These instruments were the Missouri Children's Picture Series, the Children's Self-Social Constructs Tests, and the Behavior Problem Checklist.

Homeyer (1994) developed a survey instrument to identify play behaviors of sexually abused children. The survey was field tested and 140 items of play therapy behavior were developed into the survey instrument. This instrument in its entirety can be found in the dissertation.

Subotnik and Callahan (1959) reported that they used tests administered at varied times before, during, and after the play therapy sessions in their research. In the study designed to evaluate outcome of play therapy for institutionalized mentally retarded boys, they used the Children's Anxiety Pictures, Auditory Memory for Digits, Vocabulary, Draw-a- Person, and Bender Gestalt.

Herd (1969) used the following tests in her assessment of play therapy outcome: the California Test of Personality, the Vineland Social Maturity Scale, the Haggerty-Olson-Wickman Behavior Rating Schedule, school grades, and a sociometric measure. Quattlebaum (1970) used the Rorschach, the Thematic Apperception Test, and the Draw-a-Person in investigating the effectiveness of nondirective counseling and play therapy with maladjusted fifth-grade pupils. She used the assessments for pretest and, after four months of treatment, for a posttest.

Bucur (1970) used a modified version of Bower's Sociometric Index and a teacher's rating scale in his investigation of the effects of nondirective group play therapy with aggressive boys.

West (1969) used the Wechsler Intelligence Scale for Children, the Goodenough-Harris Draw-a-Person Test, the Self-Esteem Inventory, a sociometric measure, and the School Apperception Method in his study evaluating the effectiveness of play therapy.

In a study investigating the effectiveness of play therapy with other modalities in the treatment of children with learning disabilities, Siegel (1972) used the Observation Rating Form. Each teacher was evaluated in the study in order to quantify aspects of the teaching process. Truax Scales were applied to excerpts of the therapy tapes in order to assess the level of therapist-offered conditions. Siegel also used the Borke Process Scales in order to compare the clients who received the highest offered conditions to the clients who received the lowest offered conditions.

Johnson (1953a) investigated the clinical use of Raven's Progressive Matrices to appraise potential for progress in play therapy. The children, institutionalized mentally and educationally retarded, consisted of twelve boys and six girls. They were aged from 9 to 16 years old. The measures used as pre- and posttests to play therapy were the Stanford-Binet, Authur, and Raven. Johnson reported improvement in every instance in which the

Raven Z score was higher than the Binet Z score. This was evidenced in thirteen children. Twelve of the thirteen showed improvement in interpersonal relationships and a reduction of symptomatic behavior. No improvement was noted in the five children who had a lower Raven Z score than the Binet Z score. In addition, Johnson used sample histories of the play therapy responses in terms of the criteria of projection, insight, and working through to illustrate and support findings.

Johnson (1953b) investigated the sensitivity of Raven's Progressive Matrices as a clinical predictor of play therapy progress, conceived as a function of superego potential by using the Rorschach Prognostic Scale of ego strength. Prognostic scores were computed for a group of fifteen children who had previously been reported as improved or unimproved in psychological treatment according to clinical and social criteria of behavior. As a result of the findings, Johnson concluded that while the Raven may be a more accurate predictor of play therapy responses, the use of it was incomplete. The Rorschach Progressive Scale more reliably estimated the level of improved behavior obtainable in short-term clinical treatment.

OTHER RESEARCH CONTRIBUTIONS

As discussed elsewhere in this book, Finke (1947) made a worthwhile contribution in the study of process in play therapy. She derived categories to be used in the assessment of the process as it occurs in the work with children. Because of her marriage, her scales are now labeled the Borke Scales.

Rogers and L'Abate (1969) developed a bibliography for use by persons researching the areas of play therapy, emotionally disturbed children, child development, and handicapped children. The references are comprehensive and are inclusive from 1928 to 1968.

Lebo (1953, 1955b) wrote on the status and quantification of research in the play therapy process. He summarized in a very usable way the research that was of note in the area of play therapy until 1955. This material remains valuable in that it furnishes a critical summary in a field that has been somewhat lax in quantifying. Lebo pointed to the fact that statements based on philosophy and emotionality in reference to the treatment were not enough to prove professionality in the area.

Heinicke and Goldman (1960) reviewed the child therapy research that was available at that time. They presented a detailed study of the method of comparing outcome research in the area of child therapy. They noted the difficulties of a research model in evaluating the effect of play therapy and suggested that the benefits of child therapy can be more clearly observed when research is performed in the dimension of process.

Levitt (1957, 1963) made a contribution in the area of child therapy in that he, too, pointed to the fact that quantification is necessary. His work was mainly negative toward psychodynamic philosophies and techniques. However, the stimulation he caused in the field is healthy.

Perry (1988) developed a play therapy observation instrument (PTOI). She used this in original research in 1988 and has since continued to develop the scale for use by play therapists. For a description of this comprehensive scale, the author can be contacted in Denton, Texas. The scale in its entirety is presented in her dissertation and in other writings.

Carmichael (1993) developed an inner action matrix for observation of client–therapist relationship in play therapy. The instrument is able to determine a wide range of behaviors that multiple schools of thought in play therapy have endorsed. In its final stage of development this assessment will likely prove to be an invaluable method for analyzing interactions between clients and therapists in process research in play therapy in the future.

Hellendoorn and colleagues (1979) described a classification system for play therapist activities. This system was presented in its entirety at a conference in Amsterdam in 1979 and is available in its entirety as it is referenced in the bibliography. This system of classification of play therapist activities will likely prove to be highly useful in observing for process and interaction between child and therapist.

TYPES OF DOCUMENTATION PROCEDURES

Many studies suggested that verbatim records were kept of the process in an effort to identify strategic areas and growth stages. These records were kept by observers through the use of tape recordings and video equipment.

Mende and Kauffman (1971) investigated the effects of video tape replays on the behavior of culturally different children. They used a video tape procedure of a physical education lesson, which was played back to the children immediately after the lesson. The subjects were three boys and one girl who were 4 and 5 years old and enrolled in a preschool program. The daily program consisted of three fifteen-minute instructional lessons and an eight-minute language lesson. Criterion measures used were teacher perceptions and frequency of inappropriate behavior. The Adapted Devereaux Child Behavior Rating Scale was completed for each subject by four teachers, and behaviors were counted. The results were significantly favorable toward appropriate behavior. A video tape replay may be used to change human behavior. When this technique of observation is used with young children, some consideration must be given to specific replay techniques that facilitate the attainment of the desired therapeutic goals.

Lovaas and colleagues (1965a) described an apparatus and procedure that have been developed to facilitate recordings in child observation studies. The apparatus consisted of a panel of twelve button switches connected to an Esterline-Angus pen recorder. An additional piece of apparatus was developed for training observers and for insuring interobserver agreement. Various behaviors of the child and the attending adult were defined. Each behavior corresponded with a designated button on the panel (or pen on the recorder). The apparatus kept a running account of both frequency and duration of each of these behaviors. The procedure can be used for analysis of interrelated behaviors of the child as well as for studying co-varying relationships between the child's behaviors and those of the attending adult.

The authors also described a series of studies performed on (1) reliability of the observations, (2) assessing the effect of experimentally controlled variables on various behaviors, (3) quantifications of behavior changes over time, (4) analyzing temporal relationships between various behaviors from the child, and (5) comparing the behaviors of normal and autistic children. Lovaas and colleagues suggested that by the use of the apparatus, they were able to record reliably the frequency and duration of several coinciding behaviors of children at the time of occurrence. Also included in the record was the context in which the behavior took place.

Lovaas and colleagues (1965b) described a procedure designed to overcome some of the limitations associated with traditional doll play. The apparatus centered on dolls, puppets, and motion pictures. These were designed to exemplify certain social stimulus functions such as affection and aggression.

Cline (1972) described his use of video tape as a documentation of behavioral change in children. He felt the tape offered an opportunity to re-observe every behavior of a child during the therapy session. He contended that after initial interest in the lights of the taping procedure, the clients eventually failed to pay it any attention. Haworth and Menolascino

(1967) reported the use of a standard play interview situation that was developed as an aid to the differential diagnosis of young nonverbal children. The individual sessions were recorded on video tape, which permitted immediate and repeated playback for data analysis. A six-pen multievent recorder was used to measure duration and frequency of a variety of behaviors. Checklists were developed that included negative and positive behaviors that might occur during each play sequence. An inventory of mannerisms was also used. Satisfactory interscorer and intrascorer reliabilities were obtained for each procedure.

The author used two methods in the playroom for noting progress. One is based on the medical model of SOAP (subjective findings, objective findings, assessment data, and planning) (see Appendix). The second method tracks progress, process, toy themes, and the content of the session (see Appendix).

THE USE OF PLAYROOM LABORATORIES

L'Abate (1968, 1969) described an automated playroom that was designed for the Child Development Laboratory at Georgia State College in Atlanta. It was designed for boys 7 to 12 years old, because most of the referrals received at the Child Development Laboratory were boys in that age range.

The monitored playroom laboratory consisted of a control booth and two connected playrooms, one with aggressive toys and games and the other with constructive toys and materials. The control booth contained dials that totaled the amount of time the child spent in each room and also the time spent with various toys and materials in each room. This material was automatically fed to a computer. The control booth was also an observation booth that was equipped with earphones and had one-way mirror panels. Microphones were mounted in the ceiling of the playroom. The design of the rooms was based on a slot machine model. As the child picked up a toy from each position, the timing began in the control booth and was fed to the computer. The child was taken on an exploration of the two rooms during the first session. By demonstrating, the therapist showed the child how each of the machines worked. Thereafter, the child was allowed to choose where he spent his time. This playroom is probably most useful in the area of research. Rogers (1969) and Golden (1969) made contributions in the area of play therapy using this laboratory, and other studies are in progress.

In a paper presented at the American Psychological Association in September, 1969, Golden presented the rationale for using the monitored playroom setting for research in play therapy. She stated that there are many unanswered questions about play therapy. Monitored play therapy is an attempt to discover answers to these questions. The main emphasis is on quantitative recordings and analysis of the process and outcome of play therapy. The strongest feature is the conceptual and physical separation of the stages of play into aggression and construction. The use of separate rooms for aggression and construction eliminates problems.

Because of its newness, however, monitored play therapy also has some weaknesses. Some of the weaknesses found in using this method were that the stimulus properties of the two rooms were always unequal, and that all of the activities did not take equal time for completion. Children differed in the amount of skill that they had for playing different games in the playrooms. There was also little opportunity for the child to manipulate the aggressive materials in his own way. The child could not destroy the objects nor create his own outlet for aggression.

Rogers (1969) described research that she did in the monitored playroom investigating the major stages that the children tended to go through in the process of development. She contended that through the use of the monitored laboratory and the consistent stages through which the children progressed, the therapist is able to ascertain and predict movement in the play therapy process.

A playroom designed for filming children while they play was suggested by Lee and Hutt (1964). This room was used in a hospital setting, and the children seen were often severely disordered and psychometrically untestable. The playroom was designed so that a close systematic observation could be made of such children with the use of hidden video cameras. The room was 24 feet by 12 feet, and was divided into partitions to create a waiting room and an observation playroom filming cubical. There were windows along one wall of the observation room. The floor of the playroom was covered with alternating black and grey squared linoleum. This made for easy recording of movement within the playroom. A camera tunnel was built so that the camera could view the entire playroom. The construction of this tunnel has proved to be an economical and convenient method of obtaining film records of children. It solved the problem of filming children without in any way distracting them or unduly modifying their behavior.

Landreth (1991) actively supervises and conducts research designed to measure both process and outcome. James (1975a,b) suggested that one of the major deficits of the body of knowledge in the field of play therapy was the dearth of research that had been conducted to support the development of theory and techniques described in the literature. At that time, James suggested that "on-line" research techniques were possible, viable, and should be utilized in play therapy study centers. The center that Landreth uses as a therapy/research center now contains these features.

Many of the universities that offer programs in play therapy now have fully equipped, monitored playrooms. Sessions are videotaped for future review and research. In many of the labs, multiple television screens are in one area, which allows supervisors to scan the work being done by a number of students simultaneously. *The Play Therapy Training Directory* is available for purchase through the Center for Play Therapy at the University of North Texas. It contains a list of training programs in the United States and Canada. The description of courses, workshops, program offerings, and facilities and equipment are noted in this book.

28

Evaluation Procedures

DOLL PLAY TECHNIQUE

Doll play has numerous variations, but essentially the child is presented with a set of dolls, generally a family, and a setting in which the dolls are to operate. The child is told to manipulate the dolls while he tells a story. The child has the opportunity to talk for the dolls as well as to act for them.

Doll play probably had its beginnings as a clinical procedure. It was used by Melanie Klein (1929) as a procedure for both the diagnosis and the treatment of disturbed children. Mann (1957) suggested that doll play offers a "third person" approach that allows the child to feel safer in dealing with intense material. In this technique, the child is not confronted directly with his problem, but is allowed to project his feelings onto the stage.

Levy (1939a) used a series of thirty-five case studies to describe the use of release therapy as a treatment/diagnostic method. The children described were aged 2 to 9. Levy suggested that this is a method whereby a frightening event could be restored in the child's play, and thereby the child could release the anxiety of which he had been unable to rid himself. Suggested criteria for the selection of children for this procedure are (1) the difficulty was precipitated by a specific event; (2) the problem was not too long in duration; and (3) the problem results from a past trauma, not a present pathology.

In another article, Levy (1939b) used the case study method in the description of his theory. He described the two forms of release therapy as general release therapy and specific release therapy. Specific release therapy relies on various forms of restoring the situation out of which the anxiety and its accompanying symptoms arose. An example of such a situation would be when a child has experienced a specific trauma, such as the birth of a new sibling, a divorce, or a death. Specific release therapy is designed to allow the child to release the anxiety and pain of this particular experience. Specific sets of toys are used for each situation. General release therapy is used typically when symptoms arise because of excessive demands or prohibitions made on the child at an early age. In this situation, the therapist typically would use the structured technique diagnostically. He would probably combine the structured technique with more nondirective techniques.

Levy (1933) described a standardized technique for assessing progress in play therapy. He based his diagnostic procedure on his structured technique of play therapy. In this article, he described shaping a situation wherein the child is able to express sibling rivalry in a standardized form. By using the same play material and the same stimulus words, the investigator is able to use play material both therapeutically and diagnostically. Levy indicated that this standardization does not interfere with the process of therapy.

Levy (1933) described an experiment that he conducted using this technique. It involved ten healthy children of average intelligence—six males and four females ranging in age from 5 to 13 years. Their problems included rebellious behavior (five cases), sibling rivalry (one case), and other difficulties such as feminine mannerisms, infantile behavior, stealing, and a mild assortment of behavior problems. All of the difficulties were within the nondelinquent category. In structuring the situation, the therapist said to the child, "We are going to play a game. We will need a mother, a baby, and an older (brother/sister). Mother must feed the baby, but she has no breast." The therapist then made a breast and instructed the child to make a breast and place it on the mother doll. The child was then instructed to put the baby in the nursing position. The therapist continued the game by saying, "When the sister comes and sees the baby at the mother's breast, she . . ." (p. 273).

Based on the use of this standardized way of assessing the level of the child's functioning, Levy (1933) identified definite patterns of reaction such as primitive patterns (hostility, possession, regression, and self-punishment).

Conn (1939) described the use of the structured play technique with a 6-year-old girl. He stressed using the natural tendency of children to play, which allows them to self-express during the experimental play situations. The play interview that Conn described is a regular part of the diagnostic work-up in each case treated. It is one of many procedures and is designed to supplement other methods. He felt that it contributes materials that deal with personal, emotional, and imaginative aspects of the child's behavior. The child's responses were accepted at face value. No attempt was made at interpretation, nor was transference encouraged.

Mann (1957), following the philosophical base and techniques developed by Solomon, Conn, and Levy, described his use of the structured doll play technique. He emphasized that this is a useful tool for "symptom" therapy because it allows the child to identify very quickly with his feelings in reference to a situation. This technique should be used with other, more dynamic, insightful methods in order to achieve the full effect. He further suggested that this method will tend to lose its effectiveness over a prolonged period of time if used to the exclusion of other techniques. He contended that it is appropriately used where situational factors abound, where the child's conflicts are externalized, and in situations where the parents are amenable to change.

Structured puppet play therapy in an elementary school setting was used by Vittner (1969). He suggested that this particular technique offers opportunity for the child to vent his feelings in grades kindergarten through six. This technique can be used effectively with children who have difficulty verbalizing their feelings.

Lynn and Lynn (1959) used doll play as a projective technique. They suggested that its usefulness as a clinical play projective technique has relevance for children between the ages of 3 and 11. In this procedure, dolls are used with a doll house, and a child is presented with a number of typical family and age-mate situations. The work usually lasts from thirty to forty-five minutes. The authors presented two research studies that they suggested lend validity to the use of this medium as a projective technique.

Kulla (1966) described a therapeutic doll play program with an emotionally disturbed child. The therapist used the method of storytelling where the experimenter's stories followed the theme of the child's and were also structured to broaden the possibilities for solutions and alternatives to the conflicts presented in the child's stories. Kulla conducted twenty-nine doll play sessions spread over a period of two years and nine months. He concluded that the child showed more appropriate aggressive responding and increased self-initiated and solution responding.

Doll play was used by Moore (1964) as a way of examining the chief divergences between play and reality in children. Moore, after observing the way children tend to oscillate between fantasy and realism, saw this as a way of regulating the amount of affect admitted to consciousness for assimilation by the ego in its thrust toward maturity. Three types of non-realistic play were distinguished. The child's way of relating play to reality was discussed. It was suggested that the concept of flight, whether to or from reality, is often inappropriate to zestful play. An alternative interpretation was offered in terms of an oscillatory mechanism for regulating the admission of an affect-laden fantasy to consciousness for assimilation by the ego in its thrust toward maturity. Both principles were shown to be useful in the interpretation of doll play in the individual child and for children generally.

Moore and Ucko (1961) reported that, by observing doll play, it is possible to gain insight into the feelings and fantasies that underlie behavior in areas of daily life that are producing difficulties or conflicts for the child or his parents. The authors developed the London Doll Play Technique, which is a structured technique providing an avenue for exploratory research into various aspects of the child's fantasy life. The technique involves presenting a doll family in a standard set of scenes and asking the child to indicate what will happen next. A group of 115 normal children were tested at 4 and again at 6 years of age. An investigation was carried out into the fantasies, feelings, and attitudes of boys and girls respectively, concerning certain situations of everyday life. Investigation also included assessing the ability of the child to solve in play simple problems in interpersonal relationships.

The authors found differences on such variables as ability to cope, intellectuality, emotionality, degree and kind of affect, freedom of expression, degree of socialization, constructiveness, and solutions among the different children tested. A comparatively high proportion of boys was unable to respond freely to these play situations. Many showed signs of emotional conflict (aggression, inhibition) that precluded constructive solutions.

Numerous researchers have investigated the variables to which the technique of structured doll play lends itself. Phillips (1945) investigated doll play as a function of the realism of the materials and the length of the experimental session. Pintler (1945) investigated the variables of experimenter–child interaction and the initial organization of materials on the outcome. Linder (1967) compared the effect of verbal conditioning of aggression using nursery school boys in a therapy-like situation. Sears (1947) investigated the influence of the method used as it affects the performance of the child.

In addition, Aderhold (1967) investigated the behavior of children in a doll play situation with reference to their age. Marshall and Hann (1965) examined the influence of experience as it affects the behavior of the child in the doll play situation. Robinson (1946) investigated the influence of the presentation of different types of family constellations to the child in the doll play experience. Baruch (1941) investigated the variable of aggression of children in doll play.

Levin and Wardwell (1962) suggested that because of the flexibility of the materials used in doll play and the endless situational scenes that can be staged, this technique is highly useful in the area of child study. It is influenced by a number of variables, such as the themes, the composition of the dolls, the nature of the setting, the amount and kinds of interaction with the researcher, and the directions and structure presented to the child. The chief variables investigated using this media are aggression, stereotype, and prejudice.

Sears (1947) and Sears (1951) made major contributions in this area by researching the variables related to the structured doll play technique. Some of the research in this area is briefly presented here. However, for a complete discussion of this research, the reader is referred to the excellent article by Levin and Wardwell (1962), "The Research Uses of Doll Play."

PLAY INTERVIEW TECHNIQUE

The case study of a very young child who was unable to talk was described. In relating the case, the author described how, through the observations in play, he was able to arrive at more accurate decisions and allow the therapeutic process to begin. During the process of the play, the child began to verbalize. By setting limits during the course of the therapy, the therapist helped the child begin to define reality. In this way, by using careful observation and by allowing the child to play, the therapist was able to conclude that the child was not retarded, and so he avoided making an error in diagnosis.

Personality reactions of normal children aged 2 to 5 years in a free play situation were reported by Despert (1940). A record of the verbal, motor, and affective behavior of each child was kept. The child expressed affective relations with his family in doll play and, to a lesser extent, in drawing play.

Howard (1944) investigated the use of the play interview with young children. He saw it as a technique of allowing disclosure of personal and social attitudes. The attitudes and interests of twenty-three kindergarten and twenty fourth-grade children were studied in a play interview technique. The average length of the interview was forty-one minutes. Materials used were mobile toys, house furnishings, human character figures, animals, and fish. Most of the children responded to the interview with fantasy, which was told in story or drama form. The attitudes and interests revealed by the children concerned war, illness, accidents, death, superstition, animals, and family relationships. The author concluded that the amount and the quality of fantasy material given spontaneously by the children of both age groups indicate that the play interview is an effective technique for uncovering attitudes and interests of young children.

Others writing about the use of the play interview or the free play technique as a diagnostic procedure included Harms (1948), who used the method as a pretherapy diagnostic procedure, Hayward (1949), who discussed the use that a social worker could make of the technique, and Rucker (1946), also a social worker, who described her work in this area.

Simpson (1938) stressed the diagnostic usefulness of the procedure, while Symonds (1940) used the procedure for assessing learning readiness. Weiss and Frankle (1938, 1941) and Conn (1948, 1952) used the procedure both diagnostically and remedially.

Baruch (1939, 1940) discussed a technique that can be used in child study. Forty children were each given fifteen minutes for free play with dolls. The observer was hidden. In the course of a very short span of time, much information in reference to the child's family, feelings, and self came out. Baruch stressed that this technique can be used in other settings for other purposes. Haworth and Menolascino (1967) reported a study concerned with the development of a play interview with a standard and a specified sequence of activities. This should be appropriate to the age level under consideration, and would have the potential of discriminating between diagnostic categories. It could be videotaped for immediate and repeated playback for analysis. Toys were selected for interest appeal to both sexes. A standard play interview situation was developed as an aid to the differential diagnosis of young nonverbal children. The individual sessions were recorded on video tape. A sixpen multievent recorder was used to measure duration and frequency of a variety of behaviors. An inventory of mannerisms was also used. Satisfactory interscorer and intrascorer reliabilities were obtained for each procedure. Results were reported on a sample of thirty-four cases who were 2 to 9 years old. Eight normal children and twenty-six clinical cases were used. Three patterns of play behavior emerging included: (1) a highly interactive group characterized by older normals, adjustment reactives, and familial retardates, (2) a group with variable inconsistent and immature reactions, which was seen in the younger normals, sensory handicapped, and multiply handicapped children, and (3) a group marked with stereotypy of behavior, inappropriate affect, and reactions of withdrawal and disengagement. This group included childhood schizophrenics, psychotic, and autistic children.

OTHER DIAGNOSTIC PROCEDURES
USING PLAY MATERIAL

A particular use of toys was made by a group of investigators who used the toys in a very structured way for diagnostic purposes. One such technique is the Little World Test. This term refers to that structured procedure using Little World Toys in a free play situation by a therapist. The procedure has a standard scoring for the outcome of the child's play.

Investigators differ in their use of this procedure, but it can generally be divided into three main groupings. Kamp and Kessler (1970), as a preface to the discussion of their use of this technique, gave an historical overview of the development of the technique. Lowenfeld's World Apparatus was discussed as the richest collection of materials and activities. They described this test as including play with sand and water, building with blocks and molding clay, in addition to arranging toys. They also overviewed the Scenes Test, which usually involves dolls and materials appropriate to the scene that the examiner is using. This scene might be outdoors, indoors, or any other setting. The use the child made of the doll in the scene was studied.

Another diagnostic procedure Kamp and Kessler (1970) discussed was the Worlds and Villages Test. These materials were used mainly to ascertain the child's depiction of the external world. Some use was made of spatial relations projectively in this technique. Kamp and Kessler reported that their use of this procedure was to evaluate the end product of the child's play. They assumed that the psychological state of the child during the test influences the final configuration to such a degree that it may be considered representative of a major part of the subject's activity. They suggested that this procedure is most useful for the children between the ages of 5 and 12. The procedure as they used it involved the use of 431 small toys or elements plus a table top. Most of the children, when given a free opportunity to manipulate the objects, built a world or construction.

The authors described a study in which they used the procedure, involving four groups of twenty children who were 6 to 9 years old. The toys were divided into ten categories, which were presented to the child on different trays. The categories included soldiers, people, animals, buildings, trees, fences, blocks, vehicles, and indoor and outdoor equipment. The authors hypothesized that the configurations of the end product of play made by different children vary according to the developmental level of mental functioning at the time of the testing. Four categories of configurations were distinguished: juxtapositional, schematic, depletive, and realistic. The investigators described the developmental scale of the four stages used to score the end products and to report the influence of chronological and mental age on the developmental level of the end product of the World Test. In addition, a number of other factors were explored that influence the child's performance.

Leton (1966) discussed a study involving the use of a standardized School Play Kit. Previous studies showed the kit to be a useful tool in identifying the need for autonomy and the need for structure among first-grade children. The judgment as to whether these emotional needs were frustrated or satisfied in their classroom situations was also made on the basis of the school play responses. The School Play Kit is a set of toy materials designed to represent the average classroom. It includes teacher and pupil dolls, desks, tables, chairs, blackboards, bulletin boards, books, pencils, and other representative materials. The pupils' behavioral reactions and verbalizations during structured play situations were recorded on a diagnostic record form.

Bender (1937) and Woltmann (1943) indicated that plasticine clay is a useful tool in the diagnostic area. The examiner sits with the child and tells him to use the clay to make anything he wishes to. The examiner carefully observes the process that the child goes through in the construction. He is not as concerned with the finished product as he is with the way the child forms the product.

Homburger and Erikson (1937) suggested that, through the use of toys, the child is allowed to experience space that has psychological implications for him. Through spatial configurations, the child weaves fantasies around real objects. The author used the configuration of toys and the spatial arrangements produced by the child as indications of the child's feelings in reference to the situations. For example, in the rooms, the grouping, the height of the walls, the openness of the house, the absence or presence of windows, and the location of the windows and doors are significant. These configurations were called the hieroglyphs of play, and all have definite meanings.

The use of drawings was described by Despert (1937a). She suggested that, by saving the drawings of a child over a period of time, it is possible to analyze them for stages of development in the child. Cashdon (1967) used drawings mainly diagnostically. He described five stages in the therapeutic process that can be diagnosed through the drawings of the child. They consist of presentation of the problem, defining the relationship, evidence of emotional learning, separation, and adaptation.

Nickols (1961b) described using regulated throwing of darts, suction-cupped projectiles, and pistols with appropriate stimulus as a projective technique. He felt that by providing the appropriate background stimulus, the child would use the materials to express his feelings in relation to peers, siblings, and parents.

Gerard (1948) used observation of both child and parent in a non-structured play setting for diagnostic purposes. She suggested that the etiology of the child's disturbance is closely connected with that of the mother's and that she must be observed during her interaction with the child.

Jepsen (1992) developed a play diagnostic instrument for the assessment of children with developmental delays. The author states that this a viable alternative for assessing a wide range of "untestable" children who, due to emotional disturbance and/or mental retardation, are unable to respond to a standard psychometric evaluation. The play diagnostic assessment scale and a preliminary manual and reporting forms with guidelines for use are printed in their entirety in the referenced body of work.

V

Case Material

29

Case Presentations

When I sit in my playroom, it is easy to remember the toy themes that have been played and replayed until issues were resolved. There have been buckets of spilled paint, pounds of sand on the floor, dozens of broken toys, bunches of bop bags, hundreds of painted pictures that were completed, photographed, and then discarded. There have been sad stories, scary stories, and happy stories. There have been beginnings and endings. I have lived much of my career within four walls that house toys, paints, sand, clay, dolls, and other fascinating objects. In this room, I never have had to give up my joy in acquiring a new toy. If I didn't have all of the dolls I wanted as a child, I do now. On my 48th birthday, my husband gave me a new doll house for my playroom. The excitement I felt was probably a bit developmentally out of character for a person my age, but I have never worried about societal norms and expectations. I have my playroom. I am the woman who gets to a reception late with tempera paint on my dress.

In this room, I remember the first picture painted by a child patient, Chris. Chris was brought to therapy because he was having temper tantrums in every setting in his life. He kicked holes in the wall by his bed and, even worse, he kicked his parents and teachers. During his first session, he painted a picture of the earth with a big black boot kicking it. The next drawing depicted his inadequate attempts to gain control of his behavior. He drew an entire page full of black squares. As I observed this picture I experienced the emotional hopelessness and entrapment this child was feeling. His kicking must have been an attempt to get out of those boxes of emotional pain. Later, this child could not accept that other children came to the playroom, and he sat under a small table for six sessions without talking or playing.

Amy came to the playroom with despair and left with self-confidence. When she came to therapy, she was having trouble with reading, and she thought that she was ugly. On one of her final visits, she appeared dressed in a rabbit fur coat. "Why, Amy," I said, "you seem really excited today." Amy replied, "I am the only girl in the second grade who has a fur coat."

Bill refused to respond to the limit of time. After a number of confrontations about this issue, Bill and I had a peaceful session. He responded to the time limit, told me goodbye, and walked out into the hall. After a few minutes, the janitor came to get me. The other persons in the building were in an uproar. Bill had apparently taken a whole handful of red finger paint out of the playroom and had smeared it all over the wall of the hall as he left the building.

Julie, who was 8, had been in play therapy for twenty sessions when her toy play told me that we were nearing termination. She lined up a number of toy horses and gave each one a tiny silver plate with tiny drinking glasses. In the center of the circle of horses, she put a feast of playdoh food. "Why, Julie," I said, "what is happening here?" Julie said calmly, "We've all been lost in the woods and we have found our way out. Now we are going to have a big banquet."

Carolyn was 4 years old and lived with her parents and a grandfather who was very ill. The family had not told Carolyn the extent of her grandfather's illness. However, in the playroom she said to me, "Dessie, something's going on in my house that's really scary, and I don't know what it is."

One 6-year-old girl was brought to me for therapy because her mother was dying. She had been unable to bond with anyone during her mother's long illness. During the first session, she drew a two-story house with no details. However, at the bottom of the house, she drew a tiny door. Off to the side of the picture she put a tiny dot, which she named a key. I thought to myself that even though this house has thick walls and only a small entry, this child is telling me that there is a key and she showed me where it was. During the next session she drew the same house again. This time, she drew an attic and said that this is where she keeps her Christmas decorations. During the next few weeks she painted the house over and over, each time with more details. One week she said, "In this house live a little girl and her grandmother." Toward the end of the session that day, she turned to me and said, "I have figured it out. You are sort of like a grandmother." I knew at that moment that I was in the house.

One 4-year-old child was brought to therapy because her parents stated that "she lies." This signaled a problem with attunement on the part of the parents, but I began therapy with the child without engaging the parents initially. This child painted houses destroyed by storms, trees that had been torn down, trees that had been burned, and cars that had crashed. Later, she took the same type of play to the sand pile. When I started to have parent interviews, the parents disclosed that they were in the process of a divorce and were going through decision making about division of property. They had not disclosed this to the child. This child was telling me through her play that her life was being destroyed.

Some sessions have clearly described certain issues that surface during the course of play therapy. The following describes an initial session with a child in which limits were tested from the very moment the child came to the therapy room.

One 6-year-old female child was brought to therapy because of aggression toward her parents, regression in school, and oppositional behavior at home and school. The parents of this child had recently gone through a divorce. The father had remarried and was building a new home with another woman. The children were living with their mother, who was depressed and overwhelmed with the pain in the family.

This child presented with a combination of aggression toward and clinging to her mother. She talked baby talk, tried to sit in her mother's lap, and was reluctant to enter the play therapy room. After coaching, she did enter into the play therapy room, and we began our first session. The patient indicated that she did not want to be here and would like to hurt me.

> *Therapist:* I sense that you are upset about being here, but this is our time together. You can spend your time in the toy room however you wish to, but you may not hurt me.
>
> *Child:* [Looked at therapist with her head turned to one side, then picked up the horses and a large dinosaur, placed them on one side of the play area, lined up all the sheep in the playroom, and used the horses and dinosaur to demolish the sheep. They kicked them, stomped them, tore at them, and did many vicious things to the sheep.]

Therapist: The large animals are angry, and they are hurting the sheep.

Child: [Got the large trucks out of the sandpile and, without words, systematically ran over all the sheep and then all the dinosaurs. Child then named the therapist as one of the sheep, took two large animals, and set a trap for the therapist.] Mrs. Sheep, I want you to come to the sandpile to play.

Therapist: I know you would like for me to come to the sandpile, but this is your time in the playroom.

Child: Then I will make you come to the sandpile on my own. [Child took the sheep and walked the sheep to the sandpile, where the large animals angrily bit and tore at the sheep.]

Therapist: [Did not comment on this action.]

Child: [Child picked up the wolf] If you will close your eyes, the wolf will be really nice to you.

Therapist: The wolf wants me to close my eyes.

Child: Yes, the wolf wants you to close your eyes, and he will be very nice to you.

Therapist: I know the wolf would like for me to close my eyes, but I cannot. This is *your* time to be in the toy room. [Therapist had the option of moving into more interpretation but elected to not interpret the child's anger toward the therapist and to simply allow the animals to work through the issues themselves.]

Child: I'm the boss of the playroom, and you have to close your eyes.

Therapist: This is your time in the playroom, and when you're here you're the boss of the toys. But you cannot be the boss of me. I know you would like to be the boss of me.

Child: You have to close your eyes.

Therapist: I know the wolf would like for me to close my eyes, but I will not. You can use the sheep, you can use the horses, you can use the other animals, but I will not close my eyes.

Child: [Took the wolf and aggressively began to physically attack therapist with the small plastic wolf.]

Therapist: [Set the limit again] I know the wolf would like to hurt me, but he is not allowed to hurt me.

Child: The wolf is going to bite you and scratch you.

Therapist: I know the wolf would like to bite me and scratch me. He can bite the sheep, he can bite the horses and scratch the horses, but he cannot bite and scratch me.

Child: He will bite and scratch you.

Therapist: We must put the wolf up on the shelf today.

At this point, the therapist took the wolf and put the wolf up on the shelf. The child proceeded to kick and scream in the playroom, but the wolf remained on the shelf.

One child used the sandpile almost exclusively to describe her inner life. A 7-year-old child presented with enuresis and depression. She was brought to therapy by her mother. The child spent alternate weekends with her biological parents, who were divorced. Her biological father was re-married and in a traditional marriage. On weekends, their life centered on going to church on Saturdays and Sundays, all day. They were in a nonde-nominational church that a small community of people had started. The mother was a nontraditional type of woman who worked all week, and typically stayed at home with the kids on the weekend and played with them.

This little girl played out a recurring toy theme over many sessions in which she built a wall in the middle of the sandpile. On each side of the wall, she put people, animals, cars, and a city. In the beginning session, the people on each side of the wall maintained their own lives. They went about town, they talked to each other, the animals produced milk and ate hay, the people went to school, to work, and to church.

Later in the therapy, the people on each side of the wall began to pre-pare for some sort of ominous occurrence. The child would say, "They're getting ready for something bad." At times the child would say, "We don't know what's going to happen next," but the material that the toys were acting out was that they were getting ready for a catastrophic occurrence.

In later sessions, airplanes from one side of the wall or the other side of the wall would fly over and spy on each other. Finally, as the sessions progressed, one side actually built big underground cavities in the sandpile, and the child enacted putting materials and supplies into the big "cellar." The child described elaborately how the people were going to go into the cellar to protect themselves when the other side came over with the air-planes and tried to destroy them.

My interpretation of all of this play scenario was that the sand play represented the psychological splitting within the child, in which she was trying to incorporate her mother's value system on one side and her father's value system on the other side. However, the implications for the safety of the child were deeper than this, because when I started to explore with the father in private sessions, it was determined that his religious group was moving closer to becoming a religious sect.

The mother was unaware that the child was carrying the burden of fear that she was introjecting from exposure to the religious group of which her father was a part. At that point, I recommended that both parents go into individual psychotherapy. The father agreed and started to work on his own issues. Many months later, the father and his new wife elected to build their religious life in another church environment that was less radical.

In retrospect, I believe that this child's toy play described her own psychological splitting, which she was having to undergo on a weekly basis. Finally, her toy play reflected prophetic types of material in which she sensed that tragedy was going to occur. There was also the probability that she understood at a conscious or unconscious level that the church group her father was involved with was preparing for a radical step in which they left society and went into hiding. In any event, the child's toy play possibly saved the child and her family members.

Children's lives are often controlled by the fear that their magical thinking has started. One such child was reluctant to talk about the pain that had gotten her to therapy. It was a situation in which her sister had developed a neuroblastoma with sudden onset symptoms of leg-aches. The baby sister, who was 5 years old, had been hospitalized and diagnosed with a neuroblastoma. After a few months of excruciating illness, she died.

After her death, my child patient was brought to me for therapy to work through her emotions surrounding the loss. We had many sessions together, but she never focused on the issue of death or on the issue of the loss of her sister. Her toy play typically involved denial and very strong boundaries, in which the central issues to her problems were not dealt with.

One day, at the end of the session, she said to me, "Dessie, next week I have something to tell you." I told her if that was what she wanted to do, that was up to her. The next session came, and she played almost through the whole session. Then she asked to leave the playroom and ran to the toilet where she vomited and was very sick in her stomach.

When she came back into the playroom, she crawled up in my lap and sat down and said, "Dessie, I have to tell you something. I have to tell you a secret. It was after church one morning, and Mary [her sister] and I and another kid were out on the churchyard. We had been studying about the devil in Sunday school, and my sister said, 'I'm going to fix him [the devil].' She jumped up and down on the churchyard and stomped and said, 'I hate you, Devil, I hate you, Devil.'" By that afternoon, her sister had developed pain in her leg and, by the next day, had gone to see the doctor.

Realistically, we all would assume that the child was not being punished by God or the Devil but, because of the circumstances, my patient was convinced that when she and her sister stomped on the ground, it had brought forth the forces of evil and had caused the illness in her sister. She sat in my lap and sobbed and sobbed and eventually got down and began to start to play again.

Over the course of a number of sessions, she was able to work through her own feelings of guilt and realize that the original fears were, in fact, magical thinking and were not realistic.

Another example of a session in which the child's fears were developed and maintained by his imagery was the child patient who came racing into the playroom for his session after school one day. In pain and suffering, after crying, he was able to ask:

Child: Have you heard about any train wrecks today?
Dessie: No.
Child: You've been listening to the radio all day long?
Dessie: Yes.
Child: And you've heard of no train wrecks?
Dessie: No.
Child: Oh, thank God! Yesterday, I went down and put a penny on the railroad track, and when I got to school today, someone told me that causes train wrecks. I been scared all day, sitting in the classroom. I was afraid I had caused a train wreck.

Every afternoon when I leave the playroom, I look at the toys and the room. I remember the voices, the toy themes, and the emotions that have happened here. I carefully close the door and say, "It's been a fine day in the playroom." With that, I also remember my first supervisor in play therapy, Dr. Harold T. Perry. Thank you, Dr. Perry.

Appendix

JAMES'S NURTURING ASSESSMENT SCALE
(Copyright Spring 1977)

TOUCHING BEHAVIORS	Frequently observed	Infreq. observed	Never observed
1. Gently touches abdomen and back (strokes and pats)			
2. Kisses baby on stomach, arms, feet (while dressing, sitting, etc.)			
3. Kisses baby on face (eyes, forehead, cheeks)			
4. Gently fondles hands, arms, feet, legs			
5. Gently preens baby (e.g., wipes mouth, around eyes, touches with finger around ear, hair, etc.)			
6. During free-time play, touches in a stimulating manner (e.g., pats baby's hands together, touches baby's hand to mother's face, blows on baby's arm or leg, nuzzles baby on arm or stomach)			

RESPONSE TO CRYING

	Frequently observed	Infreq. observed	Never observed
7. Comforts baby when he cries, without jabbing in pacifier to quiet the child in desperation (rocks, talks, strokes, etc.)			

(continued)

RESPONSE TO CRYING (*continued*)	*Frequently observed*	*Infreq. observed*	*Never observed*
8. Mother makes soothing motions with baby when he cries (e.g., sways back and forth, patting, rocking)			
9. Mother is effective in stopping baby from crying (i.e., tries different techniques until baby stops)			
10. Speaks to child in reassurance when he is crying (talks with baby softly, coos, hums, makes eye contact)			
11. Mother relaxes when baby stops crying (e.g., body relaxes, she smiles, etc.)			
12. Responds to baby's cries with assurance or confidence that needs will be met (doesn't bounce or jostle to keep baby quiet)			
13. Facial expression shows concern when baby cries (e.g., frowns, worried look, body tenses, sits up in chair)			

VOLUNTARY NURTURING BEHAVIORS

14. Engages in gentle talking to baby (coos, gurgles, sings, hums)			

(*continued*)

VOLUNTARY NURTURING BEHAVIORS (*continued*)	*Frequently* observed	*Infreq.* observed	*Never* observed
15. Mother maintains visual contact with infant when he is awake (watches his face)			
16. Mother holds her face close to baby's and talks to him			
17. Lays child on pad as opposed to dropping him (i.e., 3 or more inches)			
18. Smiles at baby while talking to him during activities such as feeding or changing diapers (face close to infant)			
19. Mother totally focuses attention on child and disregards the rest of the environment (e.g., touches hands, feet, talks during feeding and diaper changes)			

FEEDING BEHAVIORS

20. Watches child during feeding			
21. Strokes back for burping (i.e., does not slap on back or bounce)			
22. Holds bottle so that nipple is completely full, not half-full. Bottle is held at an angle, not straight			

(*continued*)

FEEDING BEHAVIORS (*continued*)	*Frequently observed*	*Infreq. observed*	*Never observed*
23. Holds baby over shoulder while burping (does not bounce on lap)			
24. Holds bottle during feeding so baby's mouth is close to her breast			
25. Bottle/breastfeeds, holding baby so his trunk is against her body (holds legs up in cuddle position. Places hand under bottom and legs)			
26. Bottle/breastfeeds, sitting quietly and holding baby firmly			
27. Allows bottle to stay in mouth for satisfying periods (i.e., doesn't constantly check on number of oz. taken, etc.)			

HOLDING AND PROTECTING BEHAVIORS

28. Protects baby properly (i.e., blanket over head in cold weather)			
29. When dressing baby, firmly supports baby's back and neck with arm, grasps baby's arm firmly (doesn't let head and neck flop)			
30. Mother is comfortable in hovering position			

(*continued*)

HOLDING AND PROTECTING BEHAVIORS (*continued*)	*Frequently observed*	*Infreq. observed*	*Never observed*
31. Protects baby's head and face when other children are near			
32. Holds hand so that it protects baby's eyes from the sun			

BEHAVIORS WHILE THE DOCTOR IS PRESENT

33. Stays near while baby is on bed before doctor comes in			
34. Looks and talks softly to baby as child is weighed and measured			
35. Reacts to the doctor and the child (facing them—pays attention to them)			
36. Talks softly to baby as the doctor works with child			
37. Watches quietly as doctor examines baby			
38. Stays near baby during doctor's examination to assist and soothe			

STATEMENT OF INFORMATION AND DISCLOSURE

Thank you for choosing me as a psychologist to work with your child and your family. Please take a few minutes to read the following paragraphs. I request that you sign to signify your understanding and agreement to the terms outlined. You will sign a copy and leave it here. I will provide you with a copy for your records.

AFTER HOURS CONTACT

This office is open daily from 9:00 A.M. to 5:00 P.M. Monday through Thursday except for holiday and vacation schedules. Alternate hours are sometimes arranged by appointment. In the event that you feel you have a crisis with your child that is an emergency, you may call my office number, which is _____.
This number is answered 24 hours via an answering service. At that time I will be contacted and I will return your call. In the event that I am on vacation, a professional colleague will be contacted who will be able to assist you.

CLIENT/THERAPIST RELATIONSHIP

I believe that each of us has the ability to resolve many of our own problems. However, in order to solve very complex and sometimes personally overwhelming problems, consultation is necessary. The amount of time required for desired change is different for everyone. It is not possible to guarantee results regarding your personal goals, but I will do my best to provide effective service in a professional and ethical manner.

Our relationship will be a professional one, limited to the paid sessions you have with me. Both professional ethics and Texas law govern the scope of our relationship, and both specifically prohibit a "dual relationship." Therefore, I do not enter into such relationships.

CONFIDENTIALITY

Our relationship will be private and confidential. My responsibility is to protect the confidential information that you share with me and to uphold the honoring of that information. This issue becomes somewhat more complicated in the treatment of children and/or families. These issues have to be discussed at length in session for clarification. However, I hold as confidential anything you tell me with the following exceptions:

1. In writing, you direct me to divulge information for professional purposes;
2. I determine that you are behaving in ways that are dangerous to yourself or someone else;
3. I am ordered by a court of law to disclose information.

MISSED APPOINTMENTS

I will reserve the time you request for your appointment. In the event that you need to cancel, please do so at your earliest convenience. If nonemergency cancellations occur, we will have to discuss whether it is therapeutically helpful for your child to continue in therapy with me. If we are unable to resolve the issue of missed appointments, then I will be forced to refer you and your child to another professional.

FEES

$100.00 per hour for psychotherapy, consultations, psychological evaluation, or any other professional duty.
$100.00 per hour for any court appearance—portal to portal.
$100.00 per hour for every attorney in the room during depositions.
Court appearances and consultations with schools or attorneys are not billable to insurance companies.

I expect full payment for services. Financial responsibility is yours. If your account becomes 90 days overdue, I reserve the right to declare it delinquent and relinquish it to _____ (collection services). You then will be responsible for any court fees, legal fees, and collection charges.

CLIENT RIGHTS

In the welfare and protection of the public, the practice of psychology is overseen by the Texas Board of Examiners of Psychologists (telephone _____).

When you enter a professional relationship with a psychologist, you are entitled to receive information about methods, techniques, and probable duration of treatment. You are free to seek a second opinion or to terminate at any time. If you feel that your client rights are violated, you have the right to contact the State Board at the above telephone number. The address is posted on the wall next to my credentials.

Thank you for taking time to read the information. Please sign and date in the space below.

I have reviewed the above and I sign below to indicate my agreement to the terms of this professional relationship.

_____ Date _____
          Patient or Parent   Relationship to Client _____

Read and agreed to by_____ Date _____

DECLARATION OF CUSTODY

PERMISSION TO TREAT A MINOR CHILD

In the event that the child does not live with both natural parents, it is critical that the issue of custody is established in advance of our beginning a professional relationship.

I do not see minor children who are not accompanied by the custodial parent, unless prior arrangements are made by the court, or by mutual consent of both custodial parents in writing.

If you are the biological and/or the adoptive parents of this minor child, please so indicate below:

I _____ and I _____
are the biological/adoptive parents of _____,
whose DOB is _____.

PERMISSION TO TREAT

We give you permission to treat our minor child.
_____, _____
Date _____.

If you are divorced, please describe your legal relationship with the minor child:
_____

I will need a copy of the court ordered custodial agreement for my files before treatment.

PERMISSION TO TREAT

I, we, give you permission to treat our minor child _____.
Date _____.

INSURANCE COMPANIES

If you choose to use a third-party payer, such as an insurance company, to pay in part for this treatment, please remember that you will be forfeiting rights of confidentiality. Depending upon the policies of your insurance company, loss of your rights of confidentiality and those of your child could occur in several ways. Even to submit a claim form, I will be required by the insurance company to list the diagnosis, the dates of treatment, the dates of service, and how much you have co-payed in advance.

In most cases with insurance companies, I receive regular forms to be completed about progress and prognosis. If you are a member of a PPO or HMO plan with which I am a listed provider, I will be able to discuss with you the types of forms I will be asked to complete. However, I do not know about the requirements of all insurance companies, and it is impossible for me to cover any potential areas of violation with you. I strongly advise you to discuss these issues with your insurance company in advance of treatment.

If you choose to involve an insurance company for the partial or complete payment of your therapy, then you will need to note your consent to allow this insurance company to have access to the above information. Please note that in the event I am contacted by an insurance company about the above issues, I will inform you about the nature of the information given.

I have read the above information about using insurance in partial or total payment for services here. I have been informed about the loss of privacy this will cause.

_____ Date _____
Signature of parent or guardian

Patient's or Authorized Person's Signature: I authorize the release of any medical or other information necessary to process this claim. I also request payment of government benefits either to myself or to the party who accepts assignment below.

_____ Date _____
Signature of parent or guardian

Your relationship with your insurance company is your own. By prearrangement I will accept assignment on an insurance program. However, you will be expected to meet your deductible and also your co-payment at the time of service.

AUTHORIZATION FOR
RELEASE OF INFORMATION

I do hereby authorize O'Dessie Oliver James, Ed.D., psychologist, to consult with and to release all records, reports, and other information from her files to:

_____

_____

_____

_____

in the case of _____, whose date of birth is

_____.

FOR THE PURPOSE OF:

Printed Name_____ Signature _____

Date_____ Witness_____

If your child is the client, please describe your legal relationship (e.g., parent, legal guardian):

_____

If child is 15 years or older, please have child countersign:

Printed Name_____ Signature _____

This release is in effect until_____.

Vernon L. James, M.D.   O'Dessie Oliver James, Ed.D.
Developmental Pediatrics   Psychology, #21732
Santa Rosa Children's Hospital   1250 N.E. Loop 410, Suite 231

HISTORY

(Please fill out as completely as possible)

Date _____   Person Completing Form _____
                            Relationship to Patient _____

IDENTIFYING INFORMATION

Signature _____

Name of Child _____

Address _____
                    Street   City   State   Zip Code

Phone Number _____   Present Age _____

Date of Birth _____   Address _____

Referred by _____

School Grade (present) _____   School District _____

School Now Attending _____   Address _____

Father's Name _____   Birth date _____

Occupation _____   Education _____

Mother's Name _____   Birth date _____

Mother's Occupation _____   Education _____

Legal Relationship of Parents to Patient (please check)

    Natural Parent: Mother _____   Father _____

    Adoptive Parent: Mother _____   Father _____

    Step-Parent: Mother _____   Father _____

    Foster Parent: Mother _____   Father _____

Relative: _____

Child's Doctor _____

Address _____
                    Street   City   State   Zip Code

Phone _____

Persons living in the home

Name	Age	Relation To Patient	Present School Grade or Highest Grade Completed
_____	____	_____	_____
_____	____	_____	_____
_____	____	_____	_____
_____	____	_____	_____
_____	____	_____	_____

List all major concerns about your child

DEVELOPMENTAL HISTORY

Mother's Pregnancy

Medical care was given by Dr. _____

Address _____

            Street   City   State   Zip Code

Medical care was begun in _____ month of pregnancy.

Check any of the following mother had during pregnancy and indicate at what time during the pregnancy they occurred:

Excessive nausea and vomiting	_____	_____
RH incompatibility	_____	_____
Toxemia	_____	_____
Severe headaches	_____	_____
Bleeding	_____	_____
False labor	_____	_____
German measles	_____	_____
Chicken pox	_____	_____
Virus infection	_____	_____
Other illnesses	_____	_____
Serious accident	_____	_____
Drugs or medications	_____	_____
What kind and amount	_____	_____
X-rays	_____	_____
Special diet	_____	_____
Unusual physical strain	_____	_____
Unusual emotional strain	_____	_____

Did you smoke during this pregnancy? If yes, how many packs per day? _____

Did you drink alcoholic beverages during pregnancy? _____

How much per week? _____

Hospital where baby was born _____

Address _____
           Street   City   State   Zip Code

How long was labor? _____ Type of anesthesia used _____

Birth was: Normal _____ Caesarian _____ Breach _____ Twins or more _____

Were forceps used? _____ What was mother's condition? _____

Newborn

Birth weight _____ Length at birth _____ What was baby's condition at birth?

_____

Did baby need medical assistance in starting to breathe? _____

If so, how long before normal breathing was established? _____

What means were used? _____

Was baby in incubator? _____ If so, how long? _____

Did baby receive oxygen? _____ If so, how long? _____

Check any of the following baby had in the first month of life:

Cyanosis (turned blue) _____ Deformity _____

Jaundice _____ Feeding difficulty_____

Injury _____ Swallowing or sucking difficulty _____

Convulsions _____ Excessive crying _____

Hemorrhage _____ Infection _____

Skin eruption _____

Feeding: Breast _____ How long? _____

           Formula _____ Kinds _____

  At what age was baby weaned? _____

  Was baby's weight gain unusual in any respect? _____

  How? _____

General impression of baby's development: Slow _____ Normal _____

Advanced _____

Baby's Activity Level:

Could be either active or relaxed _____ Overactive _____ Listless _____

Other (specify) _____ _____

Give approximate age at which baby first did the following:

Smiled _____ Followec objects with eyes _____

Held head up _____   Noticed noises _____

Rolled over _____   Cut tooth _____

Sat without support _____   Crawled _____

Stood alone _____   Walked alone _____

Fed self with spoon _____

Completed toilet training _____   Bowel: _____

Bladder: Day _____   Night: _____

Age of first word _____   Months: _____

List the first words:

   1. _____

   2. _____

   3. _____

   4. _____

Age at which two or three word sentences were used _____

Example:

   1. _____

   2. _____ _____ _____

   3. _____

   4. _____

Check those statements which are most typical to your child's speech development:

   Understands simple commands _____

   Understands everything said to him _____

   Speech is limited to single words and/or simple phrases _____

   Speech is mainly short sentences _____

   Converses without apparent handicap _____

   What is the average number of words in the sentences that your child uses? ___

Past illnesses (Check those the patient has had and indicate at what age. Mention any complications or exceedingly high temperatures.)

	AGE	COMPLICATIONS/TREATMENTS
___ measles (red)	___	_____
___ German measles	___	_____
___ scarlet fever	___	_____
___ chicken pox	___	_____
___ diphtheria	___	_____
___ mumps	___	_____
___ polio	___	_____
___ encephalitis	___	_____
___ tonsillitis	___	_____
___ ear infection	___	_____
___ other infection	___	_____
___ fractures	___	_____

Accidents or injuries of serious nature _____

Does your child take any medication on a regular schedule? _____

If so, what and how much _____

Has the child taken medication in the past on a regular schedule for seizures, hyper-activity, sleep problems, nervousness, etc.? _____

If so: When _____ How long _____

What kind (name) _____

Doctor's name: _____

Address: _____

    Street   City   State   Zip Code

Hospitalization:

	Address:		
Hospital:	*(City and State)*	*Year*	*Reason*
1.			
2.			
3.			
4.			

Review of Systems—Check any of the following that pertain to child and indicate at what age they occurred:

Age	*Age*
Falls frequently _____	Allergies _____
Eye or visual problems _____	Frequent colds _____
Ear or hearing problems _____	Mouth breathing _____
Bleeds or bruises easily _____	Cough_____
Asthma_____	Poor appetite_____
Abdominal pain _____	Skin rashes _____
Vomits frequently_____	Convulsions or spells _____
Constipation frequent_____	Diarrhea frequent _____
Urine dark or blood-tinged_____	Strain on urination _____
Right-handed _____	Left-handed _____
Prefers neither hand_____	Speech problems_____
Pain or weakness of muscles_____	

Explain any medical treatment given for the above

EMOTIONAL DEVELOPMENT

Check all the following as they apply to your child:

	Yes	No	Sometimes
Difficult to discipline	___	___	___
Gets upset easily	___	___	___
Has temper tantrums	___	___	___
Bites nails	___	___	___
Hurts other children	___	___	___
Hurts animals	___	___	___
Sets fires	___	___	___
Unusual tics or mannerisms	___	___	___
Has unreasonable fears	___	___	___
Has difficulty sleeping	___	___	___
Has nightmares	___	___	___
Sucks thumb	___	___	___

(continued)

	Yes	No	Sometimes
Wets bed	——	——	——
Is destructive	——	——	——
Prefers to be alone	——	——	——
Lives in a world of his own	——	——	——
Unusually active	——	——	——

Other (specify) _____

_____

During the child's early life was there anything that placed the mother or father under strain? (explain)

How old was the child when toilet training started?_____
What methods were used? _____
Who generally disciplines the child? _____
How does the child get along with members of the family? _____
Mother _____ Father _____
Sisters and brothers _____ Others _____
How does the child get along with people outside the family? _____
Does the child have a problem? _____
Is there any person outside of immediate family who has been particularly helpful concerning the child? _____
What age and kind of playmates does he/she prefer? _____

_____

Does he/she pick on other children? _____ or let others pick on him/her? _____

_____

Has either parent been away or out of the home frequently for any long period of time? _____
If so, please describe circumstances _____

_____

Was the child subject to any illnesses or uncomfortable conditions that made him/her irritable or unhappy?_____
How was child cared for in absence of parents? _____
Did child object to being left in care of others? _____
What is child particularly good at doing? _____

_____

How does child like to occupy his/her time? _____

_____

SCHOOL HISTORY

Please list schools child has attended. (Include nursery and preschool)

School	Address (Include city/state)	Age	Grade (indicate if used special education services)

School subjects with which child is having difficulty _____

What steps have been taken to help child with difficulties? _____

Please give the names of any persons who have been especially helpful or harmful to child's school adjustment _____

Has child/family had contact with the school psychologist?_____
If so, what was the nature of the contact?_____

Has child attended a special education program? _____

Has child been absent from school a lot? _____ If so, what have been the reasons for absences? _____

Sources of help used to date (other physicians, clinics, hospitals, guidance centers, social agencies, speech evaluation or therapy, etc.)

Name	Complete Address

FAMILY HISTORY

	Age	State of Health	Age at Death	Cause of Death
Patient's mother				
Patient's father				
Patient's brothers				
Patient's sisters				
Mother's mother				
Mother's father				
Father's mother				
Father's father				

Are parents blood relatives? _____

What is the national background of parents? (Swedish, Greek, etc.) _____
_____

Specify which members of the family (brothers, sisters, parents, grandparents, uncles, aunts, cousins) have had any of the following:

Allergies _____

Birth defects (specify) _____

Cancer _____

Cardiac _____

Convulsions (seizures or epilepsy) _____

Diabetes _____

Hearing loss or visual problems _____

Lead poisoning (or other poisoning) _____

Mental illness _____

Mental retardation _____

Reading Problems _____

Writing Problems _____

Math Problems _____

ADHD _____

ADD _____

Other _____

Parental comments

Parents' estimate of child's problem:

Parents' estimate of child's developmental level:

Person completing application _____

Relation to patient _____ Date _____

Parent/Guardian Signature_____

HISTORICAL TIMELINE

(an example)

1990, September	Birth, Newborn Intensive Care Unit, 15 days
1990, October	Released to go home to biological parents
1993, August	Entered preschool program
1993, December	Child referred to university for hearing evaluation by pediatrician
1994, January	No evidence of hearing loss reported by university audiologist
1994, February	Referred for Early Childhood Stimulation Program
1994, June	Female sibling born
1994, December	Seen by psychologist for cognitive evaluation, given Stanford-Binet Form M, average IQ documented, depressed scales in language
1995, January	Parents called to request therapy
1995, January 12	Parents scheduled for intake session

SOCIOMETRIC QUESTIONS TO USE

1. If you could ask three persons in your home room to work with you on a project, who would they be?
   a.
   b.
   c.
2. If you could choose three persons in your home room to eat lunch with, who would they be?
   a.
   b.
   c.
3. If you could invite three persons from your home room to eat lunch with you, who would you invite?
   a.
   b.
   c.

The child is then asked to state who the persons (a, b, and c on each list) would choose.

DR. O'DESSIE OLIVER JAMES
DAILY COUNSELING NOTES

NAME _____ DATE _____ ON PREMISES ____
MN ____CPT ____DNK; DNC; CNCLED   Y,   N; TIME _____ALONE,
WITH _____VIA _____ON TIME   Y,   N; MEDS   Y,   N;
M.D. _____ CONTACTED   Y,   N; SEDUCT. ISSUES
Y,   N; PRECAUTIONS TAKEN _____
LEGAL THREATS   Y,   N; VEILED, OVERT; ABUSE ISSUES   Y,   N;
HO; SUI;

_____

_____

S. _____

_____

O. See attached Play Therapy Observation Sheet _____

_____

_____

_____

_____

_____

_____

A. DSMIV   I.   II.   III.
CHANGED   Y,   N

COMMENTS _____

P. _____

_____

_____

_____

_____

RESCHEDULED _____

DR. O'DESSIE OLIVER JAMES

_____

KEY TO DAILY COUNSELING NOTES

MN = MINUTES
CPT = COMPREHENSIVE PROCEDURE TERMINOLOGY
DNK = DID NOT COME
DNC = DID NOT CALL
CNCLED = CANCELED
VIA = TRANSPORTED BY
MEDS = MEDICATIONS
SEDUCT. = SEDUCTIVE
HO = HOMOCIDE RISK
SUI = SUICIDE RISK
S. = SUBJECTIVE INFORMATION
O. = OBJECTIVE FINDINGS
A. = ASSESSMENT
P. = PLAN

PLAY THERAPY OBSERVATION SHEET

Child _____ Date _____ Session Number _____

Observed Mood:

Observed Physical Condition:

	Toy Themes	*Length of Time*	*Emotional Constructs*
1.			
2.			
3.			
4.			

Changes in Emotional Contact With Therapist:

Limits Tested:

Outside Content:

PEDIATRIC DEVELOPMENT PROGRAM
VERNON L. JAMES, M.D.

MEDICATION RESPONSE CHART

TARGET BEHAVIOR	If Present CHECK	Before Meds GRADE	Week 1 GRADE	Week 2 GRADE	Week 3 GRADE	Week 4 GRADE
Attention to task						
Listening to lessons						
Finishing work						
Impulsivity						
Interrupts						
Organizing work						
Overactivity, fidgety						
Peer interaction						
Makes many mistakes						
Poor follow-through						
Loses things						
Aggression						
Forgetful						
Out of seat						
Problem waiting turn						
Talks excessively						
Problem in quiet play						
Blurts answers						
Stubborn, refusals						

(grade—as you see it)..........X   5.................4.............3..............2...............1

        Worse   Unacceptable ---------------------------- Acceptable

              NO IMPROVEMENT--------------------MUCH BETTER

Check any side effects that you have noted: _____Appetite loss, _____Stomachaches,_____Stares,

_____Excessive tiredness, _____Headaches, _____Motor tics, _____Tremors, _____Shakes,

_____Irritability, _____Sadness, _____Crying, ____Insomnia, ____Withdrawal, ____Nervousness

CHILD'S NAME_____

RATER_____ RELATIONSHIP TO CHILD_____

DATE_____

Pediatric Development Program
Vernon L. James, M.D., Medical Director
Santa Rosa Children's Hospital
San Antonio, TX

TREATMENT RESPONSE CHART

TARGET BEHAVIOR	Before Treatment	Period #1	Period #2	Period #3	Period #4

Score behavior as you see it.   1........... 2.............3........... 4........... 5

(Acceptable...........Barely OK...........Not Acceptable)

Return at any time that you are satisfied that you can judge the response, the lack of response, or an unacceptable response to the treatment.

Treatment given _____

Child's name _____ Age_____

Person filling out this form _____ Relationship to child _____

Date started _____ Date ended _____

DR. O'DESSIE OLIVER JAMES
BEHAVIORAL CONTRACT

Name:

Issues	M	Tu	W	Th	Fri		

Contract:

Dr. James will pay _____ for every check.

Dr. James will charge _____ for every _____.

_____

Child's signature

_____

Dr. James

References

Abraham, K. (1953). The psycho-sexual differences between dementia praecox. In *Selected Papers on Psychoanalysis*, trans. D. Bryan & A. Strachey. New York: Basic Books.

Ackerman, H. W. (1937). Constructive and destructive tendencies in children. *American Journal of Orthopsychiatry* 7: 301–319.

Aderhold, E. C. (1967). *Doll play behavior as a function of age.* Unpublished doctoral dissertation, University of Georgia, Athens.

Adler, A. (1927). *Understanding Human Nature.* New York: Premier.

Ainsworth, M. D. (1964). Patterns of attachment behavior shown by the infant in interaction with its mother. *Merrill-Palmer Quarterly* 10: 51–58.

Alexander, E. D. (1964). School-centered play therapy program. *Personnel and Guidance Journal* 43: 256–261.

Allan, J. (1976). Identification and treatment of difficult babies. *Canadian Nurse* 72: 11–16.

——— (1977). The use of creative drama with acting out sixth and seventh grade boys and girls. *Canadian Counselor* 11(3): 135–143.

——— (1978). Serial drawing: A therapeutic approach with young children. *Canadian Counselor* 12(4): 223–228.

——— (1988). *Inscapes of the Child's World.* Dallas, TX: Spring Publications.

Allan, J., and Berry, P. (1987). Sandplay. Special issue: Counseling with expressive arts. *Elementary School Guidance and Counseling* 21(4): 300-306.

Allan, J., and Brown, K. (1993). Jungian play therapy in elementary schools. *Elementary School Guidance and Counseling* 28(1): 30–41.

Allan, J., and Lawton-Speert, S. (1993). Play psychotherapy of a profoundly incest abused boy: a Jungian approach. *International Journal of Play Therapy* 2(1): 33–48.

Allan, J., and Levin, S. (1993). Born on my bum: Jungian play therapy. In *Play Therapy in Action: A Casebook for Practitioners*, eds. T. Kottman and C. Schaefer, pp. 209–243. Northvale, NJ: Jason Aronson.

Allen, F. H. (1942). *Psychotherapy with Children*. New York: Norton.

American Psychological Association. (1992). Ethical principles of psychologists and code of conduct. *American Psychologist* 47(12): 1597–1611.

Andronico, M., and Blake, I. (1971). The application of filial therapy to young children with stuttering problems. *Journal of Speech and Hearing Disorders* 36: 377–381.

Andronico, M., Fidler, J., Guerney, B., and Guerney, L. F. (1967). The combination of didactic and dynamic elements in filial therapy. *International Journal of Group Psychotherapy* 17: 10–17.

Andronico, M., and Guerney, B. (1969). Case conference: a psychotherapeutic aide in a headstart program: Riegel Ridge Headstart Project, Milford, New Jersey. *Children* 16(1): 14–22.

Arthur, H. (1952). A comparison of techniques employed in psychotherapy and psychoanalysis of children. *American Journal of Orthopsychiatry* 12: 484–498.

Association for Play Therapy. (1996–1997). *Membership and Registration Directory*. Fresno, CA: Association for Play Therapy.

Axline, V. (1947). *Play Therapy: The Inner Dynamics of Childhood*. Boston: Houghton Mifflin.

———— (1948). Play therapy and race conflict in young children. *Journal of Abnormal Social Psychology* 63: 300–310.

———— (1949). Play therapy: a way of understanding and helping reading problems. *Childhood Education* 26: 156–161.

———— (1950a). The child's world via play experience. *Progressive Education* 27: 68–75.

———— (1950b). Play therapy experiences as described by child participants. *Journal of Consulting Psychology* 14: 53–63.

———— (1955a). Group therapy as a means of self-discovery for parents and children. *Group Psychotherapy* 8: 152–160.

———— (1955b). Play therapy procedures and results. *American Journal of Orthopsychiatry* 25: 618–626.

———— (1964). *Dibs: In Search of Self.* Boston: Houghton Mifflin.

Axline, V., and Rogers, C. R. (1945). A teacher-therapist deals with a handicapped child. *Journal of Abnormal and Social Psychology* 40: 119–142.

Baker, B. E. (1971). The effectiveness of parental counseling with other modalities in the treatment of children with learning disabilities. *Journal of Education* 154: 74–82.

Bandura, A. (1977). *Social Learning Theory.* Englewood Cliffs, NJ: Prentice-Hall.

Barbour, R. F., and Beedell, C. J. (1955). The follow-up of a child guidance clinic population. *Journal of Mental Science* 101: 794–809.

Baruch, D. W. (1939). Play techniques in preschool as an aid in guidance. *Psychological Bulletin* 36: 570.

———— (1940). Therapeutic procedures as part of the educational process. *Journal of Consulting Psychology* 41: 165–172.

———— (1941). Aggression during doll play in a preschool. *American Journal of Orthopsychiatry* 11: 252–260.

Beck, A. T., and Emery, G. (1985). *Anxiety Disorders and Phobias: A Cognitive Perspective.* New York: Basic Books.

Beck, A. T., Rush, A. J., Shaw, B. F., and Emery, G. (1979). *Cognitive Therapy of Depression.* New York: Guilford.

Beiser, H. R. (1955). Play equipment for diagnosis and therapy. *American Journal of Orthopsychiatry* 25: 761–770.

Belter, R. W., and Grisso, T. (1984). Children's recognition of rights violations in counseling. *Professional Psychology: Research and Practice* 15(6): 899–910.

Bender, L. (1936). The use of puppet shows as a psychotherapeutic method for behavior problems in children. *American Journal of Orthopsychiatry* 6: 283–299.

———— (1937). The use of plastic material as a psychiatric approach to emotional problems in children. *American Journal of Orthopsychiatry* 7: 283–299.

———— (1938). Art and therapy in the mental disturbances of children. *Journal of Nervous and Mental Disorders* 87: 418–449.

Bender, L., and Woltmann, A. G. (1941). Play and psychotherapy. *Nervous Child* 1: 17–42.

Bills, R. E. (1950a). Nondirective play therapy with retarded readers. *Journal of Consulting Psychology* 14: 140–149.

———— (1950b). Play therapy with well-adjusted retarded readers. *Journal of Consulting Psychology* 14: 246–249.

Binswanger, L. (1958). The existential analysis school of thought. In *Existence*, eds. R. May, E. Angel, and H. F. Ellenberger, pp. 191–213. New York: Basic Books.

Bixler, R. H. (1945). Treatment of a reading problem through nondirective play therapy. *Journal of Consulting Psychology* 9: 105–118.

———— (1949). Limits are therapy. *Journal of Consulting Psychology* 13: 1–11.

Bollas, C., and Sundelson, D. (1995). *The New Informants: The Betrayal of Confidentiality in Psychoanalysis and Psychotherapy*. Northvale, NJ: Jason Aronson.

Boss, M. (1958). *The Analysis of Dreams*. New York: Philosophical Library.

———— (1979). *Existential Foundations of Medicine and Psychology*. New York: Aronson.

Bradway, K. (1979). Sandplay in psychotherapy. *Art Psychotherapy* 6(2): 85–93.

Brody, V. (1978). Developmental play: a relationship-focused program for children. *Child Welfare* 57(9): 591–599.

———— (1992). The dialogue of touch: developmental play therapy. *International Journal of Play Therapy* 1(1): 21–30.

Brody, V., Fenderson, D., and Stephenson, S. (1976). *Sourcebook for Finding Your Way to Helping Young Children Through Developmental Play*. St. Petersburg, FL: Florida State Department.

Bucur, R. R. (1970). *Nondirective group play therapy with aggressive boys*. Unpublished master's thesis, North Texas State University, Denton.

Burlingham, S. (1938). Therapeutic effects of a play group for preschool children. *American Journal of Orthopsychiatry* 8: 627–638.

Butts, A. E. (1971). Communications with the elementary age child. *Elementary School Guidance and Counseling Journal* 5: 310–312.

Cameron, W. M. (1940). Treatment of children in psychiatric clinics with play techniques. *Menninger Clinic Bulletin* 4: 172–180.

Carey, L. (1990). Sandplay therapy with a troubled child. *Arts in Psychotherapy* 17(3): 197–209.

Carkhuff, R. (1973). *The Art of Helping*. Amherst, MA: Human Resource Development Press.

Carkhuff, R., and Berenson, B. (1969). *The Sources of Gain in Counseling and Psychotherapy*. New York: Holt, Rinehart, & Winston.

Carmichael, K. D. (1993). Preliminary development of an interaction matrix for observation of client–therapist relationships in play therapy. *International Journal of Play Therapy* 2(2): 19–33.

Cashdon, S. (1967). The use of drawings in child psychotherapy, a process analysis of a case study. *Psychotherapy: Theory, Research, and Practice* 4: 81–86.

Cassell, S. (1965). Effect of brief puppet therapy upon the emotional responses of children undergoing cardiac catheterization. *Journal of Consulting Psychology* 29: 1–8.

Center for Play Therapy. *Play Therapy Training Directory*. Denton, TX: University of North Texas, Center for Play Therapy.

Chalmers, T. (1966). Value of play in nursing severely subnormal children. *Nursing Mirror* 25: 12–16.

Cline, D. (1972). Video documentation of behavioral change in children. *American Journal of Orthopsychiatry* 42: 40–47.

Conn, J. H. (1939). The child reveals himself through play: the method of the play interview. *Mental Hygiene* 23: 49–70.

—— (1941a). The timid, dependent child. *Journal of Pediatrics* 19: 91–102.

—— (1941b). The treatment of fearful children. *American Journal of Orthopsychiatry* 9: 744–752.

—— (1948). The play interview as an investigative and therapeutic procedure. *Nervous Child* 7: 257–286.

—— (1952). Treatment of anxiety states in children by play interviews. *Sinai Hospital Journal* 1: 57–65.

—— (1955). Play interview therapy of castration fear. *American Journal of Orthopsychiatry* 25: 747–754.

Cowden, S. T. (1992). *The effects of client-centered group play therapy on self concept (Masters Abstracts International 31/01)*. Unpublished master's thesis, University of West Florida, Pensacola.

Cowen, E., and Cruickshank, W. M. (1948a). Group therapy with physically handicapped children I: report of study. *Journal of Educational Psychology* 39: 192–215.

—— (1948b). Group therapy with physically handicapped children: eleven evaluations. *Journal of Educational Psychology* 39: 281–296.

Cox, F. E. (1953). Sociometric status and individual adjustment before and after play therapy. *Journal of Abnormal Psychology* 40: 354–356.

Crow, J. C. (1989). *Play therapy with low achievers in reading (Dissertation Abstracts International 50/09A)*. Unpublished doctoral dissertation, University of North Texas, Denton.

Daly, M., and Carr, J. (1967). Tactile contact: a measure of therapeutic progress. *Nursing Research* 16: 16–21.

Davidson, E. R. (1949). Play for the hospitalized child. *American Journal of Nursing* 39: 138–141.

Demaago, J. (1971). *Play therapy: client-centered counseling for elementary school children* (report of study). Kalamazoo, MI: Western Michigan University.

Despert, J. L. (1937a). Technical approaches used in the study and treatment of emotional problems in children, Part III: drawing. *Psychiatric Quarterly* 9: 267–294.

———— (1937b). Technical approaches used in the study and treatment of emotional problems in children, Part V: the play room. *Psychiatric Quarterly* 9: 677–693.

———— (1940). A method for the study of personality reactions in preschool children by means of analysis of their play. *Journal of Psychology* 9: 17–29.

———— (1948). Play therapy: remarks on some of its aspects. *Nervous Child* 8: 287–295.

De Wet, W. (1993). *Therapy with the deaf child (Dissertation Abstracts International 54/11A)* (unpublished doctoral dissertation). University of Pretoria, South Africa.

Dinkmeyer, D., and Dinkmeyer, D. (1977). Concise counseling assessment: the children's life-style guide. *Elementary School Guidance and Counseling* 12: 117–124.

———— (1983). Adlerian approaches. In *Counseling and Psychotherapy with Children and Adolescents: Theory and Practice for School and Clinic Settings*, eds. H. T. Prout and D. Brown, pp. 289–327. Tampa, FL: Mariner.

Dinkmeyer, D., Dinkmeyer, D., Dinkmeyer, J., and McKay, J. (1987a). *The Effective Parent*. Circle Pines, MN: American Guidance Service.

Dinkmeyer, D., Dinkmeyer, D., and Sperry, L. (1987b). *Adlerian Counseling and Psychotherapy*, 2nd ed. Columbus, OH: Merrill.

Dinkmeyer, D., and McKay, G. (1989). *The Parent's Handbook: Systematic Training for Effective Parenting (STEP)*, 3rd ed. Circle Pines, MN: American Guidance Service.

Dorfman, E. (1958). Personality outcomes of client-centered child therapy. *Psychological Monographs* 72: 1–22.

——— (1965). Play therapy. In *Client-Centered Therapy*, ed. C. R. Rogers. Boston: Houghton Mifflin.

Drabkova, H. (1966). Experiences resulting from clinical use of psychodrama with children. *Group Psychotherapy* 19: 32–36.

Dreikurs, R. (1967). *Psychodynamics, Psychotherapy, and Counseling*. Chicago: Alfred Adler Institute.

Dreikurs, R., and Cassell, P. (1972). *Discipline Without Tears*. Toronto: Alfred Adler Institute of Ontario.

Dreikurs, R., and Soltz, V. (1964). *Children: The Challenge*. New York: Hawthorn/Dutton.

Dupent, H. J., Landsman, T., and Valentine, M. (1953). The treatment of delayed speech by client-centered therapy. *Journal of Consulting Psychology* 17: 122–125.

Eisenberg, L., and Gruenberg, E. M. (1961). The current status of secondary prevention in child psychiatry. *American Journal of Orthopsychiatry* 31: 355–367.

Eme, R. F. (1972). *Level of experiencing as a predictor of short-term play therapy outcome*. Unpublished doctoral dissertation, Loyola University of Chicago, IL.

Engebretson, D. E. (1973). Human territorial behavior: the role of interaction distance in therapeutic interventions. *American Journal of Orthopsychiatry* 43: 57–63.

Erikson, E. H. (1950). *Childhood and Society*. New York: Norton.

Ferguson, N. (1990). Confidentiality: Implications for the Child. *Association for Play Therapy Newsletter* 9(3): 6–7.

Finke, H. (1947). *Changes in the expression of emotionalized attitudes in six cases of play therapy*. Unpublished master's thesis, University of Chicago.

Flint, B. M. (1969). *The child and the institution: a study of deprivation and recovery*. Buffalo: University of Toronto.

Freud, A. (1928). *Introduction to the Technique of Child Analysis*, trans. L. P. Clark. New York: Nervous and Mental Disease Publishing Company.

——— (1951). *The Psychoanalytic Treatment Of Children*, trans. N. Proctor-Gregg, 3rd ed. New York: Anglo-Books.

——— (1954). *The Ego and the Mechanism of Defense*, trans. C. Baines. New York: International Universities Press.

Freud, S. (1938). *The Basic Writings of Sigmund Freud*, trans. and ed. A. A. Brill. New York: Modern Library.

Fuchs, N. R. (1957). Play therapy at home. *Merrill–Palmer Quarterly* 3: 89–95.

Gerard, M. W. (1948). Trends in orthopsychiatric therapy V: treatment of the young child. *American Journal of Orthopsychiatry* 18: 414–421.

Ginott, H. G. (1956). Group screening of parents in a child guidance setting. *International Journal of Group Psychotherapy* 4: 405–409.

——— (1957a). Differential treatment groups in guidance, counseling, psychotherapy, and psychoanalysis. *International Journal of Social Psychiatry* 3: 231–235.

——— (1957b). Parent education groups in a child guidance clinic. *Mental Hygiene* 41: 82–86.

——— (1959). The theory and practice of therapeutic intervention in child treatment. *Journal of Consulting Psychology* 23: 160–166.

——— (1960). A rationale for selecting toys in play therapy. *Journal of Consulting Psychology* 14: 243–246.

——— (1961a). *Group Psychotherapy with Children*. New York: McGraw-Hill.

——— (1961b). Play therapy: the initial session. *American Journal of Psychotherapy* 15: 73–89.

——— (1961c). Play therapy limits and theoretical orientation. *Journal of Consulting Psychology* 15: 337–340.

Ginott, H., Blek, L., and Barnes, R. (1959). A study in non-attendance of initial interviews in a community clinic. *International Journal of Group Psychotherapy* 9: 314–321.

Ginott, H., and Lebo, D. (1963). Most and least used play therapy limits. *Journal of Genetic Psychology* 103: 153–159.

Glass, N. M. (1986). *Parents as therapeutic agents: a study of the effect of filial therapy (Dissertation Abstracts International 47/07A)*. Unpublished doctoral dissertation, University of North Texas, Denton.

Golden, B. (1969). *Monitored Play Therapy: Conceptual and Methodological Issues*. Georgia State University. (ERIC Document Reproduction Service No. ED 033 426)

Goldings, C. R. (1972). Books in the playroom: a dimension of child psychiatric technique. *Journal of the American Academy of Child Psychiatry* 9: 52–65.

Gordor, E. (1954). *Art and Play Therapy*. New York: Doubleday.

Grant, F. F. (1950). The Kasperl Theatre as play therapy. *American Journal of Psychotherapy* 4: 279–285.

Grisso, T., and Vierling, L. (1978). Minor's consent to treatment: a developmental perspective. *Professional Psychology* 9: 412–427.

Guerney, B. (1964). Filial therapy: description and rationale. *Journal of Consulting Psychology* 28: 304–310.

Guerney, B., and Flumen, A. (1970). Teachers as psychotherapeutic agents for withdrawn children. *Journal of School Psychology* 8: 107–113.

Guerney, B., Guerney, L., and Andronico, M. (1966). Filial therapy. *Yale Scientific Magazine* 40: 6–14, 20.

Hall, C., and Lindzey, G. (1957). *Theories of Personality*. New York: Wiley.

Hambridge, G. (1955). Structured play therapy. *American Journal of Orthopsychiatry* 25: 601–617.

Hammer, M., and Kaplan, A. (1967). *The Practice of Psychotherapy with Children*. Homewood, IL: Dorsey.

Han, L. (1994). *Sand play: Meaning, method, and metaphor (Dissertation Abstracts International 55/04A)* (Unpublished doctoral dissertation). Saybrook Institute, San Francisco, CA.

Hare, M. (1966). Shortened treatment in a child guidance clinic: the results in 119 cases. *British Journal of Psychiatry* 112: 613–616.

Harms, E. (1948). Play diagnosis: preliminary considerations for a sound approach. *Nervous Child* 7: 233–246.

Harnish, P. (1983). *The effects of the children's perceptions of certain therapist expressed conditions on the process and outcome of non-directive play therapy (Dissertation Abstracts International 45/03B)*. Unpublished doctoral dissertation, University of Toledo, OH.

Harter, S. (1977). A cognitive-developmental approach to children's expression of conflicting feelings and a technique to facilitate such expression in play therapy. *Journal of Consulting and Clinical Psychology* 45(3): 417–432.

——— (1983). Cognitive-developmental considerations in the conduct of play therapy. In *Handbook of Play Therapy*, eds. C. Schaefer and K. O'Connor, pp. 95–127. New York: Wiley.

Hartley, R. (1952). *Growing Through Play: Experiences of Teddy and Bud*. New York: Columbia University Press.

Hartley, R., Lawrence, K., and Goldenson, R. (1952). *New Play Experiences for Children: Planned Play Groups, Miniature Life Toys and Puppets*. New York: Columbia University Press.

Hawkey, M. L. (1951a). Play analysis: case study of a nine-year-old girl. *British Journal of Medical Psychology* 24: 206–214.

——— (1951b). The use of puppets in child psychotherapy. *British Journal of Medical Psychology* 24: 206–214.

Haworth, M. R., and Menolascino, F. (1967). Video-tape observations of disturbed young children. *Journal of Clinical Psychology* 23: 135–140.

Hayward, H. (1949). Social worker's use of play interviews in child guidance. *Smith College Studies of Social Work* 19: 111–112.

Heinicke, C., and Goldman, A. (1960). Research on psychotherapy with children: a review and suggestions for further study. *American Journal of Orthopsychiatry* 30: 483–493.

Hellendoorn, J., Harinck, F., and Mostert, P. (1979). *The development of a classificatory system for play therapist activities.* Paper presented at the meeting of the 11th International Congress of Psychotherapy, Amsterdam.

Hellersberg, E. F. (1955). Child's growth in play therapy. *American Journal of Psychotherapy* 9: 484–502.

Henderson-Dixon, A. S. (1991). *The child's own story: A study of the creative process of healing in children in play therapy (Dissertation Abstracts International 52/09A).* Unpublished doctoral dissertation, Union Institute, Cincinnati, OH.

Hendricks, S. J. (1971). *A descriptive analysis of the process of client-centered play therapy (Dissertation Abstracts International 32/07A).* Unpublished doctoral dissertation, University of North Texas, Denton.

Hendrix, D. (1991). Ethics and intrafamily confidentiality in counseling with children. *Journal of Mental Health Counseling* 13(3): 323–333.

Herd, R. H. (1969). *Behavioral outcomes of client-centered play therapy (Dissertation Abstracts International 30/06A).* Unpublished doctoral dissertation, University of North Texas, Denton.

Homburger, E. H., and Erikson, E. (1937). Configurations in play, clinical notes. *Psychoanalytic Quarterly* 6: 139–140.

Homefield, H. D. (1959). *Creative role-playing as therapy for stuttering children, with special reference to the use of masks.* Unpublished doctoral dissertation, New York University.

Homeyer, L. E. (1994). *Play therapy behavior of sexually abused children (Dissertation Abstracts International 56/01A)* (Unpublished doctoral dissertation). University of North Texas, Denton.

Howard, R. W. (1944). Fantasy and the play interview. *Character and Personality* 13: 152–165.

Hume, K. (1970). Counseling and consulting: complementary functions. *Elementary School Guidance Counseling* 5: 3–11.

Jackson, L. (1950). Non-speaking children. *British Journal of Medical Psychology* 23: 87–100.

James, O'D. O. (1977). *Play Therapy: An Overview.* Oceanside, NY: Dabor Science Publications.

——— (1979). Infant bonding data. In *Project AIDE: Assistance to Infants' Developmental Education—Final Report* (CRS Entity 1-480561969, pp. IV-1–IV-26). Washington, D.C.: Bureau of Education of the Handicapped.

James, O'D. O. (1987). *Theory and techniques in play therapy*. Unpublished manuscript.

James, V. L. (1979). *Project AIDE: Assistance to Infants' Developmental Education—Final Report* (CRS Entity 1-480561969, pp. IV-1–IV-26). Washington, D.C.: Bureau of Education of the Handicapped.

—— (1996). Personal communication, February 15, 1996.

James-McNabb, D. O. (1975a). *A Compilation of Rationale and Research in Play Therapy*. Wichita, KS: Test Systems Inc.

—— (1975b). *A compilation of selected rationale and research in play therapy (Dissertation Abstracts International 36/05A)*. Unpublished doctoral dissertation, University of North Texas, Denton.

Jeffrey, L. (1984). Developmental play therapy: an assessment and therapeutic technique in child psychiatry. *British Journal of Occupational Therapy* 47(3): 70–74.

Jenkins, R. L., and Beckh, E. (1942). Finger puppets and mask making as media for work with children. *American Journal of Orthopsychiatry* 12: 294–301.

Jepsen, R. H. (1992). *The development of a play diagnosis instrument for the assessment of young children with developmental disabilities (Dissertation Abstracts International 53/05B)*. Unpublished doctoral dissertation, Ohio State University, Columbus.

Jernberg, A. (1979). *Theraplay: A Structured New Approach for Problem Children and Their Families*. San Francisco: Jossey-Bass.

Jernberg, A., Booth, P., Koller, T., and Allert, A. (1987). *Manual for the Administration and the Clinical Interpretation of the Marschak Interaction Method (MIM), Pre-school and School Age*. Chicago: Theraplay Institute.

Jernberg, A., and Jernberg, E. (1993). Family theraplay for the family tyrant. In *Play Therapy in Action: A Casebook for Practitioners*, eds. T. Kottman and C. Schaefer, pp. 45–96. Northvale, NJ: Jason Aronson.

Jessner, L., Blon, G., and Kaplan, S. (1951). The use of play in psychotherapy with children. *Journal of Nervous and Mental Disorders* 104: 175–177.

Johnson, E. (1953a). The clinical use of Raven's Progressive Matrices to appraise potential for progress in play therapy: a study of institutionalized mentally and educationally retarded children. *American Journal of Orthopsychiatry* 23: 391–405.

————— (1953b). Klopfer's prognostic scale used with Raven's progressive matrices in play therapy prognosis. *Journal of Projective Techniques* 17: 320–326.

Jones, J. W. (1952). Play therapy and the blind child. *New Outlook for the Blind* 42: 189–197.

Jung, C. (1965). *Memories, Dreams, and Reflections*. New York: Vintage.

————— (1966). *The Practice of Psychotherapy*. (Vol. 16 of Collected Works). Princeton, NJ: Princeton University Press.

Kalff, D. (1971). *Sandplay: Mirror of a Child's Psyche*. San Francisco: Browser.

Kamp, L. N., and Kessler, E. S. (1970). The world test: developmental aspects of a play technique. *Journal of Child Psychology and Psychiatry* 11: 113–115.

Katz, B. (1965). Do children need play therapy? *Psychology in the Schools* 2: 113–115.

Kessler, J. (1966). *Psychopathology of Childhood*. Englewood Cliffs, NJ: Prentice-Hall.

Kidd, A. H., and Walton, N. Y. (1966). Dart throwing as a method of reducing extrapunitive aggression. *Psychological Reports* 19: 88–90.

Kimmel, M. A. R. (1952). The use of play techniques in a medical setting. *Social Casework* 33: 30–34.

Klaus, M. H., and Kennell, J. H. (1976). *Maternal–Infant Bonding*. St. Louis: Mosby.

Klein, M. (1927). The psychological principles of infant analysis. *International Journal of Psycho-Analysis* 8: 25–37.

————— (1929). Personification in the play of children. *International Journal of Psycho-Analysis* 10: 193–204.

————— (1932). *The Psychoanalysis of Children*. London: Hogarth.

————— (1939). The psychoanalytic play technique. *Mental Hygiene* 22: 49–69.

————— (1955). The psychoanalytic play technique. *American Journal of Orthopsychiatry* 25: 223–237.

————— (1961). *Narrative of a Child Analysis*. New York: Basic Books.

Knell, S. (1993a). *Cognitive-Behavioral Play Therapy*. Northvale, NJ: Jason Aronson.

————— (1993b). To show and not tell: cognitive-behavioral play therapy. In *Play Therapy in Action: A Casebook for Practitioners*, eds. T. Kottman and C. Schaefer, pp. 169–208. Northvale, NJ: Jason Aronson.

Knell, S., and Moore, D. (1990). Cognitive-behavioral play therapy in the treatment of encopresis. *Journal of Clinical Child Psychology* 19(1): 55–60.

Kottman, T. (1987). *An ethnographic study of an Adlerian play therapy training program (Dissertation Abstracts International 49/01A)*. Unpublished doctoral dissertation, University of North Texas, Denton.

———— (1993). The king of rock and roll: an application of Adlerian play therapy. In *Play Therapy in Action: A Casebook for Practitioners*, eds. T. Kottman and C. Schaefer, pp. 133–168. Northvale, NJ: Jason Aronson.

———— (1995). *Partners in Play: An Adlerian Approach to Play Therapy*. Alexandra, VA: American Counseling Association.

Kottman, T., and Schaefer, C., eds. (1993). *Play Therapy in Action: A Casebook for Practitioners*. Northvale, NJ: Jason Aronson.

Kottman, T., Strother, J., and Deniger, M. (1987). Activity therapy: an alternative therapy for adolescents. *Journal of Humanistic Education and Development* 25(4): 180–186.

Kulla, M. (1966). *A therapeutic doll play program with an emotionally disturbed child*. Unpublished doctoral dissertation, University of Oklahoma, Norman.

L'Abate, L. (1968). *An automated playroom*. Paper presented at a Workshop on Newer Approaches in Psychological Assessment Techniques, Child Development Clinic, St. Louis University School of Medicine, February 29–March 1.

———— (1969). *Design for a playroom*. Georgia State University. (ERIC Document Reproduction Service No. ED 019 133)

Landisberg, S., and Snyder, W. U. (1946). Nondirective play therapy. *Journal of Clinical Psychology* 2: 203–214.

Landreth, G. (1978). Children communicate through play. *Texas Personnel and Guidance Journal* 6(1): 41–42.

———— (1982). *Play Therapy: Dynamics of the Process of Counseling with Children*. Springfield, IL: Thomas.

———— (1987). Play therapy: facilitative use of child's play in elementary school counseling. Special issue: Counseling with expressive arts. *Elementary School Guidance and Counseling* 21(4): 253–261.

———— (1988). Lessons for living from a dying child. *Journal of Counseling and Development* 67(2): 100.

———— (1991). *Play Therapy: The Art of the Relationship*. Muncie, IN: Accelerated Development Press.

Landreth, G., Allen, L., and Jacquot, W. S. (1969). A team approach to learning disabilities. *Journal of Learning Disabilities* 2: 24–29.

Landreth, G., Homeyer, L., Bratton, S., and Kale, A. (1995). *The World of Play Therapy Literature: A Definitive Guide to the Subjects and Authors in the Field*, 2nd ed. Denton, TX: Center for Play Therapy.

Landreth, G., Homeyer, L., Glover, G., and Sweeney, D. (1996). *Play Therapy Interventions with Children's Problems*. Northvale, NJ: Jason Aronson.

Lebo, D. (1952). The relationship of response categories in play therapy to aggression and age. *Journal of Child Psychiatry* 2: 330–336.

——— (1953). The present status of research on nondirective play therapy. *Journal of Consulting Psychology* 17: 177–183.

——— (1955a). The expressive value of toys recommended for nondirective play therapy. *Journal of Clinical Psychology* 11: 144–148.

——— (1955b). Quantification of the nondirective play therapy process. *Journal of Genetic Psychology* 84: 375–378.

——— (1956a). Age and suitability for nondirective play therapy. *Journal of Genetic Psychology*, 89: 231–238.

——— (1956b). The question of toys in play therapy: an international problem. *Journal of Education and Psychology* 14: 63–73.

——— (1958a). The development of play as a form of therapy: from Rousseau to Rogers. *American Journal of Psychiatry* 112: 418–422.

——— (1958b). A formula for selecting toys for nondirective play therapy. *Journal of Genetic Psychology* 902: 23–24.

——— (1958c). Theoretical framework for nondirective play: concepts from psychoanalysis and learning theory. *Journal of Consulting Psychology* 22: 275–279.

Lebo, D., and Lebo, E. (1957). Aggression and age in relation to verbal expression in nondirective play therapy. *Psychology Monographs* 71: 449–461.

Lee, D., and Hutt, C. (1964). A playroom designed for filming children: a note. *Journal of Child Psychology and Psychiatry* 5: 263–265.

Leland, H., and Smith, D. (1962). Unstructured material in play therapy for emotionally disturbed brain damaged, mentally retarded children. *American Journal of Mental Deficiency* 64: 621–628.

——— (1965). *Play Therapy with Mentally Subnormal Children*. New York: Grune and Stratton.

Leton, D. A. (1966). The factor structure of diagnostic scores from school play sessions. *Psychology in the Schools* 3: 148–153.

Levi, A. (1961). *Parent treatment and outcome of child's therapy*. Unpublished doctoral dissertation, Columbia University, New York.

Levin, H., and Turgeon, V. (1957). The influence of the mother's presence on children's doll play aggression. *Journal of Abnormal Social Psychology* 55: 304–308.

Levin, H., and Wardwell, E. (1962). The research uses of doll play. *Psychological Bulletin* 59: 27–56.

Levin, S. C. (1992). *A case study analysis of thematic transformations in nondirective play therapy (Dissertation Abstracts International 54/06A)*. Unpublished doctoral dissertation, University of British Columbia, Vancouver, British Columbia, Canada.

Levitt, E. E. (1957). The results of psychotherapy with children, an evaluation. *Journal of Consulting Psychology* 21: 189–196.

———— (1963). Psychotherapy with children, a further evaluation. *Behavior Research Therapy* 1: 45–51.

Levy, D. M. (1933). Use of play technique as an experimental procedure. *American Journal of Orthopsychiatry* 3: 266–277.

———— (1939a). Release therapy in young children. *Child Study* 16: 141–143.

———— (1939b). Trends in therapy, III release therapy. *American Journal of Orthopsychiatry* 9: 713–736.

Linden, J. I., and Stollak, G. (1969). The training of undergraduates in play techniques. *Journal of Clinical Psychology* 25: 213–218.

Linder, M. A. (1967). *Verbal conditioning of aggression in doll play: comparison of the effect of two therapeutic tools on aggression of nursery school boys in a therapy-like situation*. Unpublished doctoral dissertation, University of Minnesota, Minneapolis.

Loomis, E. A. (1957). The use of checkers in handling certain resistances in child therapy and child analysis. *Journal of the American Psychoanalytic Association* 5: 130–135.

Loomis, E. A., Hilgeman, L., and Meyer, L. (1957). Childhood psychosis: play patterns as nonverbal indices of ego functions: a preliminary report. *American Journal of Orthopsychiatry*, 27: 691–700.

Lovaas, O. I., Baer, D. M., and Bijou, S. (1965b). Experimental procedures for analyzing the interaction of symbolic social stimuli and children's behavior. *Child Development* 36: 237–247.

Lovaas, O. I., Freitag, G., Gold, V., and Kassorla, I. (1965a). Recording apparatus and procedure for observation of behaviors of children in free play settings. *Journal of Experimental Child Psychology* 2: 108–120.

Lowenfeld, M. (1935). *Play in Childhood.* London: Gollancz.

—— (1939). The world pictures of children: a method of recording and studying them. *British Journal of Medical Psychology* 18: 65–101.

—— (1950). The nature and use of the Lowenfeld World Technique in work with children and adults. *Journal of Psychology* 30: 325–331.

—— (1979). *The World Technique,* 2nd ed. London: Allan and Unwin.

Lynn, D. B., and Lynn, R. (1959). The structured doll play test as a projective technique for use with children. *Journal of Projective Techniques* 23: 335–344.

Machler, T. (1965). Pinocchio in the treatment of school phobia. *Bulletin of the Menninger Clinic* 29: 212–219.

Mahler, M., and Pine, F. (1975). *The Psychological Birth of the Human Infant.* New York: Basic Books.

Maisner, E. A. (1950). Contributions of play therapy techniques to total rehabilitative design in an institution for high-grade mentally deficient and borderline children. *American Journal of Mental Deficiency* 55: 235–250.

Mann, L. (1957). Persuasive doll play: a technique of directive psychotherapy for use with children. *Journal of Clinical Psychology* 13: 14–19.

Mannoni, M. (1970). *The Child, His Illness, and the Others.* New York: Pantheon.

Marcus, I. (1966). Costume play therapy. *Current Psychiatric Therapy* 6: 42–45.

Marshall, H. R., and Hann, S. C. (1965). Aspects of experience revealed through doll play of preschool children. *Journal of Psychology* 61: 47–57.

Martinez, K., and Valdez, D. (1992). Cultural considerations in play therapy with Hispanic children. In *Working with culture: therapeutic interventions with ethnic minority children and adolescents,* eds. L. Vargas and J. Koss-Chiono, pp. 85–101. San Francisco: Jossey-Bass.

McPherson, C. A. (1965). The value of play in meeting the emotional needs of young children in hospital settings. *Bibliographia Pediatrics* 84: 181–182.

Meeks, J. E. (1970). Children who cheat at games. *Journal of American Academy of Child Psychiatry* 9: 13–18.

Mehlman, B. (1953). Group play therapy with mentally retarded children. *Journal of Abnormal Social Psychology* 48: 53–60.

Mehrabian, A. (1968). Relationship of attitude to seated posture, orientation, and distance. *Journal of Personality and Social Psychology* 10: 26–30.

Mehus, H. (1953). Learning and therapy. *American Journal of Ortho-psychiatry* 23: 416–421.

Mende, R. H., and Kauffman, J. (1971). Effects of video-tape replays on behavior of culturally different children. *Perceptual and Motor Skills* 30: 670–673.

Mendes, L., and Maria, R. (1966). Group-analytic play therapy with preadolescent girls. *International Journal of Group Psychotherapy* 16: 58–64.

Miller, H. E., and Baruch, D. (1948). Psychological dynamics in allergic patients as shown in group and individual psychotherapy. *Journal of Consulting Psychology* 12: 111–113.

Miller, W. M. (1986). *Play therapy and parent training: the effects of the 'systematic training for effective parenting' program on children in play therapy and their parents (Dissertation Abstracts International 47/09A)*. Unpublished doctoral dissertation, University of Northern Colorado, Greeley.

Miyamoto, M. (1965). The meaning of silence in play therapy. *Psychologia* 8: 191–196.

Moore, T. (1964). Realism and fantasy in children's play. *Journal of Child Psychology and Psychiatry* 5: 15–36.

Moore, T., and Ucko, L. E. (1961). Four to six: constructiveness and conflict in meeting doll play problems. *Journal of Child Psychology and Psychiatry* 2: 21–47.

Moustakas, C. E. (1951). Situational play therapy with normal children. *Journal of Consulting Psychology* 15: 225–230.

——— (1953). *Children in Play Therapy*. New York: McGraw-Hill.

——— (1955a). Emotional adjustment and the play therapy process. *Journal of Genetic Psychology* 86: 79–99.

——— (1955b). The frequency and intensity of negative attitude expressed in play therapy: a comparison of well-adjusted and disturbed children. *Journal of Genetic Psychology* 86: 309–324.

——— (1959a). A human relations seminar at the Merrill-Palmer School. *Personnel and Guidance Journal* 37: 342–349.

——— (1959b). *Psychotherapy with Children*. New York: Harper and Row.

——— (1966). *Existential Child Therapy: The Child's Discovery of Himself*. New York: Basic Books.

Moustakas, C. E., and Makowsky, G. (1952). Client-centered therapy with parents. *Journal of Consulting Psychology* 16: 338–342.

Moyer, K., and Von Haller, G. (1956). Experimental study of children's preferences and use of blocks in play. *Journal of Genetic Psychology* 89: 3–10.

Murphy, A. T., and Fitzsimmons, R. M. (1960). *Stuttering and Personality Dynamics: Play Therapy, Projective Therapy, and Counseling*. New York: Ronald.

Myrick, R. D., and Haldin, W. (1971). A study of play process in counseling. *Elementary School Guidance and Counseling Journal* 5(4): 256–265.

Nelson, R. C. (1966). Elementary school counseling with unstructured play media. *Personnel and Guidance Journal* 45: 24–27.

——— (1967). Physical facilities for elementary school counseling. *Personnel and Guidance Journal* 46: 552–556.

Newell, H. W. (1941). Play therapy in child psychiatry. *American Journal of Orthopsychiatry* 11: 245–251.

Nickols, J. (1961a). A multi-purpose table for testing and play therapy. *Perceptual and Motor Skills* 13: 89–90.

——— (1961b). Target game technique for examination and play therapy activities with children. *Perceptual and Motor Skills* 13: 83–87.

Noll, R. B., and Seagull, A. A. (1982). Beyond informed consent: ethical and philosophical considerations in using behavior modification or play therapy in the treatment of enuresis. *Journal of Clinical Child Psychology* 11(1): 44–49.

Oaklander, V. (1988). *Windows to Our Children: A Gestalt Therapy Approach to Children and Adolescents*. Highland, NY: Gestalt Journal Press.

——— (1993). From meek to bold: a case study of Gestalt play therapy. In *Play Therapy in Action: A Casebook for Practitioners*, eds. T. Kottman and C. Schaefer, pp. 281–300. Northvale, NJ: Jason Aronson.

O'Connor, K. J. (1990). Professional conflicts and issues in child abuse reporting and treatment. *Association for Play Therapy Newsletter* 9(2): 22–23.

——— (1991). *The Play Therapy Primer: An Integration of Theories and Techniques*. New York: Wiley.

——— (1993). Child, protector, confidant: structured group ecosystemic play therapy. In *Play Therapy in Action: A Casebook for Practitioners*, eds. T. Kottman and C. Schaefer, pp. 245–280. Northvale, NJ: Jason Aronson.

Oe, E. N. (1989). *Comparison of initial session play therapy behaviors of maladjusted and adjusted children (Dissertation Abstracts International 50/ 09A)*. Unpublished doctoral dissertation, University of North Texas, Denton.

Oppenheimer, P. C. (1988). *The appropriateness of existential play therapy for children in middle childhood (Dissertation Abstracts International 49/*

07A). Unpublished doctoral dissertation, University of Southern California, Los Angeles.

Orgun, I. (1973). Playroom setting for diagnostic family interviews. *American Journal of Psychiatry* 130: 540–542.

Paul, R. (1993). *Background interpretation with a child placed under government protection by means of play therapy (Masters Abstracts International 32/02)*. Unpublished master's thesis, University of Pretoria, South Africa.

Pechy, B. M. (1955). The direct analysis of the mother–child relationship in the treatment of maladjusted children. *British Journal of Medical Psychology* 28: 101–112.

Pelham, L. E. (1971). *Self-directive play therapy with socially immature kindergarten students*. Unpublished doctoral dissertation, University of Northern Colorado, Greeley.

Peller, L. E. (1955). Libidinal development as reflected in play. *Psychoanalysis* 3(3): 3–11.

Perkins, M. J. (1967). *Effects of play therapy and behavior modification approaches with conduct problem boys*. Unpublished doctoral dissertation, University of Illinois at Urbana-Champaign.

Perry, L. H. (1988). *Play therapy behavior of maladjusted and adjusted children (Dissertation Abstracts International 49/10A)*. Unpublished doctoral dissertation, University of North Texas, Denton.

Phillips, E. L. (1960). Parent–child psychotherapy: a follow-up study comparing two techniques. *Journal of Psychology* 49: 195–202.

Phillips, E. L., and Johnston, M. (1954). Theoretical and clinical aspects of short-term, parent–child psychotherapy. *Psychiatry* 17: 267–275.

Phillips, R. (1945). Doll play as a function of the realism of the materials and the length of the experimental session. *Child Development* 16: 123–143.

Phillips, R. D. (1985). Whistling in the dark?: a review of play therapy research. *Psychotherapy* 22(4): 752–760.

Piaget, J. (1951). *Play, Dreams, and Imitation in Childhood*. New York: Norton.

Pintler, M. H. (1945). Doll play as a function of experimenter–child interaction and initial organization of materials. *Child Development* 6: 145–166.

Prestwich, S. (1969). *The influence of two counseling methods on the physical and verbal aggression of preschool Indian children*. Washington, DC: Office of Economic Opportunity.

Pulaski, M. A. (1970). Play as a function of toy structure and fantasy predisposition. *Child Development* 41: 531–537.

Pumfery, P. D., and Elliott, C. D. (1970). Play therapy, social adjustment and reading attainment. *Educational Research* 12: 183–193.

Quattlebaum, R. F. (1970). *A study of the effectiveness of nondirective counseling and play therapy with maladjusted fifth-grade pupils.* Unpublished doctoral dissertation, University of Alabama.

Rank, O. (1936). *Will Therapy.* New York: Knopf.

Raskin, N. J. (1954). Play therapy with blind children. *New Outlook for the Blind* 40: 290–292.

Reams, R. (1987). Darkness in play therapy: anonymity and a sense of control as facilitators of disclosure. *Journal of Child and Adolescent Psychotherapy* 4(2): 112–115.

Reynert, M. I. (1946). Play therapy at Mooseheart. *Journal of the Exceptional Child* 13: 2–9.

Richards, S. S., and Walff, E. (1940). The organization and function of play activities in the set-up of a pediatric department: a report of a three year experiment. *Mental Hygiene* 24: 229– 237.

Robinson, E. L. (1946). Doll play as a function of the doll family constellation. *Child Development* 17: 99–119.

—— (1958). *The form and the imaginative content of children's block buildings.* Unpublished doctoral dissertation, University of Minnesota, Minneapolis.

Rogers, C. R. (1937). Three surveys of treatment measures used with children. *American Journal of Orthopsychiatry* 7: 48–57.

—— (1959). A theory of therapy, personality and interpersonal relationships, as developed in the client-centered framework. In *Psychology: A Study of Science. Study I. Conceptual and Systematic. Vol. 3: Formulations of the Person and the Social Context,* ed. S. Koch., pp. 184–256. New York: McGraw-Hill.

—— (1965). *Client-Centered Therapy.* Boston: Houghton Mifflin.

Rogers, M. B. (1969). *The processes of monitored play therapy.* Georgia State University. (ERIC Document Reproduction Service No. ED 033 425).

—— (1972). *Therapists' verbalization and outcome in monitored play therapy (Dissertation Abstracts International 34/01B).* Unpublished doctoral dissertation, Georgia State University, Atlanta.

Rogers, M. B., and L'Abate, L. (1969). *Bibliography on play therapy and children's play.* Georgia State University. (ERIC Document Reproduction Service No. ED 035 897).

Roland, M. C. (1952). Psychotherapeutic aspects of play. *American Journal of Occupational Therapy* 6: 8–10.

Rosenweig, S., and Shakow, D. (1937a). Play technique in schizophrenia and other psychoses: I, rationale. *American Journal of Orthopsychiatry* 7: 32–35.

—— (1937b). Play technique in schizophrenia and other psychoses: II, an experimental study of schizophrenic constructions with play materials. *American Journal of Orthopsychiatry* 7: 36–47.

Rothschild, J. (1960). Play therapy with blind children. *New Outlook for the Blind* 54: 329–333.

Rucker, I. N. (1946). Outcome of play interviews conducted by social workers. *Smith College Studies in Social Work* 17: 128–129.

Schaefer, C. E., Gitlin, K., and Sandgrund, A., eds. (1991). *Play Diagnosis and Assessment*. New York: Wiley.

Schaefer, C. E., and Millman, H. L. (1977). *Therapies for Children*. San Francisco: Jossey-Bass.

Schaefer, C. E., and O'Connor, K. J., eds. (1983). *Handbook of Play Therapy*. New York: Wiley.

Schaefer, C. E., and Reid, S. E., eds. (1986). *Game Play*. New York: Wiley.

Schall, M. A. (1967). *A study of the effects of three anthropomorphic models on the social adjustment of children*. Unpublished doctoral dissertation, Arizona State University, Tempe.

Schiffer, A. L. (1967). The effectiveness of group play therapy as assessed by specific changes in a child's peer relations. *American Journal of Orthopsychiatry* 37: 219–220.

Schiffer, M. (1952). Permissiveness versus sanction in activity group therapy. *International Journal of Group Psychotherapy* 2: 255–261.

—— (1957). A therapeutic play group in a public school. *Mental Hygiene* 41: 185–193.

—— (1960). The use of the seminar in training teachers and counselors as leaders of therapeutic play groups for maladjusted children. *American Journal of Orthopsychiatry* 30: 154–165.

Sears, P. (1951). Doll play aggression in normal young children: influence of sex, age, sibling status, father's absence. *Psychological Monographs* 65: 2–42.

Sears, R. R. (1947). Influence of methodological factors on doll play performance. *Child Development* 18: 190–197.

Seeman, J. (1954). Child therapy in education, some current trends. *Education* 74: 493–500.

Seeman, J., and Edwards, B. (1954). A therapeutic approach to reading difficulties. *Journal of Consulting Psychology* 18: 451–453.

Seppa, N. (1996). Supreme Court protects patient-therapist privilege. *American Psychological Association Monitor*, August, p. 39.

Shirley, M., Baum, B., and Polsky, S. (1940). Outgrowing childhood's problems: a follow-up study of child guidance patients. *Smith College Student Social Work* 11: 31–60.

Siegel, A. E., and Kohn, L. G. (1959). Permissiveness, permission, and aggressions: the effects of adult presence or absence on aggression in children's play. *Child Development* 30: 131–141.

Siegel, A. W. (1963). Adult verbal behavior in play therapy sessions with retarded children. *Journal of Speech and Hearing Disorders* 10: 34–38.

Siegel, C. L. F. (1970). *The effectiveness of play therapy with other modalities in the treatment of children with learning disabilities*. Unpublished doctoral dissertation, Boston University Graduate School.

——— (1972). Changes in play therapy behaviors over time as a function of differing levels of therapist-offered conditions. *Journal of Clinical Psychology* 28: 235–236.

Simpson, G. (1938). Diagnostic play interviews. *Understanding the Child* 7: 6–10.

Smolen, E. M. (1959). Nonverbal aspects of therapy with children. *American Journal of Psychotherapy* 13: 872–881.

Sokoloff, M. A. (1959). *A comparison of gains in communicative skills, resulting from group play therapy and individual speech therapy, among a group of non-severely dysarthric, speech handicapped cerebral palsied children*. Unpublished doctoral dissertation, New York University.

Solomon, J. C. (1938). Active play therapy. *American Journal of Orthopsychiatry* 8: 479–498.

——— (1940). Active play therapy, further experiences. *American Journal of Orthopsychiatry* 10: 763–781.

——— (1947). Play technique as a differential therapeutic medium. *Nervous Child* 7: 296–300.

——— (1948). Play technique. *American Journal of Orthopsychiatry* 18: 402–413.

——— (1955). Play technique and the integrative process. *American Journal of Orthopsychiatry*, 25: 91–600.

Statton, J. (1990). *Adlerian counseling and the early recollections of children (Dissertation Abstracts International 51/05B)*. Unpublished doctoral dissertation, University of North Texas, Denton.

Stephenson, P. S. (1973). Working with nine- to twelve-year-old children. *Child Welfare* 52: 375–382.

Stiber, J. A. (1991). *The effect of play therapy on the temper tantrums of a seven year old boy (Masters Abstracts International 30/01).* Unpublished master's thesis, Southern Connecticut State University, New Haven.

Stockburger, M. R. (1983). *Play therapy and its effects upon problem behavior of elementary school children (Dissertation Abstracts International 44/06A).* Unpublished doctoral dissertation, University of Arkansas.

Stollak, G. E. (1968). The experimental effects of training college students as play therapists. *Psychotherapy: Theory, Research and Practice* 5: 77–80.

———— (1981). Variations and extensions of filial therapy. *Family Process* 20(3): 305–309.

Stover, L., and Guerney, B. G. (1967). The efficacy of training procedures for mothers in filial therapy. *Psychotherapy: Theory, Research and Practice* 4: 110–115.

Subotnik, L. (1966). Transference in client-centered play therapy. *Psychology* 3: 2–17.

Subotnik, L., and Callahan, R. J. (1959). A pilot study in short-term play therapy with institutionalized educable mentally retarded boys. *American Journal of Mental Deficiency* 63: 730–735.

Symonds, P. M. (1940). Play technique as a test of readiness. *Understanding the Child* 9: 8–14.

Taft, J. (1933). *The Dynamics of Therapy in a Controlled Relationship.* New York: Macmillan.

Tallman, F. F., and Goldensohn, L. N. (1941). Play technique. *American Journal of Orthopsychiatry* 11: 551–562.

Tizard, B. (1977). *Adoption: A Second Chance.* London: Open Books.

Trostle, S. L. (1984). *An investigation of the effects of child-centered group play therapy upon sociometric, self-control, and play behavior ratings of three- to six-year-old bilingual Puerto Rican children (Dissertation Abstracts International 46/05A).* Unpublished doctoral dissertation, Pennsylvania State University, University Park.

Updegraff, R., and Herbst, E. K. (1933). An experimental study of the social behavior stimulated in young children by certain play materials. *Journal of Genetic Psychology* 32: 372–391.

Vittner, D. (1969). Structured puppet play therapy. *Elementary School Guidance Counseling Journal* 4: 68–70.

Wall, L. (1950). *The Puppet Book.* London: Faber and Faber.

Waterland, J. C. (1970). Actions instead of words: play therapy for the young child. *Elementary School Guidance and Counseling Journal* 4: 180–197.

Weiss, A. B., and Frankle, A. W. (1938). Diagnostic and remedial play. *Understanding the Child* 7: 3–5.

———— (1941). Play interviews with nursery school children. *American Journal of Orthopsychiatry* 9: 33–39.

West, W. B. (1969). *An investigation of the significance of client-centered play therapy as a counseling technique.* Unpublished doctoral dissertation, North Texas State University, Denton.

Whitted, B. A., and Scott, R. B. (1962). Significance of a play program in the care of children in a general hospital. *Journal of the National Medical Association* 54: 488–491.

Winn, E. V. (1959). *The influence of play therapy on personality change and the consequent effect on reading performance.* Unpublished doctoral dissertation, Michigan State University, East Lansing.

Withall, J., and Reddenhouse, A. (1955). Child-therapy, a frame of reference. *Exceptional Children* 21: 122–126.

Withee, K. L. (1975). *A descriptive analysis of the process of play therapy (Dissertation Abstracts International 36/12B).* Unpublished doctoral dissertation, University of North Texas, Denton.

Witmer, H. L., and Keller, J. (1942). Outgrowing childhood's problems: a study of the value of child guidance treatment. *Smith College Studies in Social Work* 13: 74–90.

Wolaver, A. V. (1992). *Children's stories in play therapy: rationale, process, and implications (Dissertation Abstracts International 53/01B).* Unpublished doctoral dissertation, Union Institute, Cincinnati, OH.

Woltmann, A. G. (1940). The use of puppets in understanding children. *Mental Hygiene* 24: 445–458.

———— (1943). Plastic materials as a psychotherapeutic medium. In *Encyclopedia of Child Guidance*, ed. R. B. Winn. New York: Philosophical Library.

———— (1956). Play therapy and related techniques. *Progress in Clinical Psychology* 30: 180–196.

Index